The canoe
and white water

C. E. S. FRANKS

The canoe
and white water

FROM ESSENTIAL TO SPORT

UNIVERSITY OF TORONTO PRESS
Toronto   Buffalo   London

©University of Toronto Press 1977
Toronto   Buffalo   London
Reprinted 1978, 1979
Printed in Canada

Library of Congress Cataloging in Publication Data

Franks, Charles Edward Selwyn, 1936–
    The canoe and white water.

    Includes bibliographical references and index.
    1. White-water canoeing. I. Title.
    GV788.F72   797.1'22   77-2611
    ISBN 0-8020-2236-7
    ISBN 0-8020-6294-6 pbk.

CONTENTS

The canoe
and white water

INTRODUCTION

As a teenager I paddled a great deal – in summer work in the north, around cottages, in Algonquin Park – but it was not until after I was married and had three children that I began canoeing in white water. In not having tried river canoeing as a youth I was like many other Canadians of my generation. We were taught that the canoe could be dangerous, that there were many absolute 'don'ts,' and that one of the most important of these was *never* to shoot rapids. Then one April, as I was beginning to consider myself middle-aged, and after a long and depressing winter during which one of my closest friends was killed in a car accident, I was talked into trying white water. Challenging and surviving rapids in a fragile canoe proved an entirely new sort of experience. It put me face to face with nature, with survival. It demanded new skills and attitudes, and the experience forced me out of my depression.

Since then I have spent much of my free time in white water canoeing, and the fascination and pleasure it gives continue to grow. Most of my canoeing is done on the small rivers of southern and mid-Canada, although every three years or so I am able to arrange something further north. Like most Canadians I cannot afford the expense, or the time, of spending weeks or months each summer canoeing in the northern wilderness. But close to home I have been able to work steadily at improving my techniques. White water canoeing is not, as I thought at first, a matter of paddling with all one's strength through foaming waves and conquering the water with brute force. It involves many different abilities, including subtle tactics for handling different kinds of turbulence, a healthy respect for the forces of nature, and an understanding of the limits of man and equipment. This book is an attempt to share the knowledge and skills I have acquired. It is mainly about white water paddling in open canoes, but covered canoes and kayaks, which can be used in much more violent water, are becoming increasingly popular, and so I have paid some attention to this new branch of the sport. It is not intended to be a primer in canoeing skills. Many excellent primers have already been written. I assume that the reader knows how to paddle a canoe in a straight line, how to get into and out of a canoe, how to hoist a canoe up and carry it over a portage, and how to make a camp-fire and pitch a tent.

This book begins where primers end. It describes what my companions and I have found interesting and important in white water canoeing. It includes matters of practical use – 'reading' white water, the paddling techniques for handling rapids, canoeing safety, and planning and organizing trips. It goes on to consider some questions which have arisen over campfires and in the quiet winters. Why, for example, were Canadians taught for three or four decades to avoid and fear rapids, when in fact white water skills have for centuries been regarded as a peak of the art of canoeing, and its most excit- ing challenge? What is the history and technology of the canoe – how were canoes made? why were they designed the way they were? what improve- ments have been made to materials and techniques? As I traced the history of the canoe I came to realize that it is part of the history of Canada's economic and social development, and appreciating this has made my own canoeing experiences that much richer and more interesting. As my friends and I become more adventurous in the trips we attempt, we have found it necessary to examine Canadian geography, the geology of rivers, and the sciences which analyze turbulent water. Finally, like many other people, canoeists have become increasingly concerned over the quality of our rivers and water resources as part of the environment. All these different kinds of knowledge fit together to form my canoeing reality. I have spent some time examining each of them in various chapters.

This is not a 'complete' book on canoeing. There are far too many canoeing manuals that claim to be complete, but on inspection the reader finds that none of them really is. Like every author I have followed my own perspective and interests in writing, and doubtless I have omitted many topics that others would want to include. Nor is this book a manual of woodcraft, or a lyrical description of nature or of canoeing experiences. Many excellent books have been written on these subjects. Among the things I most regret omitting are the tranquil virtues of canoeing. The picture that emerges from the following pages is of an active, athletic challenge. There is, of course, far more to canoeing. No other water craft is so well adapted to silent wilderness travel, contemplation of the wonders of the natural world, fishing, nature photography, observing animals, or simple meditation. But all the canoe's qualities cannot be covered in a single volume.

I would like to thank all those who have helped me with this book, including my companions of CORTS (The Canadian Outdoors Rum Toddy Society) who helped provide the experience on which it is based, the persons who have read and commented on the manuscript, including Eric Morse, Sandy Lewis of Environment Canada, Hermann Kerckhoff of the Madawaska Kanu Camp, David Holmes of the Oxford (England) Riverside Centre, Stuart Ryan of the Queen's University Faculty of Law, Ken Wilson and Arthur Brebner of the Queen's Department of Civil Engineering, Bob Greggs of the Queen's Department of Geology, Bill Waters of the Department of Economics at the University of British Columbia, Craig MacDonald and Dan Brunton of the Ontario Ministry of Natural Resources, and many others. They are, I hope, in no way responsible for the faults. The dozens of persons I have corresponded with in various government departments, both federal and provincial, have been unfailingly helpful and informative, as also have been the archivists and curators of photographs and drawings at the many archives and collections I have used. I am grateful to the *Queen's Quarterly* for permission to use, in chapter 2, material which they originally published as an article. Rosa Skudra did the drawings. Mr and Mrs S. T. Franks gave me food, lodging, and a private place to work during a crucial period of writing. My family has helped at many stages, from canoeing to proofreading. Ian Montagnes of the University of Toronto Press has been a great help at all stages, and without Jill Harris' superb typing and reading of my sometimes inscrutable writing, the book might never have been completed. Publication was assisted by grants from the Canada Council and the Ontario Arts Council, and the latter body assisted the research.

C. E. S. Franks
September 1976

ONE

The canoe

The interior of Canada is a vast low-relief surface bounded on the west and east by systems of mountains. Most of it was covered by glaciers during the recent ice age until only 10,000 to 20,000 years ago – a very short time in the geological scale. These glaciers were up to two miles thick, and their weight, their motion and their debris have helped to shape the Canadian interior: the bare scrubbed rock of the Precambrian Shield, one of the oldest landscapes in the world, which still shows the gouges and scratches left by the grinding ice; the level prairies built up on the beds of ancient glacial lakes; the gentle moulding of till, moraines, drumlins and clay plains deposited by the icefields in the St Lawrence lowlands.

Within its boundaries Canada holds nearly half the fresh water of the world. Some is in huge inland seas – including the Great Lakes and the northern lakes of the Mackenzie drainage system – but much is contained in smaller lakes and in the creeks, streams and rivers which form a network over all of Canada except the western plains and mountains. The Canadian Shield, which is the surface of most of the interior, is covered by muskeg, cliffs, rivers and lakes that make travel by foot almost impossible during the summer months. Yet the terrain is barren and unsuited for agriculture. Living off it demands hunting and fishing over wide areas.

The Indian people who migrated into Canada as the glaciers retreated adopted the only logical solution to the problems posed by this territory. They turned the waterways into routes of communication. Long before Columbus visited America they had developed the canoe, for its size and weight the most efficient form of water transport that has ever been devised. The common ones of the interior were twelve to fourteen feet long, had a low freeboard, and were open for most of their length. Thus, unlike the kayaks of the Eskimos, they could carry a large payload and were flexible in loading with people or freight. They were light and easily carried around rapids and between watersheds. And they were extraordinarily handy in the water.

To the Indian, the canoe was an extension of home for half the year. This is a Cree family on the Abitibi River, about 1907.

Champlain, on his visit to Tadoussac in 1603, was astonished to discover that two Indians could paddle a canoe faster than his men could row the ship's boat. His was the first description by a European of the Indian craft:

Their canoes are some eight or nine paces [about 20 feet] long, and a pace or a pace and a half broad amidships, and grow sharper and sharper toward both ends. They are liable to overturn, if one knows not how to manage them rightly; for they are made of a bark of trees called birch-bark, strengthened within by little circles of wood strongly and neatly fashioned, and are so light that a man can carry one of them easily; and every canoe can carry the weight of a pipe [about 1,000 lbs.]. When they wish to go overland to get to some river where they have business, they can carry them with them.[1]

The landscape provided the logic for a light, easily carried boat, but the birch tree provided the essential material. The paper birch, *Betula papyrifera*, is found over all of Canada south of the tree line except the prairies and the far west, but is especially abundant and large in the eastern part of its range. Here it can reach a hundred feet·in height, with a butt diameter of thirty inches or more. The bark is made up of resin-impregnated, paper-like layers which deepen in colour from chalky white on the exterior to a light tan on the inner layer. A rind of cambium which darkens with age until it becomes a dark brown or sepia grows between the outer bark and the wood of the trunk. The grain of the outer bark runs around the tree, while that of the inner bark is parallel to the trunk. This makes the bark strong and reduces the likelihood of its splitting, so that it can be shaped and laced with some confidence that the seams will hold. For canoe construction the bark must be over one-eighth of an inch thick, and should have the rind attached. The bark should be free from blemishes, and come from a straight trunk, large enough to give reasonably sized pieces. The best is taken during winter thaws or in the spring. Birch bark is flexible when fresh or wetted, but when dry forms a hard, tough layer. Canoes were sometimes made of other barks, including spruce or elm, but these barks had a much greater propensity to split and the canoes were not so well shaped or durable.

Indians began birch bark canoe construction by shaping a large piece of bark into the canoe form in a building bed – a piece of cleared and smoothed ground surrounded by stakes which outlined the final dimensions of the craft. The inside of the bark became the outside of the canoe. This shaped bark – the basic structural element – was laced with thread made from the black spruce, *Picea mariana;* its tough, flexible roots can be twenty feet long, yet no thicker than a pencil. The gunwales were usually made out of spruce or white cedar. The ribs, which lent strength and held the forms, were usually also made out of white cedar and bent to shape. The ribs were set about one inch apart. Between them and the birch bark was a layer of planking, also made out of split white cedar. Gunwales, ribs and planking were held in place by a lacing of spruce root, and the shape was maintained by thwarts made of maple, cedar or spruce. In the west and north, beyond the range of the white cedar, planking and ribs were normally spruce. The seams of canoes were sealed and made waterproof with gum from spruce or pine, melted and mixed with grease so it would remain flexible in cold weather, and with charcoal for coloration.

The birch bark canoes of the Indians varied in length from ten or twelve feet for single hunters up to thirty feet for war parties. The ones observed by Champlain were 'family' canoes, large enough to carry husband, wife, children and belongings, yet small enough to be portaged by one or two people. Often large war canoes were roughly constructed craft of spruce or other non-birch barks, and were discarded at the end of a short voyage. Birch bark canoes could last up to five years in use.

Most Indian birch bark canoes were open craft, pointed and similarly shaped at both ends. They had no keels. Their basic cross-section was a U,

An Indian craftsman of a previous generation builds a birch bark canoe at Murray Bay, PQ. The stakes which establish the final dimensions have been driven into the ground. The sides are being shaped and sewn together, to follow the line of the gunwale which is already in place inside the canoe. Some ribs, bent and tied across the top to maintain their shape, are nearby. They will be the last major part to be fitted.

although the larger the canoe the flatter this U could become. Towards the ends the U became a sharp V, strengthened by stem and stern pieces. Within these common elements canoes varied in design quite substantially among tribes, and even within one tribe.[2] Some of these variations were caused by different customs, some by idiosyncracies of canoe builders, and some by adaptation to the special circumstances of a region. Anthropologists are only beginning to describe the wide variety of canoes and most statements about the factors which caused design differences are largely speculation. In some canoes the ends recurved and were raised well above the general level of the gunwales; in others they were low. Some craft had a marked 'tumblehome' – the sides curved inwards as they reached the gunwales. Others were flared, and reached the greatest width at the gunwales. High ends and a tumble-home were especially useful for keeping water out in the low, short waves found in small rapids. The Kootenay Indian canoes had low, ram-shaped, pointed ends. The canoes of the eastern Micmacs, which were often used on the ocean, were higher amidships than at the bow and stern. Possibly the most striking design to modern eyes was the 'crooked' canoe of the Eastern James Bay Cree Indians: its keel line formed an arc, often more than a foot higher at the ends than amidships. This highly 'rockered' design must have

The Kootenay canoe's distinctive design stems, probably, from the difficulties in shaping spruce bark, which was used to cover canoes in the west where there were no birch trees. This particular canoe, while retaining the traditional shape, appears to be covered in canvas.

been easily manoeuvered in rapids but almost impossible to steer in a straight line in any wind. It was used on the large rivers of the eastern James Bay region where there was much fast water and few large open lakes.

Many of the Indian birch bark canoes were superbly designed. They had full lines which gave excellent buoyancy and carrying capacity, had sufficient tumblehome and decking at bow and stern to keep water out but still leave sufficient open space for flexibility in paddling and baggage arrangement, were fast and manoeuverable, were made up of a minimum amount of material for volume of water displaced, and were easily portaged. Some Ojibway and Algonkian canoes were better designed for extended wilderness travel than all but a few types of modern canoe. Moulded birch bark and bent cedar imposed their own logic and discipline on shape. The tensions of ribs and planking at right angles to each other, bent to the least-work curves of undeformed wood, produced lovely compound curves, and strong craft with fine lines.

Birch bark canoe making was a skilled art, but one possessed by many Indians. In some bands specialist workers would build canoes, in others each family. Canoe making skills were as essential to survival in nomad bands as the ability to drive a car or fill out an income tax form is to us today. Among

A Micmac canoe on the Restigouche River, New Brunswick, about 1870.

12   The canoe and white water

The crooked canoe of the James Bay Cree was superbly
adapted to white water canoeing. This photograph was
taken at Fort George, on Hudson Bay, in 1888.

These Indian women are completely recovering a birch bark canoe. Most repairs were smaller than this, but if necessary the craft could be entirely rebuilt in the bush with materials and tools at hand.

A Micmac canoe being tarred.

the first trade goods Europeans exchanged with Canadian Indians were iron axes, knives and awls. With these tools instead of stone implements, canoe making was much easier, but there was no substantial change in design, materials or construction techniques.

Samuel Hearne in 1771, after observing Indians making canoes during their trek across the barren lands, marvelled that, 'All the tools used by an Indian in building his canoe, as well as in making his snow-shoes, and every other kind of wood-work, consist of a hatchet, a knife, a file, and an awl; in the use of which they are so dextrous, that every thing they make is executed with a neatness not to be excelled by the most expert mechanic, assisted with every tool he could wish.'[3] Birch bark canoes were still in widespread use in northern Canada at the beginning of the twentieth century, and the art of making them has by no means died out amongst the country's Indians.

The main weakness of the birch bark canoe was its delicate outside skin. Great care had to be taken to protect the craft from abrasion or puncturing on rocks and boulders. As many of the rivers of Canada are small and shallow, with little flow during the summer and autumn, travel on them was a mixture of paddling and portaging. Canoes were designed so that they could be carried often and easily. Even so, a repair kit of birch bark, spruce roots and gum was standard equipment and frequently used. On difficult routes the canoes needed repairs each day, and these could be substantial. A canoe split in half might be made whole again, a bow replaced, or the actual size of the craft reduced.

Birch bark canoes could not run rapids in which they were likely to hit rocks, and this limited the number of rivers on which they could be used. So did other elements of geography. The sedimentary soils and rocks of the St Lawrence lowlands hold few lakes compared with the Canadian Shield, and the streams tend not only to be small but to have shallow gradients and rock-filled beds. Many were suitable for birch bark canoe travel only in the spring months.

The craft of the Iroquois of southern Ontario were dugouts which, according to Diamond Jenness, 'were miserable vessels, little more than logs of pine rudely hollowed out and pointed at bow and stern. So heavy were they, so easily water-logged, and so ill-adapted for portaging from one lake or river to another, that these tribes frequently purchased birch-bark canoes from their Algonkian neighbours . . . '[4] But Major Samuel Strickland, in the middle of the nineteenth century, saw in the Goderich region some dugout canoes light enough to be portaged easily by one person. The largest he saw was of pine, twenty-six feet long, three feet nine inches in beam, and could carry

The beautiful sea-going canoes of the West Coast were hollowed out of single tree trunks. Only in the west did trees of such size and quality grow. Indians hunted whales in these craft.

nine barrels of pork and five paddlers.[5] He also saw dugouts made of a single black walnut tree which could hold ten or twelve persons. The dugouts of the West Coast Indians were often even larger, sea-going boats which only loosely deserve to be called canoes.

The Indians of southern Ontario, Quebec and the maritimes also made canoes out of elm bark. These were temporary, roughly-made craft normally discarded at the end of a trip. They had a frame of alder or spruce and were lashed at the ends. Some of the war parties associated with Champlain used such canoes thirty feet in length. When the Maitland River at Goderich was too rapid to ascend by boat at the time of the spring hunt, the local Indians left their birch bark canoes at home, walked to its headwaters, and brought their pickings back down river in temporary craft of elm bark. Alexander Henry also met such boats when travelling with another group of Indians from Georgian Bay to Fort Niagara in June 1764. After going up the Severn River, across Lakes Couchiching and Simcoe, and up the Holland River to the end of navigable water, the party left their birch bark craft and followed the Indian path which roughly paralleled the present route of Yonge Street to the mouth of the Humber at Toronto. There they spent two days:

making canoes, out of the bark of the elm-tree, in which we were to transport ourselves to Niagara. For this purpose, the Indians first cut down a tree; then stripped off the bark, in one entire sheet, of about eighteen feet in length, the incision being lengthwise. The canoe was now complete, as to its top, bottom and sides. Its ends were next closed, by sewing the bark together; and a few ribs and bars being introduced, the architecture was finished. In this manner, we made two canoes; of which one carried eight men, and the other, nine.[6].

They crossed Lake Ontario on the third day. Elm bark has a strong grain, and elm bark canoes could not be laced together from many pieces like those of birch bark.

The kayaks of the Eskimo are quite different from the canoes of the Indian in construction, design and function. The essential structural element is not the covering but the wooden frame, which is built first and over which seal-skins are stretched and sewn. The kayak is long and narrow; its two ends are shaped differently, and it holds only one paddler who sits slightly aft of midships in a small opening to which he is joined by a loose but watertight protective covering. This is basically a hunting craft, fast and easy to paddle, completely seaworthy, but unfit for transporting many people or goods. The division between canoe and kayak however is blurred. A few kayaks were built for two, and the large open umiaks, made for transporting goods, were

The kayak derived its strength from a rigid wooden frame, over which animal skin was stretched.

more like canoes in shape. Kayaks were often, like canoes, paddled with a single bladed paddle, and some Indians of the far north made craft which combined the features of both kayaks and canoes. The Nahanni Indians, for example, made temporary canoes out of moosehide stretched over a wooden frame. The Chipewyan Indians who accompanied Samuel Hearne across the barrens used small, light canoes which had a wooden frame more like that of a kayak than the ribs and planking of a birch bark canoe, and like a kayak they also had a long narrow covered foredeck: they were a hybrid product of Eskimo and southern Indian boat-building technologies.

The Impact of Western Technology
The advent of Europeans and the expansion of the fur trade did not at first change the design or materials of canoes, but did encourage some standardization of sizes and some canoe-building factories. There were two basic sizes of fur trade canoe: *canot de maître* and *canot du nord*. The *canot de maître* was used to transport goods from Montreal to the head of Lake Superior. It was on the average thirty-six feet long, six feet wide, and normally carried a crew of eight or ten and three tons of freight. The *canot du nord* was used on the smaller waterways north of the Great Lakes, and west and

A moosehide boat was used in the first exploration for the Geological Survey of Canada of the mountainous region between the Yukon and Mackenzie Rivers. After wintering near Christie Pass, on the border of the Yukon and Northwest Territories, the party built boats of moosehide over willow frames. This one probably took three hides: perhaps it is the flesh of one of the same animals that is drying on the rack behind it. The party descended the Gravel River (now the Keele River – named after the survey leader and photographer) to one of the trading posts on the Mackenzie River. There, like the Indians who brought furs for trading, the party would have abandoned the craft.

A *canot de maître* of 1822, painted by John Halkett. Someone has cut off the back of the picture, but the implements for mending the craft are still visible – a kettle and ladles for boiling pitch, and a roll of birchbark. This is a lightly loaded express canoe, with fourteen voyageurs and, as passengers, two officers of the Hudson's Bay Company.

north of Lake Superior as far as the fur trade stretched. It was typically twenty-five feet long with a crew of five or six, and carried half the freight of the *canot de maître.* Because of their hard use, the life expectancy of a *canot de maître* was one year. The first recorded factory for building *canots de maître* was at Trois Rivières, which enjoyed easy access by river to the parts of Quebec where large birch trees were found. There was also a factory at Grand Portage on Lake Superior which made up to seventy *canots du nord* in a year.[7] Such factories were little more than collections at a convenient spot of a few skilled craftsmen, who built canoes on a standard frame. Canoes of both sizes were also built at interior trading posts, especially after the North West Company was amalgamated with the Hudson's Bay Company in 1821 and furs were shipped through Hudson Bay rather than through Montreal. At that time the building of *canots de maître* ceased at Trois Rivières. The bark fur trading canoes gradually disappeared during the last decades of the nineteenth century, and by the beginning of the first world war the *canot de maître* and the *canot du nord* were finished 'except as curiosities – hardly even as these, for not one was preserved in a museum.'[8]

In 1957 a full-scale replica of a *canot de maître* was made by Indians of the Golden Lake Reserve east of Algonquin Park for the National Museum of Canada in Ottawa. A decade later, Charlie Laberge of the Ontario Department of Lands and Forests built two *canots de maître,* which now are on display along the historic route of the fur traders, one at Samuel de Champlain Provincial Park on the Mattawa River, the other at Thunder Bay. There are a few other replicas in museums, including one at Camp Kandalore near Minden, Ontario, where it is one of a large museum collection of canoes.

In the late nineteenth century birch bark began to be replaced as a covering for canoes by canvas – a lighter, more flexible and more durable material. J. W. Anderson, who had been a Hudson's Bay Company district manager, described the change in Quebec east of James Bay, using Indian craftsmen:

Frances Hopkins was the wife of an HBC officer, and
accompanied him on trips into the Canadian interior.
Her pictures are the most authentic of any which
depict the canoes and voyageurs of the fur trade. The
canoe in *Shooting the Rapids* (painted about 1869) is the
largest in any of her works – a 36-foot *canot de maître*.
Besides its four passengers it carries sixteen
voyageurs. There are ten banks of seats.

The thirty-foot birch bark freight canoes used by the
HBC had a capacity of four tons and six passengers.
Normally only four men would have carried a canoe of
this size.

The desired canvas canoe was not accomplished without considerable difficulty, for
the first canoes built had double canvas so tight that it ripped with the action of the
paint subsequently applied ... They eventually developed a thirty-foot canvas canoe,
capable of carrying four thousand pounds ... The method of building these early
canvas-covered canoes was practically identical with that employed by the Indian in
constructing his birch-bark craft. First the canvas was attached to the gunwales, next
the cedar planking was placed inside and finally the ribs were driven home to make
the hull taut and firm.[9]

In the 1860s all-wood canoes were developed in Lakefield and Peterborough, Ontario. These were beautifully constructed craft of carefully fitted
cedar or basswood strips strengthened by narrow, widely spaced interior ribs
of oak, and varnished inside and out. Although this type of canoe copied the
shape of the Indian birch bark, it was very much a product of western technology. It was carvel built, with the narrow strips of planking fastened edge
to edge so closely as to be waterproof. It was constructed within frames
shaped exactly to cross-sections of the canoe's exterior, so that all canoes from
the same frame had uniform dimensions and true lines. Carefully constructed
forms of this kind were economical only when large numbers of canoes were
built and sold; thus canoe construction became a centralized craft requiring

The Tyrrell camp on the west shore of Hudson Bay, October 1893. Here the wooden Peterborough canoes had to be abandoned, and the party proceeded by foot to Fort Churchill.

special skills and equipment. The product was the equal of the best racing sculls and rowing skiffs of the times. The standard all-wood Peterborough canoe was sixteen feet long, 30 inches wide and weighed about 85 pounds. It had a V-shaped hull and with its narrow width was suitable for flat water racing. It was a work of art.

Although these finely constructed craft were most often considered to be for recreation and racing rather than the wilderness, one of the last great voyages of exploration by canoe was made in them by two men from southern Ontario, J. B. Tyrrell of the Canadian Geological Survey and his brother, J. W. Tyrrell. Their craft were 'two beautiful varnished cedar canoes, eighteen feet in length, and capable of carrying two thousand pounds.' The Tyrrells also had a nineteen-foot basswood canoe.[10] They left Toronto in May 1893, for Edmonton, then started north to the barren lands. Just after reaching the Athabaska River they amazed some Indians by paddling their Peterboroughs in circles around the natives' birch bark canoes: this was a measure of the improvement caused by western craftsmanship. Their route went to Lake Athabaska, up from its east end to Lake Dubawnt in the barrens, further north down the Dubawnt River to the Thelon River, on to Baker Lake and Chesterfield Inlet, and then south along the west coast of Hudson Bay to Fort

Churchill, which they reached by foot after being forced to abandon their canoes in mid-October. They were the first white men to cover much of this route. The Tyrrells' chief steersman, Pierre, was an Iroquois from Caughnawaga who 'had made a reputation for himself by running the Lachine Rapids on Christmas day, out of sheer bravado.' Towards the end of their river trip, J. W. Tyrrell reflected that Pierre's skill and nerve in running rapids had saved them from many laborious portages: 'During the scores of times that he piloted our little fleet through foaming waters, I believe I am correct in saying that his canoe never once touched a rock; but that is more than can be said of those who followed him.'[11] It is more also than can be said of most modern white water canoeists.

J. B. Tyrrell made many more explorations in the Canadian north and west. He resigned from the Geological Survey to join the gold rush of 1897, and afterwards played an important part in opening many northern Ontario mines. He subsequently contributed more to the understanding of Canadian history than most professional historians by, among other things, discovering, editing and having published for the first time many journals of the old explorers including especially those of David Thompson, Canada's greatest map maker-explorer, whose routes Tyrrell's own journeys had retraced and crossed. Tyrrell's studies on fur traders, the fur trade and fur trading routes and their importance to the development of modern Canada lie, often unacknowledged, behind much modern Canadian economic history. He died in 1957, aged 98. His travels and scholarly works are a very real bridge between the present generation and Canada's founders of the fur trade era.

The wood and canvas canoe as it is known today combines the materials of the work canoes developed by the Hudson's Bay Company with the construction techniques developed in the southern part of the country. It was invented in Maine and first made in Canada in the 1890s by the Peterborough Canoe Company and the Chestnut Canoe Company of Fredericton, N.B.[12] Unlike the all-wood canoe, the wood and canvas canoe is constructed *over* a form, usually of metal. The construction sequence is the reverse of that for a birch bark canoe. First the ribs, of steamed cedar, are bent over the form. Next the planking is fitted and nailed on to the ribs, the nails being turned back and clinched by the metal form. Then the canvas is stretched over the canoe and the gunwales attached. Because of the standardized form and materials, the completed wood and canvas canoe has truer lines than birch bark canoes. It is a faster and better built boat.

The Chestnut Canoe Company, which absorbed its Peterborough rival in the 1960s, today has the most varied and refined range of wood and canvas

The Chestnut Prospector was the working canoe of the north for decades. This one was being poled through shallow water, about 1910, on the La Loche River of northern Saskatchewan, part of the historic fur trade route to the Mackenzie Basin.

Making a cedar strip canoe: the process is the opposite to building one of birch bark. The ribs, bent to shape over the form, come first. Once they are in place, cedar planking is nailed to them. The brass nails are self-clinching – their points are bent backwards by the iron of the form.

The Rupert's House canoe factory on James Bay,
staffed by Indians.

canoes. It offers more than forty models. The Old Town Company in Maine
also has a large selection. The smallest Chestnut, the Featherweight, is
fifteen feet long and weighs thirty-five pounds with a carrying capacity of
350 pounds. The largest Chestnut freight canoe, the Daddy, is twenty-two
feet long, over five feet wide, weighs 310 pounds, and has a carrying capacity
of two and a half tons. The seventeen-foot Chestnut Prospector has a beam
of thirty-seven inches, a depth of fourteen and a half inches, and a carrying
capacity of 950 pounds. Its ribs are three-eighths of an inch thick, two and
three-eighths of an inch wide, and spaced two inches apart. Covered with No.
8 canvas, it weighs 85 pounds. For river travel it normally is built with a shoe
keel, half an inch deep by two inches wide. Slightly rockered, with a slightly
rounded bottom and a definite tumblehome, the Prospector combines carrying capacity, speed, manoeuverability and safety in rapids with lightness and
durability. For years it was the standard workhorse of the Canadian bush.

   These canvas and cedar strip canoes are surprisingly durable. The canvas
is 'sized' – its pores filled – and painted with enamel; on Chestnut canoes this
finish is then baked for two weeks to develop an iron-hard surface. Many
wood and canvas canoes are still in service after thirty years. Constant use
in shallow rock-filled streams will wear out the canvas and break ribs and

floorboards, but this type of canoe, like the birch bark, is easy to repair. Holes in the cover can be repaired with canvas patches and glue – or spruce gum if glue is not available – or if necessary the entire canvas covering can be replaced. Pieces can be spliced into ribs and planking, or a group of ribs or planking replaced. Dried and easily split white cedar is readily available along most northern canoe routes. With an axe, awl and snare wire, virtually any repair to ribs and planking can be made. The wood and canvas canoe thus combines western technology with the best features of Indian design and materials.

There are many small makers of canvas and cedar strip canoes throughout central and northern Ontario and Quebec. The canoe-makers are, however, generally white men. Indians did not have the capital resources, the social organization or the technical skills to enable them to make canoes on standardized forms by assembly line techniques. The end of the birch bark canoe as a result meant that if Indians wanted better canoes they had to buy ones made in factories owned and run by whites. One important exception was a canoe-making factory established by the Hudson's Bay Company, using Indian canoe makers, at Rupert's House on James Bay, which for decades supplied canoes for Indians of that area.

Canoeing became a popular leisure sport in Europe towards the end of the nineteenth century. The term 'canoe' there, however, includes what Canadians would call kayaks. The reasons lie in the past. One of the main forces behind British Arctic explorations was the search for a northwest passage to the Orient, and writings on this subject attracted great interest. The journals of Samuel Hearne, the first European to travel overland to the Arctic Ocean, were published in London in 1795. They contained pictures of the half-canoes, half-kayaks of the Chipewyan Indians labelled as 'canoes.' Franklin's first expedition of 1819-22 across the barrens and down the Coppermine River used *canots du nord*, but was accompanied by Indians with some canoes much like those shown by Hearne. As a result, what Englishmen of the first half of the nineteenth century knew as canoes from Arctic explorers included kayak-like craft. Canoes built in England at the time were pointed at both ends, and had covered decks with a central open cockpit.

This sort of canoe was more a curiosity than a popular craft. Rowing, looking where one has been rather than where one is going, was then as now more the British style. It was left to John MacGregor with his canoe *Rob Roy* in 1865, to make canoeing an English national sport and to make firm forever the transatlantic confusion of kayaks and canoes. If English-speaking nineteenth century British North America could have selected an apostle of

In northern Canada canoe design and construction techniques merged gradually into those of the Eskimo kayak. There was no sharp division. This Dog Rib Indian canoe is covered with skin and partly decked. It was photographed at Fort Rae, NWT, in 1913.

canoeing for the old country, they could have chosen no better. MacGregor came from a distinguished Scottish family; was an ardent anti-papist; had won a gold medal at Bisley for marksmanship; was an eminent patent attorney. 'Lawyer, philanthropist, athlete, preacher, traveller, author, volunteer, controversialist' (according to his biographer),[13] John MacGregor helped found the Protestant Defence Committee, the London Scottish Regiment, the Royal Canoe Club and the 'Ragged Schools' for the children of London's poor.

In May 1865, at the age of 41, MacGregor conceived the idea of a canoe trip through Europe. From visits to Canada and the Asiatic coast of Russia, he was familiar with kayaks and canoes. Just over a month later, on June 27, his craft was completed. The *Rob Roy* was fifteen feet long, two feet six inches wide, and weighed ninety pounds with mast, foresail and lugsail, and paddle. It was clinker-built (the strakes overlapped) of oak with a low underwater curve, and was covered fore and aft with cedar decks, leaving an elliptical cockpit about four feet long in which the rider sat facing the bow. MacGregor used a double-bladed kayak paddle. The boat flew a silk Union Jack, and its name was painted in blue on the stern.

MacGregor left London in the *Rob Roy* on 9 July 1865. On 7 October, nearly three months later, he paddled under Westminster Bridge, back in London after a journey of a thousand miles through the rivers, lakes and roads of the Continent. He had gone up the Rhine to Freiburg, across the Alps to the source of the Danube, down the Danube to Ulm, back to the Rhine via Lake Constance, and ended his journey on the Moselle and Marne to Paris. Even for the Victorian age, MacGregor must have been an odd sight as he cruised downriver with every available cubic inch of the *Rob Roy* packed with religious tracts and leaflets and copies of the New Testament for distribution to the crowds of villagers and peasants who gathered to watch him. But in January 1866 his first book, *A Thousand Miles in the Rob Roy Canoe on*

The canoe   29

John MacGregor in the *Rob Roy* - illustrations from his
own account of his travels through Europe.

30   The canoe and white water

Twenty Rivers and Lakes of Europe, was published, and proved immensely popular. Three editions sold out within the first year. It was followed by *Rob Roy on the Baltic* and *Rob Roy on the Jordan,* both similarly popular. The books were translated into many European languages. Napoleon III was an avid reader and encouraged canoeing in France.

MacGregor also had an impact in North America, where kayaking too became a leisure sport. J. Henry Rushton in upper New York State began, in the 1870s, to make Rob Roy canoes. These were very popular, and he later added open 'Canadian' canoes to his line. Rushton's most famous canoe was the *Sairy Gamp,* used by the woodsman and writer Nessmuk. The *Sairy Gamp* weighed only ten and a half pounds empty or, loaded with gear and food for a weekend, twenty-six. Nessmuk himself weighed only about 100 pounds. But by the turn of the century, the fad for bicycles and motor cars reduced American interest in canoeing, and the kayak (Rob Roy canoe) almost disappeared from North American rivers.

Modern Canoes
Canoe design and building techniques did not alter substantially from the early years of the twentieth century until well after the second world war, when the Grumman Company of the United States began to build aluminum canoes. These craft were a product of the technology of wartime airplane production. They are made by a huge die which stamps each half of the canoe out of a sheet of aluminum clamped between hydraulic jaws. The halves are riveted together with neoprene along the seams to assure watertightness, and fitted with aluminum thwarts and seats which are riveted and bolted to the hull. A standard Grumman canoe is heat-tempered to the point that it will withstand bumps and pressures up to 35,000 pounds per square inch before denting, and impacts of up to 42,000 pounds per square inch before puncturing.

Grumman canoes come in lengths from thirteen to twenty feet, and in three standards of construction: lightweight, standard and white water. The lightweight model is made from .032 inch marine aluminum alloy and the standard model is of .05 inch alloy. The white water models are also made of .05 inch alloy, but they have extra ribs for strengthening, a 3/8-inch shoe keel instead of a full-length one-inch keel, and are 23 per cent stronger than the standard model. The seventeen-foot canoe is 36⅛ inches wide, 13⅛ inches deep, and in the lightweight model weighs 60 pounds, in the standard 75 pounds, and in the white water model 81 pounds. These weights are slightly less than those of comparable wood and canvas canoes. The Grumman is a

The all-aluminum Grumman has replaced the Chestnut Prospector as the working canoe of the north. It is also popular for white water. This is a happily short carry.

well-designed craft, with satisfactory dimensions although it does not have as good lines as the Chestnut Prospector. All its curves are convex, so that it lacks the elegant and efficient compound curves of wood canoes. It is also not so fast. Because the manufacturing process requires such a large capital investment in equipment and facilities, aluminum canoes can be produced only by large companies and in a few standard models; as a result no aluminum canoe maker has a large number of styles and there has been little variety and experimentation in design.

Aluminum canoes were first greeted with some skepticism by wilderness travellers, but quickly won over those who use canoes for work. They require no painting or maintenance, and because they cannot absorb water they do not get heavier with use as do wood and canvas craft. They are extremely strong and durable. The Hudson's Bay Company uses 17-foot Grumman canoes for their northern U-Paddle Canoe Rental Service. These canoes are now the standard work canoe of the north.

Aluminum has its disadvantages, however. Some people find it noisy in paddling because of the slap of waves in the water. It is cold to the touch in cold weather. Hard rocks dig into the soft metal, making the canoe hang up on rocks and difficult to handle. This problem is especially serious in shallow rock-filled rivers; it can be alleviated, but not completely overcome, by painting or waxing the bottom. In addition, no other aluminum canoes are as well designed or as well built as the Grumman. Many are ugly tin pigs. I have used aluminum canoes whose rivets were so soft that they wore away and fell out, whose heat tempering was so poor that they punctured on the slightest excuse, and whose thwart supports broke in the middle of a portage.

But even the worst are not as bad as the first metal canoes. One notorious such craft was built of tinned iron sheets at the military base in Penetanguishene on Georgian Bay in the early nineteenth century. E. C. Guillet reported that:

An Indian made the pattern for this boat, which was about twenty-four feet long, and capable of holding twenty barrels of flour or six passengers and their attendants, fourteen paddlers, and provisions and supplies requisite for passengers and crew. This canoe was once portaged from Holland Landing to Toronto, being hauled along Yonge Street on rollers by teams of horses. Lewis Solomon, a French Canadian *voyageur*, in recounting his experiences in the iron boat, stated that he 'made several excursions up Lake Huron in it. It was rigged for sailing but was no good in a storm, as it cut through the waves and was in danger of filling, while the bark canoe bounded over them.'[14]

The fibreglass canoe, which might more properly be called a 'fibreglass reinforced polyester resin canoe,' was the next major innovation in canoe construction. Like industrial aluminum, both fibreglass and polyester resins are products of modern science. The glass fibres, which are a third to a half a thousandth of an inch thick, are extruded in complex machines, and woven into cloth or cut into two- to three-inch length for 'chopped strandmat.' Their tensile strength can be as high as 400,000 to 500,000 pounds per square inch. Polyester resins, products of the modern petrochemical industry, are hydrocarbons which, in the presence of a catalyst, bond together to produce extended interlocking networks of molecules. By themselves, neither fibreglass nor polyesters are good building materials, but together, like steel reinforcing and concrete, or the natural web of fibres and matrix in wood, they create an extremely strong, flexible and weather-resistant material. The tensile strength of a well made polyester reinforced fibreglass canoe can be 75,000 pounds per square inch.

Like its aluminum cousin, the fibreglass canoe is a product of wartime technology, developed for the construction of housings for anti-aircraft radar antennas. Unlike aluminum, however, fibreglass and polyester resins do not require complicated and expensive equipment. Polyester resins set at room temperature with negligible pressure, and can be used with the same sort of bucket and brush technique involved in large scale *papier mâché* construction. Canoe moulds can be made inexpensively out of fibreglass or plaster, and the layers of fibreglass and polyester resin which form the shell can easily be laid by hand. It is once again possible for an individual to build and even design a canoe himself. Many commercially sold fibreglass canoes are built in basements or small factories employing two or three people, or by one person in his spare time. Although not as durable and maintenance-free as aluminum canoes, fibreglass is better in both regards than wood and canvas. Unlike aluminum it does not stick to rocks.

Fibreglass has for the first time made it possible to design a truly ugly canoe. The curves of bent cedar strips have their own inherent logic and beauty, so that any wood and canvas canoe, built within the constraints imposed by that logic, inevitably has natural flowing and graceful lines. Moulded aluminum has fewer inherent constraints on shape, but it has some and, as a result, even the worst designed aluminum canoe has some logic of form. But polyester impregnated fibreglass is as easy to shape as a wet paper towel, and as easy to make into an illogical, unattractive form. Many modern fibreglass canoes are badly designed. They are too shallow, narrow far too sharply at bow and stern, have inefficient curves from keel to gunwale, and are as lacking in utility as they are in beauty.

It is also possible to build weak fibreglass canoes. There are nearly two hundred different polyester resins commercially available, only a few of which are suitable for boat construction. An ignorant or cost-saving builder can easily choose the wrong ones. Damp, cold, and other bad working conditions also can produce a weak finished product and failure in the bonding of the layers. Moreover many manufacturers add non-glass fibrous materials to their canoes for bulk in order to save on resins and glass, and the result is a very noticeable loss in strength. In fibreglass canoes, as in most other things, the buyer has to pay to get quality.[15]

In recent years many new materials have been tried. Epoxy resins can be substituted for polyester, and the results are a tougher but more expensive canoe. Epoxies are more difficult to handle than polyesters, and require critically controlled conditions of temperature and pressure. Some manufacturers have substituted carbon fibres for fibreglass, making a lighter and stronger but also more expensive boat. Nylon cloth is sometimes used along with fibreglass and creates a more flexible puncture-proof product. Experiments with thermoplastic-foam sandwich have produced a strong canoe with built-in buoyancy. Most of these new techniques, however, like epoxy and aluminum,

The canoeists are beginners, and have been poorly
advised. Their fibreglass cottage canoe has an inferior
design and is not strongly built. Their paddles are out
of the water – something veterans generally avoid to
ensure good control and quick response.

require carefully controlled conditions and expensive equipment, and are not
suitable for the small-scale builder. Some manufacturers have combined the
best of the old and new by substituting fibreglass for canvas as the covering
for cedar strip canoes. Others have experimented with man-made fibre
coverings. These produce a light, extremely strong and durable boat, although
there is a risk of the fibreglass cover separating from the cedar strips,
weakening the canoe.

Modern canoes are used primarily for leisure, but the variety of such use
is enormous and many specialized designs have accordingly evolved. The most
important advances for river canoeists have followed from improvements in
racing craft, and most of the inspiration has come from Europe. White water
kayak slalom events began there in the thirties using 'fold-boats' of a wide
touring design made much like the Eskimo kayaks with rubberized canvas
over a wooden frame. In the early 1960s, fibreglass appeared, and quickly
dominated the scene. Specialized designs since then have developed for
slalom, downriver racing and touring, in both kayaks and in one- and two-
man canoes. These designs, brought over to North America, stimulated the
development of recreational canoeing sports here.

Fibreglass and polyester resin construction have been essential to this expanded interest. Canoes and kayaks made of the new materials can take greater punishment, and hence can be used in more waters than their predecessors. New developments are constantly emerging. There are already sixteen-foot canoes of experimental materials which weigh under twenty pounds, yet can withstand the blows of a sledgehammer.

Like the solutions to most interesting technological and human problems, the design of a good canoe is the working out of a compromise between many competing demands. There is a number of different possible solutions and no single optimum answer. To be fast, a canoe needs a long waterline and a narrow, circular or V-shaped hull, but to be stable it needs to be broad with a large expanse of flat bottom. To follow a straight line and for easy paddling, a canoe should have a long straight keel, but to be manoeuverable it should be well rockered with little or no keel. For good carrying capacity it should be wide and deep, but this adds weight and slows it down. A narrow bow and stern make a faster canoe, but one which digs into waves with the risk of shipping water on windy lakes or rapids. The more decking at bow and stern, the less the risk of swamping but the greater the difficulty of loading and portaging. A peaked bow and stern keep water out but catch the wind.

With these and many more conflicting factors to consider, a canoe designer has an enormous range of acceptable choices. Depending on his skill and the qualities he considers important, his canoes will emphasize one set of virtues at the expense of others. Some models are very light, cheap and easy to build but tippy and liable to swamping; some are fast but hard to manoeuver and poor load carriers; others are very manoeuverable but slow. Some are a good combination of features, others bad. Canoe design is an art, not an exact science.

Designs for specific uses have common general characteristics, however, and these are listed below for the most important types of modern canoes. To round out the picture of modern recreational river and lake paddling craft, kayaks are included. The modern terminology for these craft is:

C2 (open)	the traditional Canadian canoe and its variants
C2	a two-person, covered canoe
C1	a one-person, covered canoe
K1	a one-person kayak
K2	a two-person kayak

C2s (open) include what I call cottage and wilderness canoes. *Cottage canoes* comprise the large number of modern canoes which are useless for anything but playthings in safe, still water. They are normally fourteen to sixteen feet long, and are the standard appurtenance of the beach and lake. Most are poorly designed for load carrying and stability, and have a depth of twelve inches or less. They narrow sharply at bow and stern, and dig into waves. They ship water where a good canoe does not. Their low cost usually reflects low quality of design and construction. They are unsafe in anything but flat water near shore. Many have inadequate and leaky flotation provisions for protection in case of upset. Cottage canoes are made primarily of fibreglass, although there are some of wood and canvas. Makers of aluminum canoes cannot afford the capital cost and risk of building such inadequate craft. *Wilderness canoes* are designed for long distance travel. Examples are the Chestnut Prospector and the Grumman. They are normally sixteen to eighteen feet long, with seventeen feet the standard. They are 36 inches or more broad, and at least 13 inches deep. They tend to be full in shape to bow and stern, with a relatively flat to lightly rockered bottom. Of necessity, they are well built and designed to meet all the different conditions of extended bush travel: large lakes, shallow streams, white water, lengthy portages, heavy loads, light loads, one or two men paddling, many scrapes and bangs. If a person has to choose only one canoe for him and his family and many different recreational purposes, the wilderness canoe is the logical choice.

C2s (covered) are often termed 'banana boats.' This accurately describes their shape: highly rockered, completely covered craft in which paddlers kneel in cockpits with a flexible watertight sprayskirt between their waists and the cockpit rims. Competition C2s are racing machines designed for high manoeuverability in heavy white water, and are as little suited to the average canoeist as a supercharged Ferrari is to the average motorist. They are made out of fibreglass or the newer, more experimental materials. C2s have, however, been modified for cruising. Such models are well-rockered and have a slightly rounded or generally flat bottom, characteristics which give them a good combination of stability and manoeuverability. They are fifteen to sixteen feet long, and are made out of fibreglass. On some the decks have a single open cockpit in which the paddlers and their luggage sit. These, which are a cross between an open canoe and a C2, look very much like the long-nosed craft of the Kootenay Indians. Others are three-holers, with openings at bow and stern in which paddlers kneel, and one at the centre in which gear can be packed and which, for white water work, can be covered with a protective spray deck. These C2s have a pronounced tumblehome. They tend to be slow in flat water paddling, do not carry big loads, and are not suited for frequent jumping in and out, as happens during travel on small rivers. But they are admirably suited to one-day and weekend river play.

The boy in the K1 is sitting, and using a double-bladed paddle. The man in the C1 (Jim Blight, one of Canada's best C1 paddlers) is kneeling, and using a single-bladed canoe paddle. They are at a wintertime training session in an indoor pool.

A covered downriver canoe, nearly as manoeuverable as a kayak, can be used where open craft would swamp. The paddlers wear spray-skirts which make a watertight seal around the cockpits; the central cargo hatch can be protected with another watertight cover. Many canoeists now use C2s for wilderness river travel.

They are also good for distance travel on big rivers which do not involve a lot of portaging or lining.

C1s are smaller versions of the banana boats. The canoeist kneels and uses a single-bladed paddle. The craft is made watertight with a sprayskirt. C1s are normally used in downriver and slalom racing on short stretches of rapids, and most people find them tedious to paddle for long distances. They are broad and highly rockered. Most are made of fibreglass. An open variant is used for flat water short distance racing.

K1s come in the greatest variety of all covered craft. They are designed for specific different purposes – slalom, downriver racing, swimming pools, water polo, flatwater racing, touring, sea-going or surfing. Only flat water kayaks are open. In the others, paddler and kayak are joined by a sprayskirt to make a waterproof unit. The kayak paddler does not kneel but sits in a shaped bucket-like seat, and uses a double-bladed paddle. Slalom kayaks are broad, highly rockered, very manoeuverable, but slow and difficult to paddle in straight lines. Surfing kayaks are shaped much like a surf board. Seagoing kayaks are large and strongly built to withstand arduous conditions. Slalom and touring kayaks are the types most often chosen for purely recreational paddling. Most K1s are made out of fibreglass or other synthetic materials.

K2s are rarely found in modern pleasure canoeing. The real virtue of the kayak is that, with the double-bladed paddle, strokes can be made equally well on either side. Two men with single paddles in a C2 have almost as much flexibility in stroke making as two in a kayak, and have the additional benefit of increased power and control that come from being able to grasp the shaped paddle top.

The modern buyer has an enormous range of materials, designs, sizes and quality to choose from. Each person will have in mind his own priorities. My own feeling is that unless one wants to specialize in short white water trips, the best investment is a well built wilderness canoe. It is the safest and the most adaptable type for all purposes except difficult white water and slalom racing, and with a snap-on covered deck it can even be put to these uses. I have several kayaks but only one canoe – a wilderness model of cedar strip with a fibreglass covering. I have now used it for eight years of long-distance trips, white water canoeing, and general recreational paddling, and it was several years old when I bought it. I had to get fourteen ribs and several sections of plank replaced after a series of some small and one large accident, and one year I replaced the gunwales. Once a year I need to repair some of the fibreglass covering – a matter of an hour's work on a sunny day. On any trip I take a roll of gray 'duct tape' for minor repairs, as do most river canoeists. I sand, paint and varnish my canoe each spring. While working on it and paddling in it, I have often reflected that, with the pressure of growing population on the world's resources, my grandchildren might consider a wooden canoe outside a museum as much a surprise as I consider finding a usable one of birch bark.

TWO

The canoe on the water

Modern canoeists use many strokes and stroke combinations in white water. Most are the same as those used by Indians and voyageurs in previous centuries, although they have been refined and improved with the great advances in canoeing during the last few decades. The size, shape, load and durability of the canoe affects the range of paddle strokes and techniques which can be used in white water.

Indian paddles ranged in size up to more than six feet in length and six and a half inches in width. The common flat water paddling stroke was short, with a rapid cadence of thirty-five to forty strokes per minute, although some Indians used longer and slower strokes. The birch bark canoe was notoriously 'cranky' because of its rounded bottom and lack of keel, and required more skill than modern canoes to keep upright and to paddle in a straight line. But these same characteristics of rockered, rounded bottom and lack of keel made it superb in white water. It could be spun around, sped up, stopped, and paddled backwards or sideways with an ease that few other canoes even now can match.

Paddling techniques cannot be preserved in museums like paddles and canoes, and the descriptions of Canadian Indian paddling styles which have been left by early travellers are regrettably less satisfactory than their descriptions of canoes and canoe building. Europeans did not treat Indian skills in white water as techniques which could be broken down into their components and studied and learned, but rather as an art which was part of the birthright of the wilderness native. White authors were moreover passengers, not paddlers. Their accounts of how Indians guided canoes through rapids are extremely impressionistic; they tell more about what the authors felt than how it was done. Anna Jameson wrote, for example, of her trip down the rapids at Sault Ste Marie in a small canoe:

Canoe Descending Rapids, watercolour by J. B. Wilkinson. White water canoeing was part of everyday life to the Indians of Canada.

down we went with a whirl and a splash! – the white surge leaping around me – over me. The Indian with astonishing dexterity kept the head of the canoe to the breakers, and somehow or the other we danced through them. I could see, as I looked over the edge of the canoe, that the passage between the rocks was sometimes not more than two feet in width, and we had to turn sharp angles – a touch of which would have sent us to destruction – all this I could see through the transparent eddying waters, but I can truly say, I had not even a momentary sensation of fear, but rather of giddy, breathless, delicious excitement.[1]

Samuel Strickland recorded that in man-and-wife teams paddling down the Maitland River near Goderich, ' ... the squaw generally fills an office rather opposed to our nautical notion, for she is almost invariably the steerman; and, it must be acknowledged, performs her duty admirably well. In running down a rapid where there is much swell, they turn the bow of the canoe a little sideways, which causes it to ride over the waves without shipping as much water as it would if it ran straight through the swell.'[2] Doubtless the squaw was in the stern so that her husband could handle the bow. It is often preferable in tricky white water for the stronger paddler to be bowman. To go through standing waves at an angle, as Strickland describes, there should be no forward speed on the canoe, and often the canoe has to be backpaddled.

William Armstrong painted *Mr and Mrs St John
Running the Rapids, Sturgeon River* in the nineteenth
century. Mrs St John was a reporter for a Toronto
newspaper. Like all writers about white water
canoeing at the time, she was a passenger rather than
a paddler.

Strickland was evidently not aware of these tactics, even though he accurately described their results.

These and other descriptions give enough clues that the Indians' white water techniques can be inferred. They generally kept their canoes pointed downstream or, in large waves, at a small angle to the current. They would sometimes backpaddle and go slower than the current. The small size and rounded hulls of their canoes and the large size of their paddles enabled them to change speed rapidly, and to move the canoe sideways through the water to avoid obstacles. They had many moves at hand, and many were skilled in white water work.

The fur traders, and later the northern woodsmen who first explored and prospected the Canadian wilderness, adopted the Indian method of travel and became as expert as their native teachers. They had to learn white water techniques. As long as the rivers were the highways of the north and canoes the vehicles, it was inevitable that travellers would encounter many rapids, and to avoid them all by portaging would have been impossibly laborious and time consuming. White water was part of the normal work world in the northern forest that covers most of Canada until the airplane replaced the canoe as the main means of bush travel. It is still part of normal life for many woodsmen and Indian bands.

To these men, mastery of white water was the summit of the canoeist's art. It demanded understanding of the complexities of turbulent flow, knowledge of a wide repertoire of paddle strokes, and the ability to link these strokes together into a precise series of manoeuvres which would guide the canoe through danger. 'It is a beautiful sight to see veteran woodsmen negotiating a big rapids,' a canoeing manual of twenty years ago related; 'they will drop down at surprising speed, and seem to pause when complicated and difficult obstructions appear. They hover like hawks, move over into position by back sculling, and then shoot down again. This is canoeing at its best.'[3] White water is to canoeing what mountains are to hiking: an irresistible challenge, an opportunity to push both men and equipment to their limits in the face of implacable natural forces.

'It is difficult,' according to the nineteenth century English officer and explorer W. F. Butler, 'to find in life any event which so effectually condenses intense nervous sensation into the shortest possible space of time as does the work of shooting, or running, an immense rapid. There is no toil, no heartbreaking labour about it, but as much coolness, dexterity, and skill as man can throw into the work of hand, eye, and head; knowledge of when to strike and how to do it; knowledge of water and of rocks, and of the one hundred combinations which rock and water can assume.'[4] As Samuel Johnson said about hanging, the prospect of white water concentrates the mind wonderfully.

Paddling Techniques in Fur Trade Canoes
The large canoes of the fur trade were designed to carry heavy cargoes over long distances. Through trial and error routes were developed, in the interests of speed and safety, to include as much flat water paddling as possible on large rivers and lakes. A half-mile portage took the voyageurs an hour – or as much time as would be required to paddle six or more miles. The 25-foot long *canot du nord* had a depth of about 24 inches, the longer *canot de maître* 30 to 32 inches, and when fully loaded they had a freeboard of only six inches. The paddles and paddling techniques used in them were the most efficient to propel canoes of this size and shape for long distances over long periods of time. Voyageurs were often on the water before sunrise – at 2 a.m. – and worked sixteen or eighteen hours before stopping for the night at 9 or 10 p.m. It was crucial that they avoid excessive fatigue, and that they not spend too much energy over too short a period of time.

The result was that voyageurs used a small paddle, and a rapid cadence. The paddles of the six or eight middlemen of the *canot de maître* and the

A *canot de maître* is held off the bank by two men with poles while it is lined upstream by the rest of the crew. The scene on the Chats Rapids near Ottawa was painted by P. J. Bainbrigge in 1838.

three of four middlemen of a *canot du nord* were short, about four feet in length, and narrow, little more than four inches wide. In comparison, modern canoe paddles are normally five feet or more in length and at least five inches wide. The voyageur's paddle gave him 'low gearing.' He did not have to put as much energy into a single paddle stroke as a modern canoeist, but his cadence was faster. A modern canoeist normally paddles at a tempo of twenty-five to thirty strokes per minute; a voyageur made at least fifty and often sixty. His fast rhythm and easy paddle stroke were ideally suited to long hard days. The tempo also helped to maintain the momentum of the canoe, which had higher water resistance than modern canoes because of the numerous irregularities in the birch bark surface. The speed up and slow down created by the slow cadence of a large paddle would have been extremely wasteful of energy. Voyageur paddles were light, normally made out of spruce, cedar or basswood. A voyageur could make one in an hour or less with an axe and knife anywhere along the route.

The *avant*, or bowman, and *gouvernail*, or sternman, used paddles about six feet long in normal flat water, and eight or nine feet in rapids. These paddles were made of hardwood so that while thin in the handle they were strong. Even with paddles of this length, steering heavily laden canoes must have been a difficult business. The *avant* and *gouvernail* had to be as strong as oxen through the arms and shoulders. They were the most skilful and highly paid members of the crew.

The laws of naval architecture dictate that, other things being equal, a long boat travels faster than a short one. This was certainly true of the fur trade canoes. The daily distances and the speeds they achieved (see Chapter 5) cannot be equalled by even the best modern 17- and 18-foot canoes.

The speed, size and draught of these canoes also led to quirks. Alexander Mackenzie, the first white man to travel the arctic river which has been named after him, was perhaps the most accurate and detail-minded of all Canada's early explorers. His straightforward Scottish mind was not given to hobgoblins or other such flights of fancy, yet see how he described canoeing across Lac la Martre on the fur trade route between Grand Portage and Lake of the Woods:

In this part of the lake the bottom is mud and slime, with about three or four feet of water over it; and here I frequently struck a canoe pole of twelve feet long, without meeting any other obstruction than if the whole were water: it has, however, a peculiar suction or attractive power, so that it is difficult to paddle a canoe over it. There is a small space along the South shore, where the water is deep, and this effect is not felt. In proportion to the distance from this part, the suction becomes more

Voyageur paddles were shorter and narrower than
present ones, for fast easy strokes. The paddle in the
foreground is unusually long: probably it was for use in
the bow or stern. This photograph on the Red River
was one of the first taken in the west, during the
Assiniboine and Saskatchewan exploration led by H.Y.
Hind in 1858. Frances Hopkins was beginning her
series of paintings of the fur trade at the same time.
The *canot du nord* is being portaged in the normal
position, upright on the shoulders of two men.

powerful ... I have, myself, found it very difficult to get away from this attractive power, with six men, and great exertion, though we did not appear to be in any danger of sinking.[5]

Most commentators on Mackenzie's work have chosen either to ignore this passage or to regard it as evidence that even this sober, unimpressionable man was, on occasion, subject to delusions. There is, however, a much more straightforward explanation in the practical terms of naval architecture.

All surface craft create bow and quarter waves as they move through the water, and much of the energy of propulsion is dissipated into these waves. Creating the best interaction of the hull with them at various speeds is a major problem of ship and canoe design. When a moving ship enters shallow water, they begin to interact with the bottom. The waves at bow and stern increase in size and as they grow they increasingly impede the passage of the ship. The stern wave builds up to produce a trough under the quarters into which the stern sinks. These effects reduce the speed of the ship, and any increase in speed requires a great increase in propulsive force. The ship can begin to yaw and be difficult to steer. What Mackenzie observed was this 'shallow water effect.' It would have been all the more noticeable in a fur trade canoe moving from deep to shallow water in the middle of a lake, as Mackenzie's was. Modern canoes are too short, move too slowly, have too little draught, and create too small bow and stern waves to be subject to this effect on the same lake, although canoeists can experience it in water less than two feet deep, and avoiding drag in shallow water is a key to winning downriver races.

No record exists, written or related by an *avant* or *gouvernail*, of his paddling techniques and tactical decisions in running white water. Few voyageurs could read or write. The people who wrote about fur trade canoeing, like Alexander Henry, David Thompson and Mackenzie himself, were passengers in the large canoes. As a result, their descriptions of white water techniques tend to record the general facts of success or failure – whether the canoe was on top of, in, or under water at the end of a stretch – but little else. George M. Grant, the secretary to Sandford Fleming's expedition which searched for a railway route across Canada in 1872 (and a future principal of Queen's University) described shooting rapids on the Maligne River in a *canot de maître:*

Where the stream begins to descend, the water is an inclined plane, smooth and shining as glare ice. Beyond that, it breaks into curling, gleaming rolls which end off in white, boiling caldrons, where the water has broken on the rocks underneath. On

Running a Rapid on the Mattawa River, by Frances Hopkins, was used by George M. Grant as an illustration in his account of exploration, *Ocean to Ocean*. It accurately depicts the slow, careful progress down a chute. As in her painting of a larger canoe on page 21, the bowman is making a steering-cum-draw stroke.

the brink of the inclined plane, the motion is so quiet that you think the canoe pauses for an instant. The captain is at the bow – a broader, stronger paddle than usual in his hand – his eye kindling with enthusiasm, and every nerve and fibre in his body at its utmost tension. The steersman is at his post, and every man is ready. They know that a false stroke, or too weak a turn of the captain's wrist, at the critical moment, means death. A push with the paddles and, straight and swift as an arrow, the canoe shoots right down into the mad vortex; now into a cross current that would twist her broadside round, but that every man fights against it; then she steers right for a rock, to which she is being resistlessly sucked, and on which it seems as if she would be dashed to pieces; but a rapid turn of the captain's paddle at the right moment, and she rushes past the black mass, riding gallantly as a race horse. The waves boil up at the side, threatening to engulf her, but except a dash of spray or the cap of a wave, nothing gets in, and as she speeds into the calm reach beyond, all draw long breaths and hope that another rapid is near.[6]

In Frances Hopkins's meticulously detailed painting on page 21, as in the engraving reproduced on this page, the *avant* is standing in the bows and is about to perform a steering stroke. The stroke shown in the painting is called a 'cross' stroke because the paddle is on the opposite side of the canoe from where it would be in a normal paddling stroke. The *avant* could not be doing a draw, because that would not move a huge, heavily laden canoe to any useful extent. He must be doing a 'cross bow rudder.' This stroke and its opposite, the 'bow rudder' shown in the engraving, steer the canoe by the action of water deflected off the paddle blade as the craft moves forward. The canoe must have steerage way to make these rudder strokes work. The *gouvernail* in the stern is ready to make a more positive steering stroke by using his paddle as a pry with the gunwale as the fulcrum.

Loaded fur trade canoes could weigh over four tons. They were not very manoeuverable. The *avant* and *gouvernail* would have been over the route many times and would know the individual rocks and the different characteristics of the rapids at high and low water. But they did not need a great repertoire of strokes and techniques. Fur trade canoes were in effect aimed rather than manoeuvered down stretches of white water. The tactical decisions were the responsibility of the *avant*, but he could do little except point the bow where he wanted by rudder and pry strokes, with the canoe always having some forward momentum. He would be further restricted by the danger inherent in pry strokes, for his long paddle could easily catch under and damage the canoe, be damaged itself, or flip him out into the water. Many descriptions tell how in rapids the *avant* sought to keep the vessel in the *fil d'eau*, the thread of relatively smooth though fast water lying between the dangerous rocks and eddies on the one side and the equally dangerous large standing waves on the other. This demanded skill and experience. The middle men could paddle faster, or brake, but could do little to steer. The canoes were generally moved faster than the water to maintain steerage way. A very real disadvantage of this sort of paddling in white water is that it reduces the time available for corrective actions.

Fur trade canoes were very seaworthy, and could run heavy rapids which would swamp a modern sixteen-foot open canoe. In water which was too shallow or rock-filled for paddling, the large ones were guided downstream by snubbing with poles. They also often were poled upstream through fast, shallow water. But the great size necessary for efficient load carrying over long distances made them, in general, craft of limited adaptability to white water conditions, and ones in which fewer white water paddling techniques could be used than in the smaller, more manoeuverable, Indian canoes.

Many authors have misunderstood the roles of *avant* and *gouvernail*, and left the *avant* merely giving directions like a river pilot while the *gouvernail*,

Snubbing with poles was a slow, careful way to descend rapids – in this instance at Island Portage on the Missinaibi River, Ontario, in 1901.

like the helmsman in a steamboat, did the steering. Léo-Paul Desrosiers made this error in his classic, *Les Engagés du Grand Portage*. He described running rapids in a *canot de maître*: 'the second-in-command stationed himself on the gunwales in the bows to survey the course of the river from height, and from distance, to discover the best path. He moved his right and left hand in secret signals which the observer in the stern obeyed with care. The *milieux* kneeled in the bottom of the canoe, positioned in between the *pièces* [90 lb. bales of trade goods]; at command, they paddled with all their force. And the craft was propelled like a bullet between the boiling water and the eddies.'[7] Desrosiers was an editor of the debates of the Canadian House of Commons and was writing from book rather than first-hand knowledge.

Butler, who had actually been a passenger while a canoe shot rapids, was more accurate:

The Indian has got some rock or mark to steer by, and knows well the door by which he is to enter the slope of water. As the canoe - never appearing so frail and tiny as when it is about to commence its series of wild leaps and rushes - nears the rim where the waters disappear from view, the bowsman stands up and, stretching forward his head, peers down the eddying rush; in a second he is on his knees again;

A cedar strip canoe riding white water on the French River, Ontario.

without turning his head he speaks a word or two to those who are behind him; then the canoe is in the rim; she dips to it, shooting her bows clear out of the water and striking hard against the lower level. After that there is no time for thought; the eye is not quick enough to take in the rushing scene. There is a rock here and a big green cone of water there; there is a tumultous rising and sinking of snow-tipped waves; there are places that are smooth-running for a moment and then yawn and open up into great gurgling chasms the next; there are strange whirls and backward eddies and rocks, rough and smooth and polished – and through all this the canoe glances like an arrow, dips like a wild bird down the wing of the storm, now slanting from a rock, now edging a green cavern, now breaking through a backward rolling billow, without a word spoken, but with every now and again a quick convulsive twist and turn of the bow-paddle to edge far off some rock, to put her full through some boiling billow, to hold her steady down the slope of some thundering chute which has the power of a thousand horses . . . [8]

The voyageurs, like Indians and later woodsmen, found great delight in running rapids. Some white water stretches were forbidden to them by their masters because of the high risk of loss or wetting of trade goods, but nevertheless they would often run these rapids too. Thus the voyageurs, the Indians, and white woodsmen had developed white water canoeing to a high art, and modern river canoeists use age-old skills rather than recent innovations. Nevertheless, in 1950, S. C. Ells, an experienced Canadian outdoorsman, lamented that 'In Canada forty years ago the term "canoeman" implied ability to handle large and small canoes in white water. Today such is not the case.'[9] Ells was correct. White water canoeing skills had been forgotten in much of Canada by the middle of this century.

White Water Canoeing as an Aspect of Canadian Socio-Economic History

What went wrong? Why did white water canoeing techniques, once regarded as the best of canoeing and the epitome of the canoeist's skill, nearly become forgotten in Canada, the birthplace of the canoe? It was not because canoeing itself was dying out, for in 1950 thousands of young Canadians were being taught to canoe at summer camps, and white water canoeing was beginning its postwar surge in England and Europe. Many Indians and woodsmen moreover were still proficient in running rapids. The last Hudson's Bay Company fur brigades in northern Quebec had stopped only a few years earlier.

Nor did the decline occur because, as travellers of past centuries believed, the skills needed for white water canoeing were the birthright of the Indian 'races' or 'peoples' and could not be learned by whites. We now know that the gene pool of humanity is so large and mixed that there is more variety within any given 'race' of human beings than there is between 'races'. Each community of human beings begins from a similar genetic starting place; what determines human culture, technology, social structure, and to a large extent individual skills as well is not racial genetic inheritance but the processes of acculturation, socialization and training which affect the development of mature persons. Canadian Indians developed white water skills because these skills were necessary for their survival, and because they enjoyed and esteemed the challenge of white water, not because they had an inherited aptitude for white water canoeing. Northern woodsmen learned and used white water skills for the same reasons. The river canoeing skills required in the bush were not well transmitted to those who learned about canoeing as a leisure activity in the Canadian south, and who had little contact with the wilderness frontier. Canoeing and canoes became popular, but white water canoeing did not. Cultural traits like canoeing skills survive because they have a use, and are passed on to successive generations. They die out when they become obsolete and a new generation fails to learn them. The near death of white water skills was in part caused by obsolescence when the airplane replaced the canoe. It also, however, suggests a lack of contact between places and generations and is evidence of a strong discontinuity in the Canadian experience.

In large measure this discontinuity stemmed from the gap between the explorers and fur traders on the one hand, and the farming pioneers on the other. In the United States, western settlement passed through a sequence from the frontiersmen to small settlements of farmers and ranchers to the creation of the institutions of government. Over the great plains of the Mississippi and Missouri drainage basins this progress – from exploration to settlement to society – was continuous, and each phase was closely related to and dependent on the one which preceded it. But the Canadian experience was totally different. The fur trade, a specialized and highly organized form of economic exploitation, was the first white intrusion over most of the country. By the time settlement came to Ontario and the St Lawrence lowlands, the furtrade had long since left. Settlement in the wilderness of Upper Canada did not follow from the children of the fur-trade frontiersman; it came from immigration following two representatives of the Crown - the agent making treaties with the Indian and the surveyor laying out the rectangular grid of roads which still dominates the landscape. It is not far wrong to say that government came first to the Canadian frontier instead of last, as in the United States. There was little continuity between the fur trader who had travelled by canoe and the settler coming by road or ship.

Canada has had two kinds of frontier. One has been the frontier for the creation of society - the frontier of farming and settlement. The other has been the frontier of resource extraction - of fur trading, timber and mining. These two frontiers have been separate in space and time. Timber, mining, and furs belonged to the north, to the Precambrian Shield, to the country unsuitable for agricultural settlement. The fur trade began well before, mining and lumbering well after, the spread of agricultural settlement in the St Lawrence lowlands. The two frontiers have offered competing lifestyles and there has been a marked contrast in the kinds of people attracted to them. The settlers of the lowlands treated the forest as an enemy, not as a source of wealth. They cut down, burnt and destroyed some of the finest white pine and hardwood forests in North America to open the land for cultivation. Canada's timber trade developed only after these fertile lowlands were settled. The canoe was no part of this agricultural frontier. It belonged to the prospector, timber cruiser and fur trader of the north.

The fur trade was the main economic activity of the frontier for several centuries. Its expansion north and westwards established the geographical logic of Canada as a nation. But the fur trade did not lead to settlement. The route of expansion of the trade westwards bypassed the fertile lands of southern Ontario and the prairies. It went from Montreal up the Ottawa River, across the Mattawa-Lake Nippissing-French River route to Lake

By 1900 the fur trade had developed an elaborate transportation system unrelated to settlement. This photograph was taken by J. W. Tyrrell at Smith Portage during an exploratory survey between Great Slave Lake and Hudson Bay. The canoes are being carried on Red River carts, developed by the Métis on the prairies. The carts and oxen were there because this was a regular HBC route.

Huron, around Lake Superior, and on to the west. In 1821 the Hudson's Bay Company in London merged with the North West Company in Montreal. Even though in the previous years the bulk of the fur had been shipped via Montreal to Europe by the North West Company, the new coalition shipped goods more cheaply to and from the Canadian interior via the rivers of the Hudson Bay basin, further reducing the contact between settlement (in the east) and canoeing (in the north and west). Nor was the canoe used in settling the prairies. The cost of shipping farm produce and settlers' goods, even in canoes as large as the *canot de maître*, was far too high. Even for the fur trade the Hudson's Bay Company, for reasons of economy, where possible replaced canoes by York boats. Low-cost railway transport was essential before the prairies could be farmed.

Settlement in Canada's western plains was preceded by treaties with the Indians, by the railway, and by surveys for the grid which dominates the prairie landscape even more than that of Ontario. Treaty making, railway building and surveying were government activities. The one group which might have provided continuity between the fur traders and the settlers was the Métis, the cultural and blood descendants of the voyageurs and Indians. But they were defeated in war, had their settlement pattern destroyed by the surveyor's grid, and retreated into cultural isolation and economic impoverishment from which they have not yet emerged. The discontinuity in means of locomotion from fur trader to farmer was as profound as the discontinuity in language, economic lifestyle and cultural heritage.

As a result, in both Ontario and the west there was little contact between the fur traders who came by canoe and the farmers who came by road and railway. The majority of Canadians who lived in the settled south lost contact with the heritage of the fur trade era, including white water techniques and the exploits of travel in which these techniques have been employed.

Canadians were aware of the well publicized expeditions of Franklin and other Englishmen in search of the Northwest passage, but knew little of the much greater accomplishments of men like Hearne, Mackenzie and Thompson, who found the true passages to the Pacific and the north in some of the greatest overland journeys of all time. Many journals of Canadian exploration lay in oblivion in the records of the Hudson's Bay Company until J. B. Tyrrell uncovered and edited them for Champlain Society. Tyrrell, commenting in effect on the economic determinants of Canada's cultural development, suggested the reason for this neglect:

the fur trade of the country, which was its only tangible asset at that time, became centered in the hands of two great companies, and after the union of these companies in 1821, in the Hudson's Bay Company alone, which became a virtual monopoly with headquarters in London. Private enterprise was stifled, and the people of Canada, and in fact the whole of North America, lost touch with a country in which they had no commercial interest and in the trade of which they were not allowed to participate. Thus, while thrilling accounts of adventure in north-western America, such as Irving's *Astoria*, or Ross's *Fur Traders of the Far West*, might be read with interest, regardless of location, accounts of work done to promote a fuller knowledge of [Canada's north and west] were disregarded.[10]

Ignorance of Canadian history thus contributed to the lack of appreciation of the arts of canoeing.

This discontinuity, between exploration and the fur trade on the one hand and settlement on the other, was compounded by the peculiar geography of Canada. The canoe was essentially the means of communication over the lake and river laced northern wilderness of the Precambrian Shield. It was here that the white birch grew, and here that the beaver was trapped. Most agricultural settlement was to the south of the Shield, away from the land of the canoe. The cowboy on horseback has somewhat the same mythological significance to the United States as the voyageur in a canoe has to Canada, but there is a profound difference: the American farmers who first settled the

In the far north canoeing extended well into spring
and fall on the rushing water of streams and rivers,
when large lakes would be frozen. These canoeists had
reached Slave Lake and were forcing their way across.

west could see cowboys and horses at close hand around them; settlers in
Canada were many miles away from the country of voyageurs and canoes.
The continuity of experience in the United States has meant that cowboys
and horses have not only been mythological symbols, but that real horses, and
riders of horses, have continued to exist side by side with agricultural settlement. White water canoeing was only a mythological, not a visible, fact in
most of settled Canada.

Like riding, canoeing changed from work to leisure activity in the
twentieth century. But Canada, at least until the end of the second world war,
was not a fertile ground for leisure activities. In 1900, two-thirds of the population lived in the country. The demands of farming and tending animals
were so severe that little time was left for the dedicated pursuit of non-
essential pastimes: rural existence was even more than normally arduous
because much of Canada had been opened for farming at most only a few
generations before, and markets, means of transportation and farming techniques were still being developed. The first half of the century moreover was
filled with great perturbations which further impeded the refinement of
leisure activities. The first world war, as W. V. A. MacIntosh has remarked,
did not so much reorganize as disorganize the Canadian economy. It was

Canoeing became a leisure activity towards the end of
the nineteenth century. These young ladies on the
Muskego River of Ontario were obviously not
intending to run any rapids where there would be risk
of an unexpected swim.

58 The canoe and white water

followed by a brief depression. The boom of the twenties was succeeded by the depression of the thirties, and then by the mobilization of resources for the second world war which meant an almost complete neglect of leisure sport and cultural activities. While all this was going on, in the first sixty-five years of this century Canada changed from being two-thirds rural to three-quarters urban. The dislocations of this gigantic migration and readjustment again reduced the time and energy which could be directed to cultivating non-essential pleasures. It is little wonder that work skills of the northern bush like white water canoeing failed to become popular leisure activities of an economically harrassed and anxiety-ridden south. Art, higher education, science, and most sports suffered in the same way and Canadians are still paying the cost.

Guided canoeing and fishing trips became a form of recreation for well-off North Americans and Europeans but white water canoeing for excitement became more popular in England and Europe than in Canada. The persons who introduced canoeing and kayaking there, like John MacGregor with his *Rob Roy* in the nineteenth century and Gino Watkins in the twentieth, were members of an affluent class which had existed for centuries and survived the economic blows which damaged the nascent society of Canada. One of these Englishmen, R. M. Patterson, an Oxford graduate and former proba-tioner with the Bank of England, amused himself in the late 1920s by taking a sixteen-foot canoe up the Nahanni River. In the midst of the depression, when a large proportion of prairie farmers spent more in farming than they earned, Patterson took up ranching in Alberta, and for sport ran the Bow River from below the Ghost Dam to Calgary in his canoe:

Delighted with that, I ran it again – and then certain stretches of it again and again. There were some lively bits of river in that forty miles, and on them the canoe also seemed to come alive. One could come down a riffle – which is a chute through or around a shingle bar – and drive the canoe close alongside the big waves; or through them, riding wildly on the crest of the mane. On rare occasions, I would meet a Cana-dian Pacific passenger train crawling slowly up into the hills. Nobody ever used that river; and the unexpected sight of a canoe never failed to cause a furore on board the train. Cries of delight would come from the observation car and a rush would be made for cameras. That was the time to give them their money's worth – and an extra drive on the paddle would lift the fore end of the canoe far out of the water as it leapt over some big wave. Then would come the smack and the flying spray as the canoe came down again, to land on the next wave and repeat the performance. Quite apart from the fun of showing off, there is a thrill about that which I have only found equalled when riding a fast horse and trying to corral a bunch of wild and obstreperous horses.[11]

Few Canadians in the thirties, were thinking or feeling like that, or doing anything comparable. A more Canadian style, and as interesting and sensitive a document in its own way as Patterson's, is the book *North to Cree Lake*, which describes how two young brothers left their depression home on the prairie in 1932 to spend seven winters as trappers in the northern Saskatchewan bush, in an area J. B. Tyrrell had been the first civilized man to explore forty years earlier. The Karras brothers exhausted their energy in simply surviving. Running a piece of white water time and time again for the exhilaration of the experience, or to show off for the passengers on a train, was totally outside their frame of reference.

Canoeing in rapid waters did become part of leisure activity in the maritimes, especially in New Brunswick and the Gaspé, where it was an adjunct of salmon fishing. Maritime salmon fishing, however, was very much an upper class sport, and fishermen in canoes were accompanied by guides. The guide paddled, poled and portaged. The fisherman was a passenger. The sport was in the fishing, not the canoeing. In central Canada the CPR and other groups ran guided canoeing and fishing trips, but as in the maritimes the fishermen normally were passengers.

The main instrument for encouraging recreational canoeing in Canada has been summer camps for children, and it is indicative of the slow development of leisure activities in Canada that the early camps in Algonquin Park were run by Americans for Americans. Most of them were associated with private boys' schools, frequently military academies. Summer camps for Canadians, however, gradually were established after the turn of the century, and have expanded greatly in recent decades.

These camps have done an excellent job of teaching the basic essentials of flat water canoeing to generations of girls and boys, and have given the same clientele some experience of wilderness canoeing; but few, with the exception of northern Ontario tripping camps, did much to teach white water techniques until recent years. Quite the opposite, the camps of Algonquin Park cautioned the same girls and boys that the canoe is a dangerous tool, and white water is to be feared. 'Safety rules in factories,' a popular canoeing manual written by a staff member of an Algonquin camp in the forties warned, 'stress the word *Don't* to keep persons from getting caught in machines or having their fingers chopped off. It is with this in mind that we list the things that a person must not do in a canoe – if he wishes some day to tell his grandchildren what a great canoeman he was.'[12] Two of the Don'ts were: 'Don't stand up in a canoe,' and 'Don't shoot rapids.' This manual overlooked the fact that standing in a canoe – to pole, or to survey white

Indian guides and fisherman near Lake Nipigon,
Ontario - the sport was in the fishing, not the canoeing,
and the man from the south had no real experience in
handling the canoe.

water – is often essential. It also ignored the great pleasure that can be found in white water canoeing. Perhaps Canadian camp leaders did not know in the thirties and forties that white water canoeing competitions were attracting hundreds of entrants in Europe, many of the same age as Canadian summer campers.

This attitude can be partly explained by the purpose and style of the Algonquin region summer camps. They were, and are, normally large organizations with room for a hundred or more youngsters who stay for only two weeks or a month. In that short period, and as only one part of their program, they teach as many campers as possible some basics of canoeing. In their own interests the camps must be assured of very low risks to children and property, must set standards low enough that the average youth can get the satisfaction of meeting them, and must teach by methods suitable for large numbers. They are in effect the elementary schools of canoeing skills. The challenge of white water is at high school level – and beyond. In contrast, the camps of the Temagami region emphasized wilderness river travel, as did many American camps that could afford a high staff-to-camper ratio to ensure safety.

The men who first taught canoeing skills to Algonquin campers were old-time guides who lived in the Park and nearby towns. Some were competent in white water, but little advantage was taken of this. Instructors at the camps took the guides' canoeing skills apart into the component paddle strokes, classified, analyzed and described them, but did not put them back together for effective practical use. As a result, Algonquin campers learned some canoe strokes which are used primarily in white water, like the draw and pry, but were told to avoid the fast water in which they would be valuable. Many other aspects of good white water technique were neglected, including the art of using eddies and currents, the manipulation with the knees of canoe balance, standing, poling, or working as a team in complicated rapids – to name a few. Algonquin Park is not a good place to learn these skills. Most rapids on the Petawawa, the main river within its boundaries, are too difficult for beginners, as are those on the two rivers closest to its southern boundaries, the Oxtongue and the Upper Madawaska. The tragedy is that, according to one recent estimate, 80 per cent of the people of Ontario who are interested in canoeing started, developed or continued their activities in Algonquin Park and, consequently, have not had the benefit of good training grounds for white water canoeing.

But lessons even more important than white water were also neglected. Like salmon fishing in the maritimes, summer camping in the Park was in large part an activity for the well-off. The founder and head of a prominent Algonquin girls' camp wrote that after her first experience in carrying a canoe on a portage she 'resolved that if I ever owned a camp, no one but a guide accustomed to the task would carry one, definitely not a camper.'[13] No one has ever said that portaging a canoe is easy, but it is not impossible, even for young girls. Many women carry canoes on portages; two or four girls or boys can carry a canoe if it is too difficult for one. These girls were learning how to be taken on a guided canoe trip, not how to make a trip by themselves. They would have had to marry strong husbands, or rich ones, if they were to continue canoe camping as adults. Much of the virtue of the canoe is its portability. Youths who did not learn that with care and patience one or two people can carry and paddle a canoe virtually anywhere were being deprived of the self-reliance and independence that go with the sport. Now, fortunately, this camp, like most others, lets campers perform their share of the work.

Contributing to the fear of white water was a misunderstanding of how to run it, shared by camp leaders, the writers of textbooks on canoeing, and many popular writers, including Grey Owl. A wilderness manual of the forties stated: 'Once you have made up your mind to run the rapids, your approach to them should not be slow – but fast – from the quiet water. The speed of the canoe must be faster than the rapids if steering control is to be had.'[14] This was bad advice. Going faster than the current is acceptable in some white water, but in much it is poor technique. Fast movement in rapids, as in car driving and skiing, makes problems more difficult to solve because there is less time to think and act between events. Speed also makes the bow of the canoe dig into waves, and leads to reliance on passive and slow steering strokes rather than quick, positive draws and pries to move the canoe sideways. This misguided approach to white water – in part a relic of the fur trade when steerage way was essential – became widely accepted in North America. Artists who wanted to depict voyageurs in white water usually copied Frances Hopkins's *Running the Rapids*, but showed the crew paddling full speed downstream rather than, as Hopkins had, moving forward with caution. Like Desrosiers, they had no actual experience with white water canoeing. Schoonover's pictures in the popular press, drawn like his canoes from his inaccurate memories, also showed the bad style of a headlong downstream rush.[15]

The combination of this misunderstanding, the geography of Algonquin Park, and the emphasis on flat water canoeing at most summer camps, has meant that for several generations most central Canadians of the class which had the leisure to explore the challenges of canoeing to their frontiers were

This over-dramatized painting, *Chief Trader McDonald Descending the Fraser*, must have been done in the studio, and the artist, A. Sherriff Scott, likely had never actually descended rapids in a large canoe. It obviously was derived from Frances Hopkins's earlier paintings. However, the canoe is being paddled far too quickly and would be likely to swamp.

instead discouraged from trying white water and wilderness river canoeing. This has gradually changed, but as recently as 1974 a book on Algonquin Park included the admonition that running rapids was 'what not to do.'[16] In the United States, camps were bolder in teaching white water skills, and many required them as part of their tests in canoeing.

White water canoeing never completely died out. In 1950, as today, some northern Indians and woodsmen still used canoes on rivers, and used them properly. Some canoeing texts, including the excellent American National Red Cross *Canoeing* (1956) analyzed and described accurately and in detail the techniques of handling a canoe in fast water. Then, in the late fifties, white water canoeing began to revive.

The Revival

An important part of the revival was a series of trips along the old voyageur routes taken by a group of eminent Canadians, among them a major general, the Dutch ambassador to Canada, the president of the Canadian Bank Note Company, the executive director of the Association of Canadian Clubs, and the future prime minister of Canada, Pierre Elliott Trudeau. Many of these trips were written up for newspapers and magazines by their participants, including the fine journalist Blair Fraser (who later died in a canoeing accident on the Petawawa). Sigurd Olson's *The Lonely Land* described a 500-mile trip taken by six of this group down the historic Churchill River. The enthusiasm of these middle-aged men in not simply enduring but enjoying long days of cold and wet, in running rapids, and in plain hard work, was a healthy antidote to the common phobia of white water. At a time when most of their contemporaries were beginning to regard tennis as hard work, this group put wilderness canoeing in its proper perspective. 'There were no heroics in our travel and we took few chances, believing that desperate adventures were the result of lack of knowledge and foolhardiness,' Olson commented. 'To those who have never been in the bush or traversed the wilderness hinterlands by canoe, our expedition might seem like a formidable undertaking, while to old-timers just as to the voyageurs of the past, it would be merely a routine trek.'[17] Such accounts also linked Canadians of the present to the age of the voyageurs. Eric Morse's *Fur Trade Canoe Routes of Canada/Then and Now*[18] was one of the products, and has encouraged Canadians to explore their history and land. After a half century of adversity, the thirty years of relatively uninterrupted prosperity which have followed the second world war created, for the first time in Canada, a fertile ground for the cultivation of leisure activities.

But the real stimulus to modern white water canoeing came from Britain and Europe. The man who first showed the British that kayaks could be used for more than straightforward paddling was Gino Watkins, an adventurer of the same mould as Franklin and Scott. Watkins organized and led his first Arctic expedition before he graduated from Cambridge. Later he led expeditions to Labrador, which he explored by canoe, and to Greenland where, between 1930 and 1933, he learned from the Eskimos the art of handling a kayak. Watkins' adventures added less to knowledge of geography than those of men like J. B. Tyrrell, but they achieved great renown largely, one suspects, because they were conducted in a good British style of casual, effortless superiority. Watkins may be the only man who has succeeded in preserving an Edwardian elegance while in a kayak. His main contribution to Arctic exploration was that he, like Stefansson and Hearne, adopted the ways of the Inuit. This enabled him to travel light and to live off the land and sea in a way that Franklin's ill-fated expeditions could not. He was one of the first Europeans to learn to do the Eskimo roll in a kayak. The publicity he received encouraged others to explore the possibilities in rough water of kayaker, kayak and paddle operating as a close-fitting, completely co-ordinated unit made watertight by a spray skirt joining man to craft.

The second world war slowed kayak development, but in 1949 the first world kayak white water slalom championships were held on the Rhone at Geneva. Slalom racers at first used normal flat water strokes. Wide beams and low centres of gravity made the kayaks stable. Little thought was given to improving paddling techniques until 1953, when a Czech paddler, Milo Duffek, adapted the traditional draw strokes of Canadian canoeists to kayaks in a revolutionary way. Duffek had been a world champion in covered C1 slalom racing. After he adapted the racing C1 strokes to the kayak, he became the world champion in kayak slalom as well.

The Duffek kayaking strokes leave one paddle blade waving high in the air, while the kayak itself is tilted so that it turns rapidly on its sharply rockered side. The paddle is used as an instrument of stability during sharp turns and in rough water. These techniques, combined with specially designed fibreglass slalom kayaks, made possible the modern white water style of sharp leans, fast turns into and out of eddies, and the utilization of eddies and standing waves to help the kayaker manoeuver in heavy water. In fact, it is not strictly accurate to call this style 'modern,' for many Indian bands in northern Canada had used the techniques of leans for centuries. The Duffek approach has however been brought to Canada by immigrants from Europe. In other words, techniques first developed by Indians in this country have reached Canadian canoeists by a circuitous route via Europe and kayakers.

Under the stimulus of new blood and new ideas, clubs and other groups have begun to explore the possibilities of white water canoeing in the settled south. Today's adventurers are not the MacGillivrays and Mackenzies of old, but the Mascheks and Kerckhoffs. Canoeing to them does not always mean arduous long-distance travel into the wilderness. They now actively seek out white water as the most interesting and challenging sort of canoeing, and often find their favourite waters close to home. Slalom races can be held only close to civilization where strong support staff and good safety precautions can be provided.

With this healthy impetus, canoeing has become more varied. Like mountaineering routes, canoeing routes are now graded and the skills, experience and safety are related to level of difficulty (see Chapter 4). To many families, and to youngsters at many summer camps, white water canoeing now is a source of great pleasure and children play in rapids that would have made yesterday's campers tremble. Clubs and schools have winter training practices in swimming pools, where canoeists from high school age up learn to do the Eskimo roll and to move canoes and kayaks around slalom gates in complicated patterns which demand advanced strokes and techniques. Groups like the Ontario Voyageur's Kayak Club maintain a regular schedule of weekend trips from April to October, on rivers within a few hours' driving distance of Canada's largest centres of population. Many races are held throughout April and May in southern Canada when the swollen rivers are best for white water canoeing.

There are still too few qualified and experienced instructors, but this is changing. Canoeing has become more democratic and less the preserve of the classes which can afford summer camps for their children. It is not an expensive sport. Expanded incomes and increased time for leisure have made it possible for most Canadians to own, and use, a canoe or kayak. Increased activity has improved the sport, much as the postwar popularity of mountaineering encouraged the development of new techniques and better training there. Because the modern canoeist knows and understands white water and his own strengths and limitations better than his predecessors did, canoeing has become more interesting and safer.

The new white water techniques and stronger fibreglass canoes have opened up new frontiers for canoeing close to the largest cities. A provincial government report on the Moira River Valley, west of Kingston, Ontario, stated in 1950 that 'There are few attractive canoe routes in the watershed, due to the steep gradients of the rivers. The Black River falls 650 feet in 36 miles, the Skootamatta 740 in 46 miles, and the Moira 850 in 90 miles.'[19] Now the Black, the Skootamatta and the Moira are considered among the best spring canoeing rivers in southern Ontario. The same qualities of fast water, rapids and drops which made these rivers unsuitable by the standards of 1950 make them attractive today; each May a downriver race is held on the most difficult part of the Moira. But the rivers of the north also have become more crowded than they were even in fur trade days. Many hundreds of people canoed down the historic Albany River to James Bay in 1974. There are now more canoes in Canada, and more Canadians canoe, than ever before.

Technology and social organization in Canada have advanced to the point where most people can choose to devote a large portion of their time and energy to voluntary leisure activities. The Canadian and North American custom has been to exercise these choices in the direction of expanded consumption of consumer goods, and in activities like motor boating, air travel and downhill skiing, which necessarily entail a large consumption of resources and energy. Worldwide shortages of resources, the energy crisis, and the environmental problems caused by large-scale resource consumption all indicate that this pattern of economic growth cannot continue. One of the dangerous absurdities of modern economics is that activities like canoeing and cross country skiing, which do not consume much in the way of goods or services, are not adequately accounted for in measures of economic welfare like the gross national product. As a result, a worker who takes a week off to go canoeing, instead of working overtime to buy a second television set, counts as a loss to the GNP regardless of the value of his choice to himself or to the world. Nevertheless, white water and wilderness canoeing are taking their place as ways of using leisure to achieve satisfaction on many different levels. Canoeing makes it possible for Canadians to recreate, for themselves, part of their heritage; it lets them see their countryside from a different angle; and it enables them, if they want, to explore new frontiers in themselves by developing their physical and mental capacities to the utmost. The resurgence of canoeing is a healthy sign of growing maturity in Canadian social and economic values.

Paddle Strokes for White Water

White water paddle strokes for open canoes have two functions: to move the canoe sideways, and to turn it. They do not move the canoe forwards through the water, nor do they usually steer it.

Modern white water paddles have huge blades for extra power. This one is made of fibreglass and epoxy resin and is stronger than steel.

Modern white water canoeists tend to use paddles with larger blades than those of touring canoeists. Often the blade is as much as nine inches wide by twenty-two inches long, with an overall paddle length of five or five and a half feet. The large blade gives the paddler the power he needs to move the canoe quickly with as few strokes as possible. White water paddles are not good for touring, however, and it is not unusual for canoeists on river trips to carry two sets of paddles for the two different kinds of water. Because at least one extra paddle is essential as a safety precaution, this adds only the weight of one more paddle. White water kayak paddle blades usually are slightly smaller than canoe paddle blades, but are much larger than those of Eskimo kayakers, which were about two inches wide and two feet long. Eskimoes would paddle their kayaks fifty miles a day in hunting seals, and a small blade was suitable for steady long distance paddling for them, as for the voyageurs. Modern white water paddles are made out of laminated wood, aluminum and plastic, or fibreglass and resin. Canoeists look for the best mixture of durability and good feel. Wood is still a favourite. Some of the best paddles are made of fibreglass and epoxy, with shafts of aluminum tubing covered with epoxy-fibreglass. They are stronger than steel, and as expensive as they are strong.

White water paddle strokes are quick and positive. They are not generally steering strokes which rely on the action of moving water hitting the paddle blade to move the canoe, but active strokes which move the canoe through the water by the force of the stroke. In executing some the paddler leans far over the side of the canoe – to the point where he would fall over without the positive force of his stroke against the water as a support. Balance and support during stroke execution are essential parts of the art. The canoe, paddler, paddle and water form a series of interlocked stresses, supports and forces. The canoeist controls the canoe with his knees (which in covered craft are held in place with straps) and moves it to or away from his paddle in the water. Canoeists always kneel in their canoes in white water. Kayakers sit with their feet braced against a footrest, their knees braced by straps or supports, and their bottoms tightly fitted into a bucket seat.

Most white water strokes are used in both one- and two-man craft. In two-man canoes, the strokes are used in combinations. Bow and stern can paddle in the same direction to move the canoe sideways through the water, for example, or in opposite directions to turn the canoe around. Paddlers use a variety of strokes in sequence to guide their craft in rough water, and good paddlers select the appropriate sequences so that the finish of one stroke leaves them prepared for the next. This avoids the delays involved in stroke preparation – and time saved can be crucial when fast manoeuvering is needed. Good canoeists also try, if possible, to avoid shifting their paddles from one side to the other in white water so as to save the time needed to move the paddle over the top of the canoe, and they tend to keep their paddles in the water so as to be always ready to make a stroke.

The same paddle strokes have been given different names by various experts. The total number of different strokes in books is over two dozen, with very fine differences between some. This confusion is understandable because good white water paddlers not only have command of a full range of strokes but also vary the execution of each stroke depending on water conditions, the strokes which went before, and those to follow. Many strokes can shade imperceptibly into others: a draw can be a brace, a low brace a reverse sweep, a rudder a draw.

This is my own preferred short list of white water strokes for open canoes for thinking about, learning, and practising.

Back Paddling This is simply paddling the canoe backwards, in reverse. White water running frequently demands extended back paddling, during which the canoe must be kept on a proper heading – either parallel to or at a

A bow draw stroke.

slight angle to the current. A bow and stern team who intend to run white water should practise back paddling in still water and easy river stretches until they are thoroughly familiar with the problems of steering a canoe in reverse.

Draw The draw stroke is used to pull the canoe towards the paddle. It moves the canoe sideways. The blade is parallel with the canoe, and the paddler leans out to the side, puts the paddle nearly vertically into the water, and pulls it towards him. He must be careful not to catch it under the canoe at the finish of the stroke. The paddler can lean well out of the canoe while doing a draw, and rely on the power of the stroke to support him. A well-done draw stroke has a strong righting and stabilizing effect on the canoe. Often canoeists open the blade of the paddle towards the bow when making a draw while the canoe is moving forwards in the water. This produces a rudder action which further helps move the canoe, and slows it down. The draw is an important and powerful stroke for any sort of white water canoeing. It is used by both bow and stern. Recovery is either just above or under the water. In open canoes the paddler often will have to make a sequence of several draw strokes before the canoe has moved to where he wants it.

CANOE

Bow

Stern

Indicates angle of paddle blade
and direction of its motion

Draw Stroke

Pry

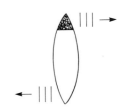

Sculling draw

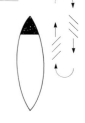

Hanging draw

72   The canoe and white water

Cross Draw The cross draw is a draw stroke made on the opposite side of the canoe, without changing the position of the hands on the paddle. It fulfils the same function as a draw, but because it is difficult for the canoeist to lean out in a cross draw the stroke has less supporting or bracing virtue. A bowman moving from draw to cross draw in white water with his paddle flashing from side to side in the sunlight is a handsome sight. The cross draw is a common white water stroke. It has disadvantages however: it is not generally as powerful as the draw, it does little to stabilize the canoe, and it creates delays and problems of adjusting balance as the paddle moves from side to side. The cross draw is a bow stroke.

Pry In the pry the gunwale or side of the canoe is used as a fulcrum and the paddle as a lever to move the canoe sideways. Power is put on the side of the blade which normally faces forward (the wrong side) as opposed to the normal power side (right side) which is used in draw strokes. In effect the pry is the opposite of a draw, moving the canoe away from the paddle. The pry tends to dip the gunwale of the canoe towards the water, and at the beginning or end of recovery from the stroke the paddle can get caught under the canoe. Pry strokes are safer, and more common, for the stern than the bow, but many bowmen favour the pry over the cross draw because with the pry there is no need to shift sides. A bowman should not use the pry in shallow water where the paddle may catch on rocks or the bottom, because this can easily lead to a quick upset.

Sculling Draw The sculling draw is a sequence of short forward and backward underwater strokes made with the paddle at an angle to the water, the combined effect of which moves the canoe sideways towards the paddle. It is especially useful for a single canoeist or a sternman who wants to move sideways slowly and carefully. It can have a strong supporting effect – so much that kayakers and C1 canoeists can put their elbow, shoulder and ear in the water while doing a sculling draw. Because the blade is always in the water, and always moving, it leaves the canoeist well prepared for a change of stroke. It can also move the canoe forwards or backwards. It is a right side of paddle stroke.

Hanging Draw This is primarily a stroke for a single paddler or stern man. The paddler leans well out and back, and draws the paddle towards him at an angle. A single stroke can move the canoe three feet sideways or more. The hanging draw has a strong supporting action. It is especially effective

Low brace

High brace

Sweep

Reverse sweep

74   The canoe and white water

when the canoe is moving through the water, or when it is used to move the canoe sideways through a current differential into a small eddy. It is a right side of paddle stroke.

Low Brace The low brace is a support stroke. It is a wrong side of paddle stroke, in which the paddle is extended at right angles to the canoe and thrust down with the outside hand. This gives enormous leverage which is used to balance the canoe and upright it when an upset is impending. The low brace can be a quick slap on the water. The stern man especially gains great power to use his knees to adjust the lean of the canoe. It is one of the most important recent additions to white water canoeing.

High Brace The high brace is very much like the draw except that its purpose is to right and support the canoe rather than move it sideways. The blade is put into the water at more of an outward angle than for the draw. It is a right side of paddle stroke. The high brace is especially useful in singles covered canoeing and kayaking, where it melds into draw, steering and combination strokes.

Sweep In a sweep stroke the paddle is extended forward, parallel to the canoe, and the right side of the blade is moved in the arc of a circle towards the stern. The sweep is primarily a turning stroke, but it also imparts some forward motion to the canoe. A single paddler can move his paddle through 180 degrees during a sweep. In doubles the sweep is normally used by the bowman, who moves his paddle 90 degrees until it is at right angles to the canoe. The paddler can lean towards the paddle as he makes a sweep, and when tilted on its edge the canoe, because it has more rocker, turns very easily and quickly.

Reverse Sweep This is the opposite of a sweep, and is used, in a double canoe, by the stern man. It is a wrong side of paddle stroke which begins with the paddle extended behind and parallel to the canoe. The paddle is then moved forward in the arc of a circle. A single paddler can move his paddle 180 degrees, the stern man in a team 90 degrees. The reverse sweep has the opposite effect from the sweep. It also slows the canoe down. If the bowman and sternman perform a sweep and reverse sweep at the same time on opposite sides, the two strokes complement each other to spin the canoe around. A reverse sweep can be combined with a low brace by the sternman to produce a stroke which lifts the stern of the canoe and moves it sideways. In Britain this is sometimes called a 'low telemark.'

Steering Strokes Canoeing books often include many varieties of 'cuts' and 'rudder' strokes in which the paddle is held in a constant position and angle, and the canoe is steered by the action of moving water against a stationary blade. These strokes require fast forward canoe motion through the water to be effective. They have their place, but they are not good basic white water strokes in open canoes. They are slow, passive, and demand steerage way. They have no stabilizing effect: to the contrary, those which push the paddle against the canoe, especially in the bow, can lead almost inevitably to upset if the blade catches on the bottom. Steering strokes had their use for the voyageurs in their huge unwieldy fur trade canoes, but the world would be a better place if modern canoeists did not learn them until after they had mastered every other stroke.

Many other strokes and combination strokes are used in white water canoeing in covered canoes and kayaks. One of these, the original 'Duffek' stroke, is called the 'high telemark' by British writers. It is a high draw-brace-steering stroke in which the craft is leaned strongly and turned, taking advantage of current differentials in moving into an eddy. The Colorado Hook, a kayak stroke, begins with a cross-bow rudder followed by a low telemark on the same side with the other paddle blade, concluded with a bow draw which leaves the kayaker ready for a strong forward thrust after his fast 180-degree turn. Modern racers prefer a forward sweep-Duffek combination to the Colorado Hook. Paddlers in slalom canoes and kayaks can turn their craft quickly and easily, and tend to emphasize the steering component more than do paddlers in the heavier open canoes. Paddlers right a kayak after an upset by using an Eskimo roll, which is easy to learn in a few hours with good instruction. The roll can be done in covered C1s and C2s, but is harder to learn for these craft than for a kayak. The ability to do an Eskimo roll makes practice in any sort of water safer and pleasanter, and learning the roll is now an essential early part of kayak and C1 training.

A reverse sweep. The paddler is Gisela Grothaus, three-times woman world champion downriver kayaker racer.

Learning to do the Eskimo roll in a winter pool training session. This time the paddler did not right himself, but after a few hours' practice he could. The roll is not difficult, and it makes paddling much safer and easier.

THREE

Turbulence and river tactics

White water occurs when a combination of turbulence and obstacles mix the river water with air. Sometimes the mixture can be as much as sixty per cent air, which impairs flotation and paddling. Obstacles are usually rocks – hard and easy to understand. Turbulence on the other hand is a complex phenomenon that is not well understood even by scientists.

Turbulence means both violent motion and disorganized motion. These are not always the same thing. Violent turbulence in rivers can be very organized and clearly patterned or it can be disorganized and confused, and disorganized turbulence can often be found in apparently tranquil flow. The kind of turbulence of most concern to the canoeist is the violent kind, organized or disorganized. Turbulence, furthermore, can rotate about both vertical and horizontal axes, giving complicated movements of the water in three dimensions. In rivers the flow of water is always turbulent, and the wide range of variations in configurations of river bed and volume and speed of water creates the equally wide variety of turbulence encountered by canoeists in white water. The kind of turbulence found in little streams and brooks is the same in causes, patterns and effects on floating objects as that found in the largest cataracts and rivers. Large rivers have only bigger, not different, turbulence. A canoeist can learn a great deal about flowing water and objects in it by floating leaves and twigs down brooks too small for canoeing – making them, in effect, his own scale models.

A fundamental distinction between 'streaming' and 'shooting' flow is important. Anybody who has used a fast motorboat, sailed a fast dinghy, or water skiied knows that there is an enormous difference between the interaction of the hull of the boat with the water when it is plowing through the water at low speed and when it is planing over the surface at high speed; or between the skiing when the water skis are pushing through the water as the skier starts and the way they skim over the surface when he is up. At the lower speeds the water streams around the boat or water skier and fills

Artists (in this case Cornelius Krieghoff) who do not understand turbulence and have no experience of rapids make white water into a seething, formless maelstrom. That is how it looks to them. Canoeists must learn to 'read' white water – to discern the underlying patterns of the different kinds of turbulence that make it up.

in behind; at the faster speeds the water does not flow around but under the boat or skis. This difference in the behaviour of water at low and high speeds is important in canoeing, not because a canoe can plane like a motor boat – it can't because paddlers cannot produce enough power – but because it creates much of the complex turbulence of rapid and white water. When the water in a river or brook is moving slowly it runs around rocks and other obstacles, but when it is moving faster it climbs up and over them. The speed of the water itself (just as the speed of the boat or skis over still water) reaches and passes a critical velocity at which, in the language of fluid dynamics, it goes from a *streaming* to a *shooting* mode of behaviour. The flow in rivers is usually in the streaming phase. It changes to the shooting phase when the water reaches a high velocity over sharp drops or in rapids.

The differences between the behaviour of water in its shooting and streaming phases, and the kinds of turbulence created when water moves from one phase to the other, are crucial in reading rapids. Most books on white water state that rocks lying just below the surface will hump up the water flowing over them. But only when the water is in its less common shooting phase will it 'hump up' and create rock-stuffed pillows and cushions of water. When it is in its more usual streaming phase its level is actually

The canoeists are running rapids below Oxford House,
an HBC post in northern Manitoba, in 1910. The water is
changing from sub-critical to critical as it drops into
the hole in the centre. The white water below the little
drop marks where it returns to sub-critical, and it
remains sub-critical as it enters the pool below the
rapids. The canoeists are following a clear channel on
the right of the white water. This they could pick out
from above the rapids because it would look like a
smooth, down-pointing vee of black water. It looks as
though there is also a channel to the left of the white
water. The canoeists are about to hit some standing
waves where the water in their channel loses velocity
at the bottom of the rapids.

This water is super-critical, in its shooting phase. Notice the curious, dark, pock-marked surface of the water, and how it shoots up to the wader's knees even though it is only a few inches deep. The water's velocity, from right to left, was more than four miles per hour.

lowered by an obstacle. Moreover, at the point where the flow moves from streaming to shooting the water's level is lowered, and the level is raised when it returns. The two phases can be identified by eye. Where there is white water and confused surface turbulence the flow is sub-critical and streaming. Where it is smooth and black, and the surface turbulence apparently disappears, it has reached its super-critical shooting phase. The flow returns to streaming phase abruptly, with great churning, standing waves, and white water. The white water, which is sub-critical, moves slowly, and the fastest parts of the flow are in the accompanying deep black chutes and channels in the shooting phase.

In the study of fluid dynamics, whether the flow is in a 'sub-critical' streaming phase or a 'super-critical' shooting phase depends on the value of a dimensionless parameter known as the 'Froude Number' after a pioneer Victorian naval architect. The formula which determines the value of the Froude Number is $F = \dfrac{V}{\sqrt{gD}}$ where

F = Froude Number
V = velocity
g = gravity (32 ft/sec^2)
D = depth of the water

A Froude Number of 1 is the point at which water changes from streaming to shooting. The water does not need to be moving fast to reach this point. With a depth of one foot the critical velocity is only 3.8 miles per hour, with a depth of two feet 5.5 miles per hour, and with a depth of ten feet 12.2 miles per hour. Such velocities are often reached in rivers, and speeds of four to six miles an hour are common in rapids. Flows of ten miles an hour are very rare, however, and the top speed recorded is only slightly over twenty miles an hour. Even in waterfalls the top speed, because of air resistance, does not exceed twenty miles per hour. These calculations, which can be easily supported by studying actual flow, help to explain why rapids are so complex, for in them, in countless places as it falls over ledges and down inclines and rushes over and around rocks, the flow moves back and forth between streaming and shooting phases, between sub- and super-critical velocities.

A canoeist sees only the surface of the water as he inspects a rapid, but turbulence is not just a surface phenomenon. The patterns on the surface are visible products of the complex movement of water in three dimensions, and give only bare suggestions about the conditions below, the speed, turbulence and depth of water, and the location and size of rocks and other obstructions. At different depths in the same spot water can not only be changing velocity but even be moving in opposite directions, and a canoeist must be aware of such complicated patterns because it is their cumulative impact that determines what happens to canoe, paddler and paddle. Paddling on one side of a canoe in some forms of turbulence can easily lead to a quick upset, while paddling on the other has a strong bracing effect. One good way to learn to understand the complexities of turbulence is to walk or even swim through easy rapids. But the only way, ultimately, is through canoeing experience.

River Tactics

The many varieties of turbulence encountered in rivers can be reduced to a small number of typical situations, each of which demands its own appropriate tactics. The white water canoeist must learn to 'read' the water. This means that he must be able to identify, from the patterns he sees on the water's surface, what is happening in the three-dimensional movement of the water below, and classify it as one of the typical situations. He must also look for a linked series of situations which show him where he can manoeuver through the rapids. If he is in an open canoe he will normally be concerned primarily with finding a safe passage so that he can run the rapids. Good paddlers in covered craft like to linger in the rapids, and so are apt to look especially for the kinds of turbulence in which they can play. The art of reading water is gained by trying, and through experience developing understanding of the inner significance of the outward and visible signs that flowing water presents to the onlooker. The ability and the experience is usually purchased at a high price, and few good canoeists or kayakers have not on occasion damaged their craft seriously or often found themselves unexpectedly dumped into the river. Scrapes on the bottoms of canoes and kayaks are badges of honour earned in the field.

The proper procedure when running a new piece of river is to land above a stretch of rapids and get out and look it over before deciding whether to run, line (guide the craft down the rapids by means of a line from the shore) or portage (carry it overland). Sometimes experienced canoeists can, without landing, look over a rapid while the canoe is safely above it and pick out a path through one piece of fast water to a pool or eddy below, where the canoe can rest while the next stretch is studied. Three or four short runs may be made in this way before a portage proves unavoidable or the rapids ends. Standing up in the canoe is helpful and even necessary to identify dangers and clear passages.

In a two-man canoe, the bowman is normally the tactician. He is closest to and can best see the patterns in the water in front of the canoe, and he moves the bow sideways with pries, draws and sweeps. Normally a two-man open canoe is kept parallel to the current, facing downstream, and the stern man moves his end of the canoe sideways in response to the initiative of the bowman. With two experienced paddlers, it is largely a matter of individual preference who takes bows and stern. But when one paddler is experienced and the other is a novice, even in rapids the novice should go into the bows. The sternman always has better control over the movement of the canoe as a whole, and can generally see clearly enough to decide whether the canoe should be in the centre, left or right of the river.

If there is any doubt whether a piece of river should be run at all, this should be resolved through discussion. There is a logical tendency to let the owner of the canoe have the final choice. In a party of several canoes the most experienced crew usually runs a doubtful piece first, and then waits at the bottom to observe and help the others. Often some canoes will run, some will line, and some portage a given stretch.

In choosing a channel through fast water, several conditions must be satisfied before it is safe to run:
1 It should have enough water to float the canoe.
2 It should not have any unavoidable and dangerous rocks or other obstructions.
3 There should be enough room to manoeuver the canoe around obstacles.
4 It should lead to a spot where it is easy to get out of the canoe and portage

if necessary, or to where the fast water ends in a safe pool.

5 The turbulence should not be so great that it will swamp the canoe.

The standards are not the same for all canoeing occasions. The nature of the craft and skill of the canoeist must be matched with the challenge of the water. A covered kayak is more easily manoeuvered and can handle much greater turbulence than an open canoe. Expert paddlers often play in dangerous turbulence which most canoeists will wisely avoid.

The following sections describe some of the warning signs to recognize and techniques to use in typical river situations. The concentration is on the tactics to be used by two persons in an open Canadian canoe. Paddlers in covered canoes and kayaks use these same tactics, but have many additional moves in their repertoire because of the manoeuverability and watertight security of their craft; and some reference to the advanced manoeuvers of covered craft will be made in this chapter, to indicate the levels of skill and enjoyment that can be achieved. *The following sections, it must be cautioned, cover only the elementary aspects of white water situations and tactics. They are only a beginning.* Before he becomes an expert, a canoeist needs a great deal of practical experience – and this should be good practical experience, with the opportunity to learn from skilled and careful veterans. Rushing water is powerful and dangerous. Join a canoe club. Take organized instruction. Find a group of competent canoeists from whom to learn. These are the only sensible ways to begin white water canoeing.

Downstream Vees As a general rule black water is deep and fast. White water indicates turbulence and obstructions. The canoe is more likely to be safe in the black water. The channel into the rapids is often marked by a downstream pointing vee of smooth dark water which has obvious turbulence on either side. A linked series of these downstream pointing vees usually indicates a good, safe channel.

Upstream Vees Underwater obstructions like rocks create a visible pattern in the shape of an upstream-pointing vee of turbulent water. Canoeists should avoid these vees, which indicate rocks close to the surface. They are often hard to spot. When the water is fast and deep over the rock they can start three or four feet downstream from where the rock actually is, which makes it doubly important for the bowman to keep a close watch for them. The canoeist must move the canoe out of danger well before it gets near the vee. The bowman moves his end to the clear water at the side of the vee by using draw or pry strokes; the sternman moves his end in the same direction

The canoe is going down the middle of the vee. It is taking the small standing waves at their centre, as that is where the deep water is and the waves are too small to swamp the canoe. An upstream pointing vee of rough water indicates rocks or other obstructions in the foreground and just astern of the canoe.

so the canoe does not go broadside into the underwater rocks.

Eddies and Eddy Turns A rock in a stream channel, a bend, or a widening after a drop, creates a turbulent eddy. These are horizontal rotations in the water alongside the main flow. They are marked by a pronounced difference in the direction of the current between the main flow and the eddy. Often, as the eddy line is crossed, the water's flow will change within a few feet from a downstream rush to a fast upstream motion. Eddies are relatively tranquil. Canoeists use them in moving upstream – paddling furiously from one eddy across the current to catch the eddy from a rock further upstream, moving up on the eddy, and then darting across again. Fish move upstream in the same way. Eddies give the paddler a chance to pull out of the main current and stop to catch his breath, and to look over the next piece of water. Good paddlers delight in playing with eddies – in moving from them into the main

EDDIES BEHIND ROCKS

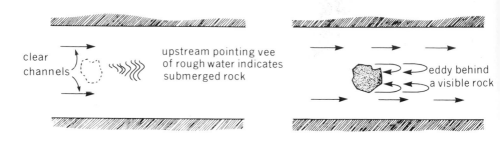

clear channels

upstream pointing vee of rough water indicates submerged rock

eddy behind a visible rock

DOWNSTREAM VEE, STANDING WAVES, EDDIES

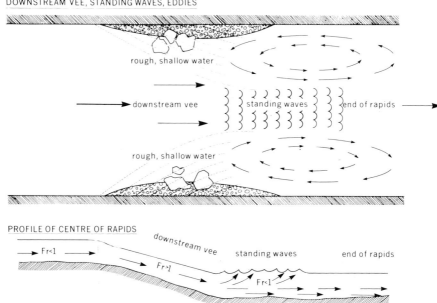

rough, shallow water

downstream vee   standing waves   end of rapids

rough, shallow water

PROFILE OF CENTRE OF RAPIDS

downstream vee   standing waves   end of rapids

Fr<1   Fr>1   Fr<1

current and back again, at the same time using the current differentials to help to turn the canoe and re-direct it. The differentials also can be used to help turn canoes and kayaks in slalom play, and the gates of slalom courses usually are arranged so that competitors must be aware of and take advantage of the changes in water speed and direction eddies provide. Playing with eddies teaches canoeists much about the complexities of flowing, turbulent water. Open canoes are also fun to manoeuver into and out of eddies, although because they are liable to swamp and are often loaded and heavy they should be used only in easy ones.

In a kayak the normal approach to an eddy is bow first, with the paddler drawing the kayak into the eddy with a sweep followed by a Duffek stroke, a bracing draw (on the upstream side of the river – in effect the 'downstream' side of the eddy) forward of his sitting position. The kayak is leant so that its bottom is facing the upcoming current of the eddy. In leaving the eddy, the bow of the kayak is placed into the current, with the paddler braced on the downstream side, and the speed of the current is normally enough to turn the kayak; if not, a sweep followed by a brace or Duffek will move the stern around.

These manoeuvers have their counterpart in an open two-man canoe. In entering an eddy from the stream, the bowman can draw on the upstream side or pry on the downstream side. The sternman can execute a low brace on the upstream side, or a Duffek on the downstream side. Similarly, in entering the main current from an eddy, the bowman can draw on the downstream side or pry on the upstream side, and the sternman also can draw on the upstream side, or brace on the downstream. The paddlers should normally be on opposite sides of the canoe. The safest manoeuvers are those in which the bowman is drawing rather than prying, but experienced crews who want to manoeuver quickly and do not want to be continually changing sides will often use the pry in the bow and the low brace in the stern combinations. Like a kayak the canoe should be leant so that its bottom faces the current.

These manoeuvers are also used in embarkation and disembarkation in fast water. The normal put-in spot in fast water is in an eddy, and the canoe is loaded facing upstream. It is then paddled out and into the current, being turned to face downstream at the same time. The opposite manoeuver is used to leave the current and reach the shore.

Often paddlers in open canoes will enter and leave small eddies facing downstream, without the turn. They then use a combination of back paddling with draw strokes, in order to maintain alignment as the canoe crosses the eddy line. A hanging draw by the sternman helps move the canoe into an

EDDY TURN

Moving into an eddy

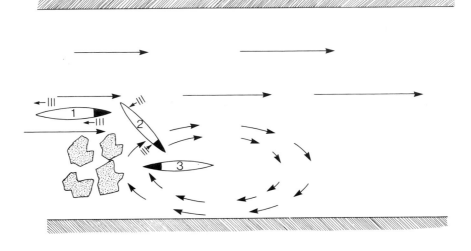

EDDY TURN

Moving out of an eddy

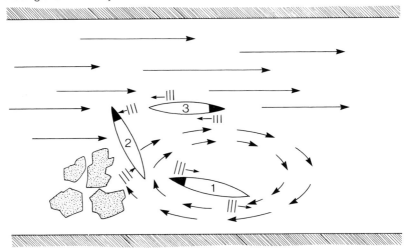

EDDY TURN

Moving behind a small rock

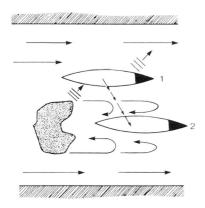

eddy. Once in the current (or eddy) the padders change from back paddling to normal forward motion. When the current differential is large, this manoeuver is dangerous because the canoe enters the current (or eddy) at an angle that encourages an accidental broadside out-of-control turn. In easy rapids the technique is particularly useful for unwieldy large canoes, since it avoids the need for leans and sharp turns. But it is not nearly so elegant as the eddy turn.

On trout fishing rivers, a canoe can be parked in a eddy and kept there by one paddler while the other fishes. Beginning canoeists, however, will find that when they try to place the canoe in the eddy behind one rock, they will be lucky if they succeed in settling behind another rock twenty or thirty feet downstream. The current moves the canoe so quickly, and the novice canoeist's strokes are so slow, that the canoe's response is that many feet too late.

There are many varieties of eddy turns and ways of playing with eddies that have not been mentioned here, but most of them are for advanced paddlers in covered canoes designed for white water work. The patterns and forms of moving water are infinitely varied; white water paddlers are still discovering the best ways of responding to its different nuances.

In heavy water, eddies sometimes lose their tranquility. They surge and

Poling up the Abitibi River in the James Bay Region, about 1907. The downstream eddy behind the rock in foreground is obvious. The canoe was poled upstream in this eddy and has just been moved out into the current so it can be poled past the rock, after which the Cree canoeists will seek another eddy to help them in their upstream travel. The smooth water behind the rock in the centre of the river indicates another eddy.

boil, and the canoe is tossed around unpredictably. In very heavy water, large boils, whirlpools and ridges come and go along the eddy line and in the eddy. They can be several feet high, and can swamp an open canoe and upset a covered one. They can be dangerous. Paul Kane in 1847 was likely describing this sort of turbulence at the 'Little Dalles' on the Columbia River:

It is here contracted into a passage of one hundred and fifty yards by lofty rocks, on each side, through which it rushes with tremendous violence, forming whirlpools in its passage capable of engulfing the largest forest trees, which are afterwards disgorged with great force ... On arriving at the head of the rapids, the guide gets out on to the rocks and surveys the whirlpools. If they are filling in or 'making,' as they term it, the men rest on their paddles until they commence throwing off, when the guides instantly re-embark, and shove off the boat, and shoot through this dread portal with the speed of lightning. Sometimes the boats are whirled around in the vortex with such awful rapidity that it renders the management impossible, and the boat and its hapless crew are swallowed up in the abyss.[1]

Rock Gardens Often a stretch of rapids is strewn with rocks, some protruding above the water's surface, some identifiable only by upstream pointing vees. These stretches are called 'rock gardens.' Eddies, conflicting currents, and the need for precise quick action, make rock gardens a challenge. Sometimes in Canada's Precambrian Shield, as at the *Portage des roches* on the Mattawa, rock gardens are filled with almost perfectly rounded stone spheres two to four feet in diameter, piled like marbles in the river bed. It is almost impossible to run this sort of obstacle at low water levels. The paddler must often jump out to lift his canoe off rocks, and often too he must give up paddling altogether and wade along the river, guiding his craft. It is much easier to jump in and out of open craft than covered ones, which is one of the reasons why open canoes retain their popularity for wilderness travel in Canada.

Rock gardens, if they have enough water flowing in them, can also be fun. The canoeist faces an exacting challenge in picking a path. Where the flow is super-critical in some places and sub-critical in others, some rocks will be hidden in pillows of water, while others will be concealed under a level or depressed surface. The bowman must read the water quickly and accurately. The paddlers must work together as a team, and move the canoe quickly to avoid obstructions. Usually, when a rock protrudes above the surface, the water flows around it and the canoe will move with the water around the rock. But the currents may urge the two ends of the canoe to go to different sides of the rock – and if the paddlers do not correct it the canoe will go broadside into the rock. This is one of the most common causes of difficulty in this type of water. Skilled canoeists use a wide variety of stroke combinations in rock gardens, in order to take advantage of eddies and current differentials. They try to link their strokes together in sequence so that each manoeuver leaves them in good position and prepared for the next.

Ferry Gliding Often paddlers must move the canoe across the current to the opposite side without letting it make much headway downstream. This might be necessary when the channel down one side of a stream is blocked by several rocks which cannot be manoeuvered around by a few draw or pry strokes. In these circumstances the appropriate technique is the ferry glide.

In a downstream ferry glide, the canoeists backpaddle strongly and point the canoe at a small angle to the current, with its stern in the direction towards which the craft should move. The river current moves the canoe downstream. The backpaddling moves it upstream. These two motions cancel each other out. The fact that the canoe is at an angle to the current imparts sideways motion. The tactic is called the ferry glide because ferries (more commonly in Europe than in North America) cross rivers by the force of the water acting on their angled hull – the ferries running along a cable across the river.

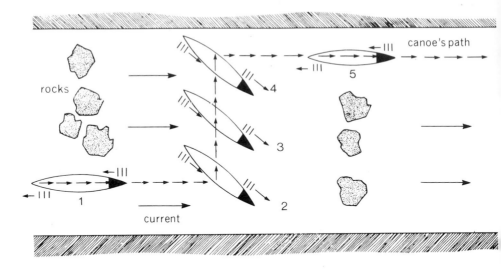

A proper ferry glide requires skill and practice. If the canoe is at too great an angle, the current will turn it broadside and it will be vulnerable to obstacles. If the angle is too small it will not move across the river. If the backpaddling is too weak, the canoe will be carried too far downstream. If the paddlers cannot maintain course almost anything can, and probably will, go wrong. Canoeists should practise the ferry glide in easy, unobstructed channels, and gradually work up to difficult situations where it must be used. Only through trial and error can paddlers learn what the appropriate angle to the current is, when the ferry glide will work, and how to keep the canoe on course while backpaddling. In very fast, shallow water the ferry glide is difficult to use because of turbulence created by the interaction of hull, current and river bed. In some teams the bowman takes over the steering in the downstream ferry. I have found it preferable for the sternman to retain control, although the bowman does a sort of backward J stroke to help keep the canoe pointed in the right direction.

Covered kayaks and canoes are easy to turn, and paddlers in them often spin around to face upstream in ferrying across the current. Where a wide channel has to be crossed, it is often easier in an open canoe also to turn upstream and paddle forwards to ferry glide. The upstream ferry glide is a stronger tactic than the downstream, because canoeists can paddle more strongly forwards than backwards.

Trees Fallen trees and log jams protruding into, or across, a river are some of the most dangerous obstacles a canoeist is likely to meet. Water flows around rocks, and the current helps to carry the canoe around them. But water flows through fallen trees, and the current carries the canoe into them. There is a natural tendency to hold on to branches when a canoe goes under a tree, but hanging on makes the canoe extremely unstable. Fallen trees must be avoided. If a tree lies across a stream, get out and carry past. If the tree protrudes only part way into the stream, ferry glide around it.

Going Around a Bend When the river is wide and the current is slow, curves present no difficulty to the canoeist. But when the river is narrow and the current fast, curves and bends become a challenge because the current does not follow the shape of the curve. Water travels around a curve in a corkscrew pattern, moving on the upper levels towards the outside of the curve, and then down, under and back. At the same time, the deepest water in the channel is at the outside of the bend, and that is where the canoe should be. Yet if the canoe stays at the outside of the curve, it will be pushed towards the outside shore by the current, and here is danger – the current is fastest, the bank is steepest, and there are most likely to be obstructions, including trees that have fallen from the bank. Thus the canoe must be kept away from the outside bank. Draw strokes, or furious paddling, do not solve the problem when the current is fast.

The right way to go around a bend is to backpaddle, with the canoe pointed downstream but angled towards the outside of the curve. The canoeists paddle backwards fast enough to keep the canoe away from the outside shore. The current carries the canoe around the bend. In covered craft, the paddler can point the canoe or kayak away from the outside of the bend, and paddle forwards. This is a faster way to negotiate a bend, but it is less safe for open canoes than the backpaddling approach.

Standing Waves This term describes various kinds of turbulent flow which produce wave-like patterns on the surface. One sort of standing wave is formed at the bottom of a rapids, where the fast flow coming down the rapids meets the slower, deeper flow at the bottom. These series of standing waves rise and fall in a regular, quick succession, and are often called 'haystacks.' When the river bed is irregular, another sort of standing wave is formed,

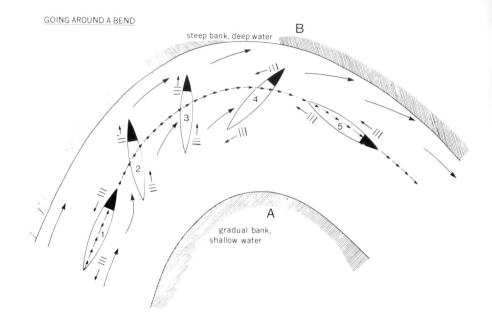

which tends to remain stationary. When the flow is sub-critical, the waves form over the holes between obstructions; when it is super-critical they form over the obstructions themselves. In rapids where the flow varies, as it often does, between being sub-critical and super-critical, it is easy to mistake a rock-stuffed pillow for a deep standing wave. All these standing waves involve turbulence with rotation about a horizontal axis. Within them the water is moving downstream, but the rotation makes the water move downstream at a faster velocity deep within the wave than on the crest. Sometimes, when the standing waves are steep and short-based, a curl much like the whitecaps on ocean waves will form as the top of the wave falls back upstream.

As long as they do not conceal rocks, standing waves normally indicate deep water and a safe channel. When they are not too big, the proper course is right down the centre. As they become larger, they present more risk because they will come over the sides and swamp an open canoe. One way to handle big ones is to find a safe course at their edge, along the shoulder. Such shoulders may be found when the standing waves occur in a vee-shaped ridge down the channel. There are likely to be eddies at both sides of these standing waves, but between these eddies and the largest standing waves is often a relatively calm section of downstream moving water in which an open canoe can survive. Sometimes the waves will be head high on one side of the canoe while the water is almost flat on the other. This is the path the voyageurs called the *fil d'eau*. Captain George Back described his voyageur guide leading them down this path on what is now known as the Back River in the Northwest Territories:

I had this day another opportunity of admiring the consummate skill of De Charlôit, who ran our ricketty and shattered canoe down four successive rapids, which, under less able management, would have whirled it, and every body in it, to certain destruction. Nothing could exceed the self-possession and nicety of judgment with which he guided the frail thing along the narrow line between the high waves of the torrent and the returning eddy: a foot in either direction would have been fatal.[2]

A second way of dealing with large standing waves is for the paddlers to move towards the middle of the canoe. The bowman sits behind the front seat, and the sternman behind the centre thwart. Moving the weight towards the centre in this way allows the bow and stern to bob up and over the waves. A single expert paddler sitting in the centre of a canoe can ride bigger standing waves than two paddlers. If the canoeists backpaddle until their craft is moving slower than the current, the bows will have extra time to ride up and over the wave rather than dig in. Backpaddling can also be used to ferry the canoe in picking the best channel through a series of standing waves. In large rivers, expert canoeists frequently will turn the canoe at an angle to the waves and go over them angled to the current. A downstream lean and careful balancing with knees and paddle keeps the canoe from swamping even in very large waves with this technique.

As the canoe is turned across the current, it is important to compensate for the vertical turbulence within standing waves. If the paddle is placed deep in the water on the upstream side, there is a strong pressure against the blade from the fast deep water, and the canoe may tip over upstream. The paddle therefore should be used on the downstream side, and the canoe should be tipped with the knees so that its bottom is facing upstream. Paddling on the downstream side, with the canoe tilted so that its bottom faces the current, is the proper approach to standing waves and fast water in covered canoes and kayaks as well. Kayakers take great delight in playing in large standing waves. They surf from side to side across the upstream side of the wave, and dart in, around and over haystacks. They suffer many upsets in learning to respond to the demands of the water. Open canoes can also surf across standing waves, and this gives one of the quickest upstream ferries imaginable.

The canoeists are following the *fil d'eau* between the
main flow with its heavy turbulence on their right and
the eddy on their left. The bowman in the lead craft is
using a cross-bow stroke to move his canoe into the
centre of the channel to avoid the current which sweeps
in towards the left-hand shore. The two stern men are
sitting on the gunwales for better vision – their large
canoes are very stable.

Open canoes, however, swamp easily and are generally much bigger and more difficult to rescue than covered canoes and kayaks. When there is a good deep pool nearby downstream in which the canoe, even if submerged, is not likely to hit a rock, and rescue crews are ready, then the open canoeist can experiment and test his skills in standing waves.

There is no absolute limit to the height of standing waves which an open canoe can negotiate. Long canoes usually ride big standing waves better than short ones, but this very much depends on canoe design and wave form. When the waves are steep, and the distance between their crests is short, any canoe is more likely to ship water. Three-foot height can be the limit in short, steep waves. In comparison, on the big rivers of the west, where the standing waves are long and huge, open canoes have been used in waves more than ten feet in height.

Hydraulic Jumps It is possible for the water in a river to move from a lower to a higher level as the river progresses downstream. This change takes place abruptly, over a short distance, in a phenomenon known as a 'hydraulic jump' to engineers, and variously as a 'hole,' 'souse hole,' 'weir slot,' or hydraulic jump to canoeists. A hydraulic jump occurs when the flow goes from super-critical to sub-critical – when water that has been in its shooting phase slows up quickly, and changes to streaming on reaching a pool at the bottom of a bit of rapids. The kinetic energy of the shooting water is changed into potential energy in the abrupt rise in height of the water level.

The shape of a hydraulic jump depends upon the slope of the drop over which the water falls and on the configuration of the bed of the river following the drop. When the drop is over a gently sloping sill and the following river bed is also gently sloping, the water will often follow a smooth unbroken line until it has created one standing wave, although the subsequent waves will be more irregular. At the opposite extreme, when the drop is steep and the water changes abruptly from shooting to streaming phase, the hydraulic jump can have a powerful reversal current, or upstream eddy, on its surface. The first kind of hydraulic jump presents no problems to canoeists except the power of the water and the size of the waves. The second kind, however, can be a serious and perilous obstacle. These dangerous hydraulic jumps have a vertical eddy in which the top surface rolls upstream and the downstream-moving water is found only deep below the surface. Associated with the hydraulic jump is a 'hole' between the shooting flow and the roller. A lot of the white water in rapids is caused by this sort of hydraulic jump. Sometimes the upstream roller will extend more than twenty feet downstream from the jump.

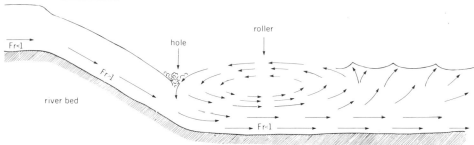

This hydraulic jump does not have a dangerous hole in it, although there are nasty upstream rollers, and hidden rocks, in the white water at either side of the channel of dark water in which the canoe is centred. The bowman is kneeling behind the front seat. Both paddlers are backpaddling and will soon change this to a quick forward stroke to lift the bows over the hump of water below the hydraulic jump. This is about the limit of short, sharp drop which can be safely handled in an open canoe.

When a canoe, going downstream, enters the upstream eddy at the bottom of these jumps, it feels as though a giant hand (or as canoeists sometimes call it, the 'muncher with a thousand teeth') has grabbed the canoe. The canoe slows down abruptly and loses buoyancy in the aerated foam. Paddles have to thrust deep to get enough purchase to move the craft. The paddlers must work hard. The roller tends to hold back the canoe and turn it into the hole; but if the canoe is allowed to broach, turn sideways and get caught in the hole, both the canoe and paddlers are in danger. An open canoe can easily swamp by being filled from the higher water on either side. If that happens there is a strong tendency for the canoe – and the paddlers – to be turned over and over in the roller, in a circular motion with a cycle of a few seconds. The canoe can be damaged and the paddlers drowned before they can escape the hole. Logs caught in rollers below dams will often stay in them for days, being ground to match sticks or until some change enables them to continue downstream. Many canoes and kayaks are broken up each year in the same way. Often rescue boats, coming upstream, also get caught in hydraulic jumps with fatal consequences. A hydraulic jump that extends across a river must be avoided by both open and closed canoes. It is simply too dangerous to be played with: even a hole four or five inches deep can be enough to hold a canoe or swimmer. These sorts of holes are often caused by weirs or other man-made obstacles.

Many factors can make a canoe broach in a hydraulic jump. The keel can get caught on the shallow water of the ledge, slowing the canoe down so that the bow gets caught in the upstream current of the roller and pushed sideways. The less buoyant water of the roller can make the bows of the canoe dig in and the stern swing around. The paddlers can fail to paddle fast and hard enough to climb out of the hole.

Canoeists should always consider portaging around hydraulic jumps. If one is run, it should be with a powerful forward motion, so that there is no chance of the canoe catching on the ledge and broaching. This is one of the few important exceptions to the general rule of backpaddling in dangerous water. Forward motion should be maintained until the canoe is well out of the roller, ten, twenty or more feet downstream.

Sometimes the worst happens and the canoe is caught sideways in a hydraulic jump. The canoeist must then remember to lean downstream. If the roller is small, he can try to pull the canoe up and over it with his paddle by digging deep on the downstream side in the lower downstream flowing water. He can try to paddle his canoe along the hole and out at one of the ends. If his canoe upsets he can dive down to the downstream flowing water and get out below the roller, but to do this he must remove his life jacket.

Sometimes he can stand up and dive out past the roller. In a covered craft he can intentionally roll over on the upstream side, hold his paddle out while upside down, and hope to get caught and pulled out by the powerful lower current.

Between the hydraulic jumps which have no back current and those with dangerous reversals are countless variations. The most common, which occurs when the slope is moderately steep and the bottom moderately shallow, has a single reversing wave at the bottom of the hole. This is called a 'stopper.' If the stopper is small, a canoe can be paddled right through it. Stoppers do not have the holding power of full-scale reversals, and are not as dangerous.

Holes with safe exits at the ends can be play spots for covered canoes and kayaks. The paddlers slip into them sideways and balance while bracing on the downstream side, trying to stay in the hole without upsetting. They can practice rolling in the hole – the downstream flow deep under makes rolling easy. They can try balancing without a paddle, or while they are twirling their paddle over their heads with one hand. They can let their paddle slide under their kayak, and catch it with the other hand on the downstream side. They can slide in slowly from the upstream or downstream side, and let the lower current catch the end of their kayak as they flip up and do an 'ender' or 'pop up.' All these are great fun, but only in a covered craft and only for a competent paddler.

Horizon Lines Sometimes when he looks downstream the paddler will see a sharp line across the river. The water on the far side often does not look significantly lower, but these sharp lines mean that the river drops abruptly at that spot. They are called horizon lines. Weirs and rock ledges can cause them. It is impossible to tell from upstream what is happening below a horizon line. There might be a dangerous hydraulic jump, or the river might break up on many sharp rocks. Canoeists in both open and covered craft should stop well upstream of a horizon line and scout. The situations they indicate are always uncertain, and often unrunnable. The Tyrrells encountered a horizon line on the Athabasca River on their expedition of 1893. As they rounded a bend ' . . . old Pierre suddenly stood up from his seat in the stern; . . . and we likewise were gazing at what looked like the end of the river. Right before us there extended a perpendicular fall . . . We braced ourselves for the plunge, and in a moment were lost to sight in the foaming waters below. But only for an instant. Our light cedars, though partly filled by the foam and spray, rose buoyantly on the waves, and again we breathed freely.'[3] They were lucky that their canoes were not loaded; otherwise the expedition could have ended right there.

Playing in a hole – a famous one near the Madawaska
Kanu Camp in Ontario. The water is rushing from the
right, and the seething foam on the left is the return
flow of aerated white water below the hole. This is not
a particularly dangerous hole, because it has exits at
both ends, but it would swamp an open canoe.

Portaging and Lining Learning the borderline between runnable and unrunnable water comes with experience. When a piece of rapids is reached which
the paddlers do not wish to run, they have the choice of portaging canoe and
gear around the obstacle, lining their canoe through it, or using any combination of carrying, paddling and lining.

The portage is the surest method of avoiding dangers and obstructions. The
canoe is taken to shore, emptied, and it and the gear carried. The paddlers
share the carrying. If they are strong, gear and canoe can be carried in one
crossing; if they are not strong or the load is large, two or more crossings will
be necessary. At the beginning of a long wilderness trip, when many
hundreds of pounds of supplies must be carried, three or four crossings might
be necessary. There are many portages which are a mile or more in length,
and these can be divided into shorter stages. With time and patience,
virtually any crew can make any portage, regardless of its length. The
voyageurs would cross portages at a dog trot carrying 180 or more pounds
by means of a tumpline across their foreheads. An out-of-shape city dweller
will find even a 60-pound canoe difficult to carry and might want to rest
every quarter mile. One man can pick the canoe up and move it onto his
shoulders in portaging position with a neat flick, but if he is tired, or the
canoe is heavy, it is sensible for the other paddler to help. If the team is not

strong, two persons can carry the canoe. This means slower travel, but there are no medals for racing across portages. Sometimes portage trails are hard to follow. Then the person who is not carrying the canoe should go first and pick the route. Or both paddlers can search for the route before any gear is portaged. Portages are often feared, but they should not be. By circumventing obstacles and hazards, and by permitting travel between watersheds, they are the means of opening the wilderness to canoe travel. They are a necessary part of canoe routes.

In downriver work the canoe can often be lined instead of portaged. In lining, the paddlers get out and guide the canoe down the rough stretch by means of a rope. Many guide books recommend using two lines – one bow and one stern, attached by bridles – so that the canoe can be steered by adjusting the angle it makes to the current through lengthening and shortening the lines. I have found this method helpful in lining a canoe upstream, but not in going downstream. Going down a river, pulling on two lines makes it all too likely that the canoe will broach broadside and fill with water, or will fight instead of going with the current. I use a 100-foot, quarter-inch braided nylon rope attached to the stern. I let the canoe drift with the current, and move it sideways with a steady pull or by flicking its stern from side to side with jerks of the rope. Often I use all hundred feet of line. Sometimes, on a long stretch of lining, the crews of two or three canoes place themselves along the edge of the rapids, and move the canoes down one by one. Lining can save the time and effort of a portage. But canoes can be lined only in water slightly more difficult than that which can be canoed. There is only a dismal future in trying to line over a waterfall.

Modern canoes can stand a great deal of abuse, and consequently rapids which would have required a formal portage with the more fragile canoes of earlier years will often be run today, perhaps with some bad parts lined; the loaded canoes may even be lifted and carried around the worst obstacles. Sometimes canoeists will wade, pushing, pulling and dragging the canoes along with them. Often the gear will be carried around the rapids, while the paddlers run the canoes through. This the voyageurs called a *décharge*.

Poling When canoes were the basic means of transportation and freighting goods in the north, they were frequently poled, both downstream and upstream. Going downriver the pole, instead of paddle strokes, could be used to fend the canoe off rocks; in steep drops dangerous to run, the poles could be snubbed to the bottom to let the large canoes down slowly and safely. Fishermen, including salmon fishers in New Brunswick and Indians netting whitefish in the rapids at Sault Ste Marie, held their canoes in position in

The canoe is being lined, with a single stern line, down
some difficult rapids. This piece of water could have
been run, but there was only one canoe in the party and
so the safer course was chosen.

Wading downstream while guiding the canoe is very
common on shallow, rock-filled streams, in this case the
Sturgeon-Weir River in Saskatchewan. Canoeists also
may walk their craft down the edges of rapids too
difficult or dangerous to run.

the rapids by a pole snubbed on the bottom. The most important use for poling, however, was in going upstream. In shallow fast-flowing water a canoe can be poled upstream faster than it can be paddled or, when the shore is rough, than it can be lined. Woodsmen used spruce poles twelve to fourteen feet in length and about two inches in diameter at the butt. The best ones were dried on the stump. An iron shoe was attached to the lower end to help the pole grip. Modern canoeists sometimes use aluminum alloy or fibreglass poles built much like those of pole vaulters.

Poling is not used much in modern downriver canoeing, although recently it has been undergoing a revival. In the United States there are many poling competitions in which the canoeists must manoeuver around buoys while going upstream, downstream and across the current. In these short races, polers use repeated jabs, or quick changes from side to side. The more usual technique, and the only one which can be sustained for a long time, is the traditional hand-over-hand, climb-the-pole style, much the same as Oxford students use in punting on the gentle branches of the Thames. Punting at Oxford was all the experience R. M. Patterson had when he embarked on his solo canoe journey up the Nahanni, and he recalled later that 'strangely enough I never doubted that I could [do it], though exactly what I proposed to use in place of experience has since often puzzled me. I was extremely accurate with a punt pole and could place a punt where I wanted it to an inch, but the art of handling a canoe had been acquired entirely on the Cherwell and the Isis – a very gentle school of rivercraft.'[4] The canoeist must stand up in his canoe to pole, and in so doing break one of the misguided rules of canoeing safety. Covered canoes and kayaks cannot be poled.

In all downriver canoeing, the paddlers must decide not only on the tactics they should use in a particular piece of wild water, but also whether they should portage or line instead of running it. This last is the most important choice of all. Here the canoeists must exercise their judgment.

FOUR

Canoeing judgment

Good judgment in downriver canoeing ensures safety while maximizing excitement and challenge. It comes with experience, which is gained partly at the expense of damaged canoes because, like bridge and dam builders, canoeists improve by learning from their mistakes. But there are sensible and foolish mistakes. And knowledge of rivers, skills and safety measures can help avoid the foolish ones.

River Grading

A river grading scale helps canoeists planning a route to assess the difficulties they will have to face. The International River Grading System, much like that used for mountain climbing routes, includes six levels.

Grade I. Very Easy Waves small, regular. Passages clear. Sandbanks, artificial difficulties like bridge piers. Riffles. Obstacles are easy to avoid. *Beginner's water.*

Grade II. Easy Waves up to one to two feet. Rapids of medium difficulty, with passages clear and wide. Low ledges which are easy to negotiate. The best passage is generally easy to negotiate. *Requires basic white water skill.*

Grade III. Medium Waves numerous, high (up to three feet), irregular. Rocks, eddies. Rapids with passages that are clear though narrow, requiring expertise in manoeuver. Inspection usually needed. *The limit for open canoes. Requires sound white water skills.*

Grade IV. Difficult Long rapids. Waves powerful, irregular. Dangerous rocks. Boiling eddies. Passages difficult to reconnoitre. Inspection mandatory first time. Powerful and precise manoeuvering required. *Requires advanced to expert level of skill.*

This particular piece of water – the Five Finger Rapids on the French River – looks to be grade II, although it could be grade III if it were followed by another piece with medium standing waves and obstacles which demanded precise manoeuvering.

Grade V. Very Difficult Extremely difficult, long and very violent rapids, following each other almost without interruption. River bed extremely obstructed. Big drops, violent current, very steep gradient. Reconnoitering essential but difficult. *Requires absolute expertise.*

Grade VI. Extraordinarily Difficult The difficulties of Grade V carried to extremes of navigability. Nearly impossible and very dangerous. For teams of experts only, at favourable water levels and after close study with all precautions. *Even experts avoid this kind of water if possible.*

In this condensed form, the international rating system appears simple. The grade assigned to a rapids depends largely on its gradient, volume of water, and the shape of the river bed and obstructions in it. But in use the rating system is far from simple, for three reasons: difficulty changes with changes in water flow; there is inevitably a subjective element in grading; and dangers as well as difficulty must be considered.

The grading of a river usually describes its difficulty at 'normal' volume of water flow. But what is 'normal' is often unclear. The flow in rivers varies tremendously, especially in the cultivated parts of southern Canada where land clearing and swamp draining have increased the spring floods and reduced the capacity of the drainage basin to store water to augment the summer flow. The Moira River which empties into Lake Ontario at Belleville has reached more than 15,000 cfs (cubic feet per second) in spring flood, and a low of 15 cfs in September. At 15,000 cfs the Moira is too dangerous for open canoes, while at 15 cfs it can only be walked, not canoed. Even within a week the changes can be dramatic.

On many popular U.S. and European white water canoeing rivers, water levels are measured at strategic spots and guide books give the grade for different water levels. Some guide books also suggest a local person who will report the water level by phone before the canoeist leaves home. Sudden rainstorms and flash floods can make even this sort of information unreliable, however. In Canada, many rivers have scarcely been graded at all, let alone for difficulty at different water levels. Some, like the Madawaska south and east of Algonquin Park, are regulated by dams for power production and can vary tremendously in flow and difficulty from day to day. As a result, river grading – especially in Canada – is only a rough guide to what a canoeist might encounter.

Normally a river becomes more difficult as the flow increases. The standing waves become larger, the current faster, the eddies and holes more turbulent and more dangerous. The resting places become fewer and smaller. In peak flood some rivers are dangerous and should not be canoed: the debris contained in their muddy waters can create risks which even the most expert paddlers cannot avoid. Others become interesting only in flood conditions. This is especially true in the farming regions of southern Ontario and Quebec, where rivers that are chains of stagnant scummy pools in summer become exciting grades II to IV white water for a short time in April or May. River grades in these areas refer usually to the heavy spring flows. But because flow is so variable, on the same weekend in two different years or on succeeding weekends in the same year the difficulty can vary by as much as two grades. Sometimes rivers increase in difficulty as the flow decreases and ledges, drops and rocks which were deep under water become hazards which require precise manoeuvering. Because of the variability of water flow, and because of frequent uncertainty about the water flow a written description refers to, paddlers on an unfamiliar river should be doubly certain to reconnoitre and study rapids.

The subjective element in grading comes from the wide variations amongst good paddlers in levels of skill, confidence and local knowledge. When there are several possible paths through a stretch, a guide book might refer to the

This is another stretch of the French River in Ontario. It is difficult to tell from the picture what the overall rapids grading would be. At least grade II. The steep drop upstream at the left suggests that there might be tough rapids which the canoeists have just come through. Or perhaps they have portaged to the large eddy pool from which the canoe is exiting. The canoe is in the safe channel between the heavy, standing waves in the centre channel and the small, shallow hole to the canoe's right.

easiest path, which would be well known to some people but not at all obvious to strangers. Familiarity tends to make rapids less difficult. The dramatic improvement in paddling techniques during the past decades, especially for covered craft, has also tended to reduce the measured degree of difficulty of white water. Many stretches have been downgraded from V to IV, or from IV to III, over the years. In Europe a river is often demoted from VI to V once it has been run successfully, and in time it may even reach IV. These gradings have changed largely because of improved skills, but also because of better canoe design and more durable construction. All this again emphasizes the

The size of the river and the need for precise
manoeuvering around problems like the hole to the left
of the canoe make this piece of rapids grade III. The
canoe is a Chestnut Prospector.

This gorge on the Pukaskwa River above Lake Superior
stretches for a mile, and although many of the little
rapids can be run in an open canoe others, like this one,
cannot. It could be run in a kayak, but after a short and
relatively tranquil pool the river drops over a fifty-foot
waterfall. It is consequently quite dangerous. This
stretch is grade IV. We lined open canoes along the far
bank, but with great difficulty.

This small, rock-filled gorge, on the Skootamata River in Ontario, is not canoeable.

importance of knowing who graded the river, and when and under what conditions. Even knowing this, canoeists must still make their own evaluation of each stretch of rapids. The subjective element is unavoidable.

Different styles of grading have developed in eastern and western North America. In the west, heavy water which would be v in the east is often graded as IV or even III. The western assumptions are that the paddler can, and will, take the easiest passage through the rapids and the grades discount side eddies and holes which might be extremely dangerous but not difficult to avoid. Westerners also assume that kayakers have a perfect roll and can quickly recover from upsets. Some water that is graded as III in the west is *not* runnable in open canoes.

Three factors which affect danger are: first, the temperature of the water; second, the accessibility of the river; third, where resting spots occur. A rapids may be easy to negotiate, but if the water is cold, the river in the wilderness, and there are miles of unending white water without resting places, it is inherently dangerous. Spring is the best season for white water canoeing, but spring also has cold water. When dumped into water below 10°C (50°F) a person loses body heat very rapidly. The effects of exposure (hypothermia) can come within minutes, and it catches its victim without warning. In the final stages, hypothermia creates unconciousness and conditions of shock, but long before that a canoeist upset and in the water will lose strength and his judgment will be impaired. This can happen within a few minutes in water at 0°C (32°F). (See the section on Accidents.) The canoeist's assessment of river grade should take into account all the elements of danger. A canoeist should be more cautious in spring than in summer, in cold northern rivers than in the south, in the wilderness than near home, and on big rivers than on small.

One of the best aids to grading individual rapids and sections of rivers was prepared by the Guidebook Committee of the American White Water Affiliation. This is reproduced in the following chart. A close study of it gives an understanding of the many factors involved. Obviously grading is complex – and some further factors not on the chart are also important. For instance, on many Canadian rivers the lumbermen in bygone days blasted channels for log driving. The rocks left in the river bed are unnaturally sharp. Even a light bump on them can puncture a fibreglass canoe: the danger level is consequently increased. Old broken dams often have sharp iron spikes protruding from them. Log drives are still encountered on many rivers. The works of man nearly always increase danger.

The overall grading of a river is usually lower than that of its most difficult rapids because rapids and falls can almost always be avoided. Portages can reduce rivers with grade IV, V or even VI rapids to grade II or III in overall difficulty, especially in the Precambrian Shield where rivers often consist of long slow-moving pools or even lakes connected by short, sharp drops. Trails around these drops, perhaps originally created by big game, have existed since prehistoric times. Many of these rivers of eastern and northern Canada can consequently be canoed safely by persons with only a few white water skills but with the good sense to look for and use the ancient portages. Many rivers of the west, however, have long stretches of difficult rapids which cannot be portaged. For these rivers, the true difficulty rating of the overall river is that of these difficult rapids.

The system for grading rivers was developed primarily for covered canoes and kayaks, and does not adequately take into account the kinds of problems met in open canoes. Paddlers in the traditional Canadian canoes must read between the lines of descriptions oriented towards covered craft, and rely on their own on-the-spot examination and judgment. They must ask not only what difficulty there is for safe navigation, but also what is likely to happen, and how difficult rescue will be if something does go wrong. River difficulty ratings should be treated much like mountaineering ratings: they refer to

Difficulty rating chart for river sections or individual rapids

Primary factors: affecting both success and safety

OBSTACLES: ROCKS, TREES	WAVES	TURBULENCE	RESTING OR RESCUE SPOTS	POINTS
none	few inches high; avoidable	none	almost anywhere	0
few; passage almost straight through	low (up to 1'); regular; avoidable	minor eddies		1
courses easily recognizable	low to medium (up to 3 ft); regular; avoidable	medium eddies		2
manoeuvering required; course not easily recognizable	medium to large (up to 5 ft); many; regular; avoidable	strong eddies; cross currents	a good one below every danger spot	3
intricate manoeuvering; course hard to recognize	large, irregular, avoidable; or medium to large and unavoidable	very strong eddies; strong cross currents		4
course torturous; frequent scouting required	large; irregular; unavoidable	large-scale eddies and cross currents; some up and down currents		5
very torturous; always scout from shore	very large (over 5 ft); irregular; unavoidable; special equipment required	very large-scale strong up and down currents	almost none	6

Secondary factors: related primarily to success in negotiating

BENDS	LENGTH IN FEET	GRADIENT FT./MI.	POINTS
few; very gradual	less than 100	less than regular slope	0
many; gradual	100-700	5-15; regular slope	1
few; sharp-blind; scouting required	700-5000	15-40; ledges or steep drops	2
	over 5000	over 40; steep drops, small falls	3

112   The canoe and white water

Secondary factors: related primarily to safe rescue

WATER VEL. MI./HR.	WIDTH/DEPTH	WATER TEMP. °F (°C)	ACCESSIBILITY	POINTS
less than 3	narrow (<75 ft) and shallow (<3 ft)	above 65 (18)	road along river	0
3-6	wide (>75 ft) and shallow (<3 ft)	55-65 (13-18)	less than 1 hour's travel by foot or water	1
6-10	narrow (<75 ft) and deep (>3 ft)	45-55 (7-13)	1 hour's to 1 day's travel by foot or water	2
over 10 or flood	wide (>75 ft) and deep (>3 ft)	less than 45 (7)	greater than 1 day's travel by foot or water	3

Calculating difficulty

TOTAL POINTS FROM CHART	RATING	APPROXIMATE DIFFICULTY	APPROXIMATE SKILL REQUIRED
0-7	I	easy	practised beginner
8-14	II	requires care	intermediate
15-21	III	difficult	experienced
22-28	IV	very difficult	highly skilled (several years with organized group)
29-35	V	exceedingly difficult	team of experts
36-44	VI	utmost difficulty: near limit of navigability	team of experts taking every precaution

Based on a chart prepared by the Guidebook Committee, American White-Water Affiliation – H. J. Wilhoyte, 12 February 1956 *perfect* conditions, and any worsening of conditions – such as high or cold water, or unfamiliarity – may increase the effective difficulty by a grade or more. These changes are especially important to paddlers in open canoes, to whom a stretch of white water that is interesting grade III under optimum conditions becomes impassible grade IV with increases in flow, or in the more difficult channels.

Paddler Grading

Paddler grading is even more difficult and subjective than river grading, and depends very much on the kind of canoeing involved. One component is the paddler's skill in handling canoes and kayaks in different white water situations and degrees of difficulty. A second is the paddler's judgment, including his ability to assess river difficulty and danger, and his knowledge of safety and first aid measures. Others are the paddler's ability to make the right decisions in situations of stress and pressure – as when an accident has occurred – and his leadership abilities under both normal and stress conditions.

The elements of judgment and general competence are especially important in wilderness travel by open canoe. Rapids which would be run without hesitation but with risk of swamping in the south are portaged and lined in the north. The level of skills required for grades IV and V water are not needed. Leadership, good judgment, camping skills and clubability are more important. But in the settled south, and especially on group trips like those of the Ontario Voyageur's Kayak Club, or in slalom competition, extensive safety precautions are taken and the comforts of civilization are close at hand. Here the elements of judgment become less important in individual grading, and paddling techniques and white water experience correspondingly more so. Most group trips on difficult rivers see many spills, rescues and damaged kayaks and canoes. These sorts of mishaps, which could be fatal in the wilderness, are run-of-the-mill and expected in the south. Paddlers in this sort of canoeing are graded largely by their white water skills.

There is a generally accepted classification for paddlers in the south. Novices can run grades I and II water, while intermediates in covered craft can handle grade III and, perhaps with a high risk of upset, grade IV. Experts have proven ability in rapids of grade IV difficulty. Expertise in open canoes includes the good sense to know when not to attempt a rapids. There is a wider range of skills between intermediate and expert for closed than for open canoes, and the expert category itself contains as much range as the

There are thousands of small rivers like this in Canada. Grade III skills are needed to manoeuver a canoe through the rapids without getting hung up on rocks, but as long as elementary safety precautions are observed this sort of white water challenge offers little danger apart from scrapes and bumps.

other classes, from competent weekend paddlers to Olympic champions.

A simple guideline applicable to the whole range of canoeing challenges is this: The more important the elements of danger and the less the elements of difficulty in the river grading, the more important the elements of judgment and the less the elements of white water skills in paddler grading.

Safety Measures

White water canoeing can be dangerous, but so can crossing a city street. Alcohol and tobacco offer greater long-term risks than canoeing to life and health. One of the delights of running white water is the element of risk-taking and danger. Some canoeing manuals elevate safety measures and caution to the point of paranoia. Contrary to common safety rules, experienced paddlers in open canoes often stand up, canoe alone, shoot rapids, don't wear life jackets, and sit instead of kneeling. In most conditions these cautious rules are sensible. Standing up can lead to instability, canoeing alone is less safe than canoeing with others, fast water can be dangerous, sometimes life jackets are essential, kneeling is necessary in rapids. But they are not inviolable laws which apply to all canoeing in all times and all places. The canoe is not a dangerous weapon. Knowledge, training and experience are the basis of good canoeing, and as these are gained the safety measures which are appropriate for the inexperienced can and should be relaxed. Standing up for poling or looking over rapids, sitting or not wearing life jackets for comfort, solitary canoeing for peace of the soul, and shooting rapids for speed, for excitement, or because they are unavoidable, are all parts of the sport.

A thorough knowledge of safety precautions is, however, essential for good canoeing. Only when a person is aware of and can take all safety measures is he or she in a position to know when and how to relax them. There is a big difference between book knowledge and actual canoeing experience. Practical experience – and frequently many minor accidents – are the only ways to learn the habits of planning, and quick and appropriate responses that minimize potentially dangerous mishaps.

The Ability to Swim All white water canoeists will find themselves in the water at some time. Obviously anyone who wants to engage in this kind of travel should be able to swim. In retrieving canoes and gear, the side stroke and breast stroke are better techniques than the crawl. In turbulent rapids a swimmer should float on his back with his feet pointed downstream. This gives him a built-in shock absorber, and minimizes the chances of bumping his head. A good rule is not to canoe in rapids you are not prepared to swim in. Sometimes a canoeist should try to swim down rapids just for fun and the experience.

Most fur trade voyageurs and Indians could not swim and this caused many deaths. Some difficult stretches of rapids were marked with as many as thirty crosses for those who drowned there. But nowadays there are ample opportunities to learn to swim. I make it an absolute rule that people who cannot swim don't go on canoe trips with me.

Life Jackets More often than not on hot summer days, I do not wear a life jacket in a canoe. But in any sort of cold spring canoeing, and in tough rapids at any season, the wearing of life jackets is an essential safety measure. Canadian law requires that each canoe carry one life jacket for each person in it. The more I canoe, and perhaps the older I get, the more I use life jackets. In covered canoes and kayaks, life jackets should be worn in rapids at all times.

The problem is what kind of life jacket. The best kind from a safety viewpoint is a bulky horse-collar type with plenty of flotation over the chest and behind the head so that the head and face of a weak or unconscious person will be kept out of water. But these can be uncomfortable for paddling. Most canoeists choose vest-type life jackets like those used by sailors or water skiers. The best are made with solid plastic-foam flotation sewn into an abrasion-resistant nylon cover. Cheaper ones have small sealed vinyl air cells which puncture with age and use. Both kinds are comfortable and can be worn for warmth in fall and spring. Kapok life jackets, and inflatable ones, should be avoided because they rely on a few plastic or rubber-covered compartments for the ability to support, and one or two punctures – which can easily happen in a few seconds on sharp rocks in rapids – make them worse than useless. Belt-type life jackets should not be used. The minimum buoyancy for an adult life jacket should be 15 pounds. The horse-collar life jackets do have one advantage in that they protect the neck and shoulders during long portages of open canoes. This benefit would doubtless be laughed at by hardened old-time woodsmen, but to a soft-skinned city dweller who spends eleven months of the year behind a desk it can be a godsend.

Skills and Knowledge of Them There is nothing more dangerous in canoeing than the mismatch of ignorance and inadequate skills with difficult rapids and wilderness problems. Part of good canoeing is knowing the limitations of one's own skills, and avoiding water and trips which are beyond them. This sort of knowledge can come with experience – especially the experience of several severe accidents – but wise novices often have better judgment than hare-brained intermediates. Before running any potentially difficult piece, a canoeist should ask what can go wrong, and what is likely to happen if something does go wrong. If there are the slightest doubts he should ask further whether with this crew, at this time, and in this place, the risk is worth taking. Finally, canoeists, like wilderness travellers in general, should know that fatigue and cold not only reduce physical competence but can also impair judgment. The time to run long hard rapids is not at dusk after twelve hours on a hard river on a cold spring day. Fatigue at the end of the day leads to bad judgment, which leads to accidents, which lead to further cold, fatigue and worse judgment. Such cumulation of adverse factors precedes many serious canoeing accidents. The ability to assess one's own physical and mental capacities when these have been affected by hours of gruelling work and the stress of cold and wet also is developed by experience – sometimes painful – recollected in tranquility. It can also be developed in other endurance sports like backpacking, cross-country skiing and mountain climbing which, like canoeing, lower blood sugar levels, exhaust the body's reserves, and create risks of hypothermia.

Scouting Canoeing is not like skiing. Once the canoe has begun a piece of rapids, it must finish it, either on top of, in, or under the water, and with

Scouting a rapids before running it. Notice the safety measures: crash helmets, life jackets of excellent quality with solid foam support in a nylon vest, grab loops on the craft. The one in front is a K1, the other a C1.

paddlers in the canoe, or in the water, or both. A skier can usually choose to end his run and walk, or sideslip out, but often canoeists do not have this choice. It is all the more important, therefore, that the canoeist knows what is ahead of him and is committed to and ready for the challenge. Even a familiar river, or one for which a good guide has been written, can change because of fallen trees, disturbances to the river bed, or changed water levels. A close, careful look beforehand, and an awareness of every challenge, are essential to safety. Scouting is especially important on rivers which have not been properly graded, and this includes nearly every river in Canada.

Equipment All equipment should be in good repair. Wooden canoes are naturally buoyant, but aluminum or fibreglass canoes should be tested to see if they float when filled with water: often their buoyancy chambers spring leaks and help the canoe to sink rather than float. Each canoe should have lines attached to bow and stern. I normally have a twenty-foot line attached to the bows, and my hundred-foot tracking line attached to the stern. These lines are useful for rescue, and also for guiding the canoe if the paddlers have to jump out to avoid an upset. The lines should be neatly coiled and should be ready to use with one end free to run. Each canoe should have a spare paddle – there are few things more futile than trying to use the broken stump of a paddle in the middle of a stretch of rapids. Some canoeists tie in their spare paddle, but I prefer to leave mine loose so either paddler can grab it without difficulty.

Canoes should not be overloaded. At least six inches of freeboard is needed for safety. Especially in badly designed fibreglass canoes this limit is reached with surprisingly small loads – as little as 450 pounds for some 16-foot models.

Canoeists should also have a repair kit. The most elementary and probably the most useful item is a roll of gray 'duct' tape, a cloth-backed waterproof adhesive tape about two inches wide which will stick to the dry surface of any kind of craft, and is almost as durable as canvas. On longer trips, parties with fibreglass canoes should carry fibreglass repair kits that can cover at least a square yard. Aluminum canoes can usually be repaired, at least temporarily, by pounding the dent straight and covering small holes with duct tape. A small kit including snare wire and rivets is useful for repairing canoes and other equipment. Canvas and cedar strip canoes are nearly as easily repaired as birch bark ones if the canoeists know the techniques. And even modern canoeists sometimes resort to spruce gum – mixed with fat – to glue on pieces of shirt or handkerchief when they have run out of other materials for repairs. Part of the soul of a cedar strip canoe comes from this ability of its owner to repair it in the wilderness with his own hands and skills and with materials he understands, has collected and shaped.

A first-aid kit, maps and a compass are essential. Clothes should not hamper swimming unduly – as ponchos do – and should, in cold weather, help to insulate. Kayakers in the cold spring season often wear skin divers' wet suits and, although paddlers in open canoes require less protection, canoeists on the cold northern rivers are also beginning to use wet suits. These suits normally consist of a jacket with short sleeves, and short pants. In cold weather canoeists should have clothes which help, after an upset, to retain a layer of warmed air near the skin. The best are wool underclothes covered by a windproof jacket and pants. Footwear is needed to avoid cuts. Canvas basketball shoes or sneakers are good except on rough portages. Canoeists should avoid footwear which would make swimming difficult.

Some manuals argue that canoes should never have seats – only thwarts – so that the canoeists are forced to kneel. Most canoeists prefer sitting to kneeling, however, and will sit on thwarts if there are no seats. Since sitting on a thwart is unstable, it makes more sense to have good seats in a canoe, slung a few inches below the level of the gunwales, but still high enough that the feet and calves can be put under them when the canoeist is kneeling in rapids but can be removed easily.

Paddlers in kayaks and closed canoes normally place six-inch grab loops at

This is the traditional way of repairing canvas canoes, and can still be used when gray duct tape or other repair materials run out. In this photo, taken in 1921, pitch has been heated in a skillet, with some fat, and now is being spread over the hole. A piece of an old shirt or other cloth can be pressed on over the pitch as reinforcement.

bow and stern, and install large inflatable vinyl flotation bags in the bow and stern compartments of their craft. The paddlers are joined to the kayak by a water proof spray skirt, which has a safety release loop, and they wear good quality hockey helmets or helmets especially designed for white water.

A knife is essential survival gear in the wilderness. In 1796 David Thompson and his canoe went over a waterfall on the Black River near Lake Athabaska. His two Indian companions were on shore at the time. Most of the supplies and goods in the canoe were lost, but Thompson had the presence of mind, as the canoe went over the falls, to put his clasp knife in his pocket. As they recovered the gear after the accident the Indians were astonished when Thompson drew the knife out. 'They whispered to each other, how avaricious a white man must be, who rushing on death takes care of his little knife; this was often related to other Indians who all made the same remark. I said to them, "If I had not saved my little knife how could we make a fire? You fools go to the birch trees and get some touchwood," which they soon brought. A fire was made; we repaired our canoe ... '[1] Possibly the Indians could not swim and the preservation of the knife consequently would have made no difference to their certain death, but Thompson could swim and the knife was the margin by which he and the two Indians survived.

In good canoeing every detail of equipment and procedure should enhance safety. Constant experimentation and attention to detail is necessary in selecting and using equipment. Durable and safe gear is the cheapest in the long run regardless of the initial cost.

Trip Organization Parties of canoeists on white water rivers should have a designated and accepted leader. His decisions on what rapids should not be run, and who should or should not run them, must be final. Like all good leaders, he should consult with his colleagues and work by co-operation and consent. Small groups, whose members know each other well, can usually operate on consent without commands, but the structure of leadership must still be there even if it is hidden. If an accident or emergency occurs, leadership and organization are essential.

One of the leader's tasks is to ensure that the right safety precautions are taken. He must make certain that each canoe has the right equipment for the weather and the rapids, and that it is in good repair. He must assess the canoeists' skills, and see that all members of the group know the plans for the day's run. In dangerous waters he must ensure that the canoeists keep together and that each canoe watches out for accidents to the one behind. He should ensure that a rescue canoe is stationed at the foot of a dangerous rapids and, if needed, at other strategic spots along it. The greater the risks that are being attempted by the canoeing group, the more important competent leadership and organization become.

Accidents

White water canoeists try to improve their skills and to extend the range of challenges which they can handle, and in this play and practice their canoes will on occasion go out of control, ground, hit rocks or swamp. There have always been small accidents in river canoeing. At every stop Indians and voyageurs would turn their birch bark canoes over to look for scratches and punctures. These they would cover with pitch. An old well-used canoe was often completely black along the bottom from repairs. Modern white water canoeists use their duct tape and fibreglass kits in the same way to make daily repairs. Canoeists who never have accidents are obviously canoeing well within, and not extending, the limits of their ability, and there is considerable justification for suspecting that they lack adventurousness and perhaps competence as well. Some spills and groundings are a necessary part of training and practice. It is important, therefore, to learn how to handle these small accidents and how to keep them from becoming big ones.

A rescue canoe should be stationed at the bottom of every difficult stretch. It was not needed here, but is often the difference between a slight and a serious accident.

There are some basic rules for handling small accidents. First the paddlers should try as far as possible to keep the canoe from broadsiding across the current because broadsiding exposes much more surface to danger. This may happen easily when the canoe grounds on a rock. The sternman normally tries to get it off: he can stand up in the canoe and push off the rock with one foot, or he can get right out and stand in the water to lift the canoe off. Sometimes both paddlers get out. If a canoe begins to broadside it is often best to let it do a 180-degree turn, and for the canoeists to paddle backwards, or to turn around.

Second, the paddlers should stay on the upstream side of the canoe. A canoe filled with water can weigh a ton, and the pressure of the rushing water against it can be two tons. Many little accidents have turned into big ones when canoeists got their legs or bodies caught between canoe and rock.

Third, when a canoe hits an obstruction the canoeists should ensure that the canoe is leaning downstream so that its flat bottom is exposed to the impinging water. This keeps water out of the canoe, and the angle at which the water hits the canoe also helps to lift it up and off the obstruction. Leaning downstream – not only in an accident but also while paddling – is as close to an absolute rule as there is in white water canoeing.

Fourth, canoeists should empty water out of the canoe as soon as possible. Water in a canoe is dangerous. Water is heavy. It makes the canoe harder to steer. It increases draught, making it more likely that the craft will ground on rocks. It reduces freeboard, making it more likely that water will be shipped. And, because it has a free surface, water slops around in the canoe and drastically reduces its stability. If water gets into the canoe at the beginning of a long series of standing waves, the canoe may finally sink after a bit more water is added with each successive wave. Water should be dumped out, or bailed or sponged out, at every possible opportunity.

If a canoe dumps, the canoeists should stay with the canoe, try to keep it parallel to the shore, move to the upstream end, and get it to shore as soon as possible. They should hold onto their canoe and paddles unless there is other danger to life – like cold spring water or an imminent waterfall – when the rule of protecting persons becomes an absolute priority.

There are many techniques of rescuing swamped and overturned canoes. Common but nearly useless are the training drills at summer camps, in which a capsized canoe is emptied while it is still in the water by splashing and shaking the water out or by pulling the canoe upside down over a second canoe. On a stormy lake, where upsets are likely to occur, the water is often too rough and choppy for these tactics, and in a rapids it is better to try to pull the canoe to shallow water or to shore as quickly as possible than to try to empty it while it is floating. Every second a water-filled canoe stays out of control in a river increases its chances of hitting a rock and sustaining serious damage. Canoeists should practise getting canoes filled with water to shore, throwing lines to swimmers in rapids, and getting a rescue canoe out quickly to help in an upset. This experience creates the right sort of automatic response. It is a good way to prepare for the unexpected. In groups that specialize in white water canoeing, rescue techniques, including nosing an overturned kayak towards shore, or using lines and even winches to retrieve sunken craft, are almost a normal part of the sport.

Hundreds of kinds of accidents can occur, and most of them can be kept as minor incidents. The ways of handling them are as varied as the accidents themselves. But the rules of safety measures and equipment, and the general principles of dealing with minor accidents, remain constant and must be mastered and observed.

Canoeing also has risks of more serious accidents, although they are often exaggerated. The *White Water Handbook* of the Appalachian Mountain Club states that in every fatal white water canoeing accident 'one inevitably finds at least two of the following – inexperience, very cold water, failure to use a life preserver, or absence of a support party.'[2] This is a useful list, although there are other causes of fatal canoeing accidents. In world championship kayaking competitions more than one competitor has been killed because he had been so tightly strapped and wedged into his kayak to improve performance that safety measures were neglected and he couldn't get out when he overturned. In the Canadian wilderness the loss of vital equipment can make an otherwise trivial accident into a serious one when a party is days or weeks away from the nearest outposts of civilization.

Doctors used to refer to the loss of body heat because of cold weather or water as 'exposure,' but in recent years the term 'hypothermia' has become generally used. Hypothermia means a lowering of the temperature of the body's core, which in turn leads to uncontrollable shivering, followed by increasing clumsiness and loss of judgment, and then by descent into unconsciousness and death. In mountaineering hypothermia is insidious because it can occur gradually, and the progressive deterioration of physical and mental capacities is not perceived until too late. Water is a much more efficient means of transferring heat than air, and the problem in canoeing is not that hypothermia creeps up unperceived and slowly, but that immersion in cold water can lead to hypothermia so quickly that the canoeist is unable to take avoidance action before his abilities are impaired. The following table illustrates how short the time is that a lightly clad person can survive in cold water:

Water temperature, °c	Time immersed before exhaustion or unconsciousness
0°	less than 15 minutes
0° –4.5°	15-30 minutes
4.5° –10°	30-60 minutes
10° –15°	1-2 hours

These are maximum times. Immersion in Arctic waters can be fatal in as little as ninety seconds, and immersion for more than three minutes is nearly always fatal.

Hypothermia is particularly dangerous to white water canoeists in the early spring when the water is close to the temperature of melting snow. It is also dangerous at all seasons to canoeists in the mountains of Canada's west and Arctic, where large rivers rarely warm up to more than 5°c. The safeguards against hypothermia are to dress appropriately – including wet suits if there is any likelihood of prolonged immersion, and wool clothing at other times – to be in good physical condition, to eat well, and to avoid prolonged immersion in cold water. When hypothermia threatens the rule is: first rescue the paddlers, then the canoes. Once a paddler is out of cold water, he needs heat to balance his losses. Heat can come from a hot fire, hot food, hot water, hot bodies, or exercise. It should be applied immediately and in large quantities. In the treatment of hypothermia alcohol, contrary to many outdoors manuals, is bad – it lets the blood from the body's core flow to the extremities and hence cool the core, aggravating the hypothermia.

Some fatal canoeing accidents are the products of grossly bad judgment. In May 1974, eight youths drowned on the Willow River near Prince George, BC. This is a small river in mountainous terrain, so difficult of access that mountain climbers had to descend on ropes to rescue the few remains that were found of the party. The group had not scouted the river, and it probably could not have been scouted. The river was swollen with cold spring floods from melting snow. The group had little or no experience in river running. The eight youths were dropped off on a Friday and hoped to arrive at Prince George on Saturday. Rescue teams began to search for them on the Sunday, using aircraft, helicopters, four-wheel drive vehicles and expert mountaineers. The rescuers found fallen trees blocking the river. Weeks later some bodies were recovered. This river was, at that time of year, beyond grade VI in danger. In effect it was not canoeable. That party did nothing correct. They were inexperienced, didn't scout, didn't have adequate support staff, and were canoeing in a flood-swollen frigid stream. They suffered from a presumption common to far too many Canadians – that simply because they shared the Canadian heritage and had done some (flat-water) canoeing, they were competent to tackle a difficult river.

In June 1975, each craft – four canoes and a kayak – in a British army adventure training party of thirteen men, led by a qualified canoe instructor, upset on the North Saskatchewan River in Banff National Park. One soldier drowned and the rest were strewn along a mile of riverbank. This piece of river is classed as grade I, although the rapids are grade II to VI. The grade VI piece consists of a high ledge with a twelve-foot drop followed by an awesome chute with a twenty-foot drop. It can be easily portaged. The canoeists apparently upset in fast water above this place, missed the take-out to the portage, and were carried through the drops. The accident occurred because of a severe error in matching the skills of the canoeists to the risks of the river – even though the river is classified as grade I, beginner's water.

When in doubt, portage, however painful it may be.

In spring wild water canoeing races, the overconfident persons who come bereft of experience and safety equipment usually prove the most difficult and obstinate to deal with. They refuse to accept the limitations of their knowledge and ability. The open canoe part of the Jock River race near Ottawa in the spring of 1975 was curtailed after the near death of a young boy who was trapped against the pier of a bridge for twenty minutes before being rescued. The previous day another man had drowned in an unauthorized practice run. He had worn a heavy overcoat, rubber boots, a defective life jacket, had no river experience or support crew, and, it was suspected, had been drinking alcohol. The Jock River is classified as grade II, and perhaps at most severe flood can reach the grade III category.

In urban civilization, many of the risks and challenges are interpersonal confrontations where bravado and bullying can win the day, but this sort of braggadocio counts for nothing in confrontations with the implacable impersonal force of flowing water. The river is real, not an image. So is the numbing shock of cold spring water, and swimming down a rapids with pieces of your canoe as company. The river still flows after the canoeist has finished his trip or drowned. It doesn't care either way. Courage is needed in white water canoeing, but courage must be balanced with skill and knowledge.

Beginning white water canoeists often have a blind foolhardiness that lets them run extremely dangerous pieces of river which even experts shun. After a few accidents, bruised bodies and broken canoes, this wild daring is replaced by excessive caution. Then, if the canoeist perseveres, with the development of skills and expanded canoeing experience a more mature courage develops. The canoeist who achieves this level can assess both difficulty and danger, choose the risks he wants to take and serenely bypass the water which he feels is beyond his competence or unnecessarily dangerous. At this point, in balancing daring and discretion, the paddler has developed good canoeing judgment.

Some people like to think they are competing with the river in white water canoeing. This is a very one-sided competition. The river cannot lose. In reality the paddler is competing with himself. He is trying to improve his ability to read and understand the water, his skills in handling difficult white water, his judgment in determining what he cannot safely do, and his courage to try, to persevere and to improve. In this relationship, as in a happy love affair, there are no losers, only winners.

Yet accidents can happen even to expert canoeists. Gino Watkins, the brilliant young English explorer, died while seal hunting on an expedition to Greenland in 1932. He had been kayaking alone. His kayak was found floating in the water and his clothes were lying on an ice flow, but his body was never recovered. He had been as skilled as the Eskimos in seal hunting but even the Eskimos rarely hunt alone. Cautious explorers minimize risks. Vilhjalmur Stefansson, whose explorations were even more impressive than Watkins', felt that 'Having an adventure is a sign that something unexpected, something unprovided against, has happened; it shows that someone is incompetent, that something has gone wrong.'[3]

Blair Fraser died in a canoeing accident on the Rollway Rapids of the Petawawa River in May 1968. He was with a group of the 'Voyageurs,' all experienced canoeists who, since 1951, had in innumerable trips covered thousands of miles of Canadian wilderness, including much river canoeing. Fraser and his canoeing partner missed the takeout for the portage; the canoe shipped water and sank in the first few standing waves. His partner survived, but Fraser drowned. They were wearing life jackets, and the party was large enough to be of adequate support. The only factor on the AMC list was cold spring water. It was the kind of error which no amount of experience or preparation can be guaranteed to avoid. Blair Fraser once said that if he could choose his own death, he would choose to drop dead at the bottom of the Flying Mile at Mont Tremblant on the last good day of spring skiing.

'Drowning in the spring torrent of the Rollway Rapids, on that bright sunny May Sunday morning,' his son concluded, 'had a dignity and suddenness about it that would have appealed to him. He died in the land he loved; the land had made him very happy. But, as he said once about his own father's death, after a slow and humiliating decline: "There are no happy endings".'[4]

Some risks are unavoidable in white water canoeing, but the risks tend to be exaggerated because the failures, not the successes, are publicized. Scientists who have studied human desires for, and responses to, high-risk physical activity have found that taking part in these sports produces a state of well-being in the participant which can approach euphoria. The sense of satisfaction and personal competence arising from successfully completing an arduous and challenging canoe trip can last for months and helps put the rest of life in perspective. Meeting and overcoming physical risks is still a basic human need.

In modern western society life has a much higher value than it has in other places, or has had at other times. The hardships endured not only by wilderness explorers but by the average traveller on the major fur trade routes less than a century ago would be unacceptable in Canada in the 1970s. So also would be the risks of fractures, infections, hernias and drowning the voyageurs faced. Life was cheap, and often short, in those days. Now there is a tendency to condemn physical risk-taking in sports as foolish. But one of the few important certainties in human life is that we are all going to die. Modern medicine has increased the possibility of dying a passive death at the end of a lingering and painful terminal illness. Sports like white water canoeing slightly increase the chances of a quick and active death. Many doctors take up white water canoeing – more in proportion than lawyers, accountants or engineers. Dr Walt Blackadar, possibly the most adventurous white water canoeist in the world, commented at the beginning of his most dangerous trip: 'I'm not suicidal but get depressed watching so many patients with incurable diseases.'[5] He and many other people have found that in a strange but powerful way, risk-taking in sport is an affirmation and celebration of life.

FIVE

Canoe trips

The pleasures and satisfactions of a canoeing trip are largely dependent upon the time and effort that go into planning and preparations. As his experience gradually builds, a canoeist will find that preparation takes less time, although this is often counterbalanced by the need for increased planning as he becomes more adventurous and goes on longer trips further into the unknown. A canoeist needs to consider what kind of trip is appropriate for the season, whom he wants as companions, how far he can expect to go in the time available, what food and clothing and equipment he needs. These aspects of planning and preparation are the subject of this chapter. Comparisons with the Indians, voyageurs and woodsmen of old have been included for interest. Most canoeists retracing the historic rivers of Canada are prompted to wonder how the old-timers did it, whether life was better in those days, and if present-day canoeists can still live simply off the land.

The Canoeing Seasons
Spring, from late March until May, with its combination of high water, warm sun and absence of black flies and mosquitoes is the best river canoeing season in southern Ontario and Quebec. Many rivers can be canoed only then when, for a while, they are raging torrents which may change from grade IV to grade II in as little as two weeks as the spring floods recede. Most rivers in southern Ontario are short and best suited for day or weekend trips, but being close to large centres of population they are ideally located for such short expeditions. Nearly every weekend during this period, as well, at least one downriver canoe race takes place in southern Ontario, sponsored by a local club or group: the first, which attracts hundreds of competitors, is traditionally on the Credit River west of Toronto and is organized by the Ontario Voyageurs Kayak Club. To the many canoeists who are not interested in such racing, spring river canoeing permits the settled parts of Ontario to be explored from an unusual vantage point. Each year I try to canoe a few new

The start of the Credit River race in late March. This is the beginning of the canoeing season in Ontario for several hundred competitors.

rivers as well as to revisit old favourites.

In the second half of May the rivers of the south begin to dry up, but the rivers of the near north – of the Laurentians draining into the Ottawa and St Lawrence, of the north shores of Georgian Bay and Lake Superior, and of the Algonquin Park region – are at their best. By then they have usually passed their dangerous peaks of spring flooding and are clear of ice. The sun is high and bright, the weather is approaching 20°C (68°F) and insects are still scarce. In a few more weeks dozens of small wilderness rivers will dry up. But in the meantime they are open and within a day's drive of Toronto and Montreal. Many canoeists extend the May long weekend to make a five-day canoeing trip down one of them.

By mid-June, unless the spring is exceptionally delayed and wet, canoeists must begin to look to larger and often more distant rivers. June also brings out the blackflies. Sensitivity to fly bites varies with exposure. At first people are extremely sensitive, but after thousands of bites the body ceases to react.

Spring is the only season in which hundreds of rivers of southern Canada can be canoed. Spring trips allow the canoeist to observe the countryside from a unique vantage point.

The old-time voyageurs and woodsmen were so hardened by years in the bush that they were immune to and scarcely noticed the bites of blackflies and mosquitoes. They had no mosquito nets, and no repellents except bear grease. Few modern city dwellers reach this level of tolerance, and they find the small rivers of the forested mid-north of Canada a hell during June; even fly repellents and head nets can be inadequate. For this reason many canoeists restrict their June canoeing to large rivers swept clear of insects by wind or spend this period at home planning later mid-summer trips.

River canoeing during the mid-summer is restricted to large rivers which do not dry up or which have a regular flow because they are controlled by dams. This is the season which opens up to the canoe all northern Canada, where many lakes and rivers become passable only in late June or even July because of lingering ice. Summer thus is the season for long wilderness river trips. The weather is at its most benign, the large rivers are in good flow, and if a canoeist makes the effort to drive or fly thousands of miles he can have a trip to remember. July and August are the only months suitable for canoeing in the Yukon, while in the Northwest Territories the season is even shorter and a canoeist on lakes risks having to drag his canoe over candling ice until mid-July, and polar gales begin by the end of August. Overcrowding on canoe routes is becoming a hazard, however. The Ontario Ministry of Natural Resources is limiting the daily number of canoeists and campers entering Algonquin Park. So far this is the only place in Canada where canoeing must be rationed, but permit systems are in force on an increasing number of American rivers.

Autumn, like May, is a fine canoeing season in mid-Canada, although low water restricts most activity to lakes and large rivers. Canoe routes are almost deserted after Labour Day weekend, which still to many people marks the end of summer. But the weather stays warm until mid-October and there are by then few insects. Colours of fall begin to dapple the monotonous greens of midsummer. Towards the Canadian Thanksgiving weekend in mid-October the near-north, like Algonquin Park, changes from early to late autumn, and after that date frost and snow can be expected. The days become crisp and the woods have a stark beauty when the leaves have fallen. Good canoeing continues until the lakes become ice-covered in early December. However, it is wise to avoid canoeing during deer hunting season except in protected areas like Algonquin Park: it isn't pleasant to have hunters sight at you along their rifles (one hopes they are using the telescopic sight only to study the craft more closely); to hear surrounding artillery like the start of a war; or to have the feeling that a hunter might be musing that it's an odd-looking deer which wears a bright orange life jacket and paddles a canoe down the river.

Racers in covered craft have their first and biggest season in spring. Competitions continue during the summer and early fall, but are restricted to the rivers which do not dry up – like those of the western mountains – and to those which can be assured of a regular flow because they are controlled by dams. In exceptionally dry years, even dam-controlled rivers can be unfit for competition because of inadequate water. This happened in 1975 during the world championships in Yugoslavia, and in the same year in Canada at the annual summer races of the Madawaska Kanu Camp.

Some white water canoeists continue practising on open stretches of rivers throughout the winter, and more train in indoor pools. Most, however, adopt another outdoor recreation during the winter – increasingly it is cross-country skiing – and their canoeing then is limited to reading catalogues of outdoor equipment and planning the trips for the coming year. There are always exceptions. In February 1974, the Canadian Press carried this story from Port Erie:

At 1:20 a.m. Sunday, a Niagara Regional policeman had to radio somewhat sheepishly for help – his cruiser had just been rammed by a canoe.

Constable Edwin Gilmore was checking a noise complaint when he spotted some happy tobogganers swooshing down a hill in a canoe.

He parked his car at the bottom of the hill to find out what was going on. Several minutes later his car was clobbered broadside.

About $50 damage was done to the cruiser and the canoe will never float – or toboggan – again.

Police say no charges were laid because they could not find a section of the Highway Traffice Act which covered careless canoeing.

Companionship

Canoeing alone has its special delights of nature-watching, fishing, solitude, introspection and extraspection, but white water canoeing is normally, and should be, a group activity. The open Canadian canoe is handled best in white water by two men. Also, there is safety in numbers.

Beginning white water canoeists should make their first trips with more experienced companions. These can often be found through local outdoors and canoeing clubs, YMCAs, church groups, or other organizations. Provincial canoeing organizations can usually give the names of clubs that, like the Ontario Voyageurs Kayak Club, run a schedule of trips at all levels of difficulty, and often also run winter training sessions in swimming pools.

Often, over the years, a small group of like-minded individuals will find that they enjoy canoeing together and will form a sort of informal, unorganized canoeing club. The 'Voyageurs' who explored so many of the historic fur-trade routes in the fifties and sixties was of this sort. My own group of canoeing companions has coalesced over more than a decade. Its name, which was suggested after one particularly enjoyable fall trip in Algonquin Park, is the 'Canadian Outdoors Rum Toddy Society' (CORTS for short). Members of CORTS live in Toronto, Montreal, Ottawa and elsewhere, and two or more of them happily get together many times each year. On some trips, usually the more rugged, only CORTS members are invited; other trips will have up to fifteen canoeists, including women, children, friends and acquaintances. The big group trips are relaxed holidays and are training and recruiting grounds, but they nurture companionship in their own right, including parent-child relationships.

Canoeists on any but the shortest trip are in contact with one another twenty-four hours of the day, and may be isolated from most other human contact. Trips act as a sort of pressure cooker in human relations, where people get to know, like or dislike one another extremely quickly. The further into the wilderness a trip goes, and the greater its duration, the more important is care in choosing companions. Quirks and personality traits that are merely amusing in civilization and on brief trips can begin to irritate after a week or two in the bush, and many one-time friends have wanted never to see or talk to each other after festering rancour has accumulated during a long trip. Conversely, the compatability and mutual understanding that builds up can be deep, lasting and rewarding. Before going on a long trip, a group should make certain that they are compatible on a short one.

Distance, Endurance and Motivation

In planning any trip, a canoeist must be realistic about the distance that can be covered in a single day. Few of us today can begin to equal the feats of the voyageurs. Because of their long waterlines the large craft of the fur trade move more quickly than modern canoes but even so the distances they covered were prodigious. On well known routes the voyageur's day began at 2 or 3 am, and continued until 8 pm, although when the day's work began with a portage or an unfamiliar rapid the start would be delayed until daybreak. The canoe would stop for breakfast at dawn, and for lunch about 2 pm. Supper came after camp was set up for the night. While they were on the water the voyageurs would paddle steadily at five to six miles per hour, and about once an hour would stop for a *pipe*, or pipe of tobacco – part of each voyageur's provisions was fourteen pounds of tobacco. Distances were often measured by time intervals of *pipes* rather than by miles or hours. During their fifteen to eighteen hours of paddling the voyageurs could, on flat water, make more than seventy miles. Going downstream they covered even greater distances. Alexander Mackenzie, on his exploration of the river that now bears his name, travelled the more than one thousand miles between Great Slave Lake and the Arctic Ocean in thirteen days, nearly eighty miles per day, even though he made several prolonged stops to meet Indians. Sir George Simpson, general superintendent of the Hudson's Bay Company, in his 'light' canoe (a *canot du nord* with a picked crew for speedy travel) averaged more than ninety miles per day on some downriver routes. The seventy miles of the French River from Lake Nipissing to Georgian Bay, which includes two portages and which takes three days for modern canoeists, was only a single day's travel to the voyageurs.

Because they had to carry two or three loads across each portage, voyageurs

While on the trail the voyageurs began at dawn, as in this further painting by Frances Hopkins. One man is using his blanket to protect him from insects. Rocks are actually more comfortable to sleep on than sand.

could cover only about half a mile an hour on land. Long portages were divided by *poses*, a quarter to half a mile apart, at which the voyageurs would put down their loads and return for more. A load was normally two *pièces* of ninety pounds each, and each voyageur was responsible for six *pièces*. Exceptionally strong men would carry three, four or five in one load. Alexander Mackenzie had known voyageurs at the Grand Portage to 'set off with two packages of ninety pounds each, and return with two others of the same weight, in the course of six hours, being a distance of eighteen miles over hills and mountains.'[1] The pay was a 'Spanish dollar' for each *pièce* carried.

Even when there were many portages the voyageurs covered remarkable distances. Archibald McDonald, who led Simpson's party in lightly loaded express canoes from York Factory on Hudson Bay to Fort Langley on the Pacific in 1828, recorded that the total travelling time for the 3,181 miles was sixty-five days, an average of fifty miles per day, and much of the trip was difficult upstream travel. Alexander Mackenzie took thirty-seven days to retrace upstream a thirteen-day downriver trip in 1789. Most of the time the current was too fast for paddling, and his men tracked (lined upstream) their canoes along the river's edge. Their speed at tracking was less than two miles

Men who spent their lives in wilderness canoeing developed tremendous strength and endurance. The man on the left is carrying his huge load solely with a tumpline across his forehead.

per hour, yet they averaged twenty-seven miles per day.

These distances were achieved by picked crews in light canoes. Loaded freight canoes were slower, but the hours of work were as long. The feats of the voyageurs during the six to eight weeks they were on the trail were possible because of hours of work longer than modern canoeists are prepared to endure, years of conditioning in as hard physical labour as humanity has ever known, and a willingness to allow men by early middle age to exhaust their physical vitality through grinding travail. Father Jean de Brébeuf told prospective Jesuit missionaries: 'All the fine qualities which might make you loved and respected in France are like pearls trampled under the feet of swine, or rather mules, which utterly despise you when they see that you are not as good pack animals as they are. If you could go naked and carry the load of a horse upon your back, as they do, then you would be wise according to their doctrine, and would be recognized as a great man, otherwise not.'[2]

Although the French-Canadian voyageur has received the most attention, many canoe brigades were manned by Indians and Métis who worked just as hard and long. Sir George Simpson's canoe was manned with a picked crew of Iroquois, like Tyrrell's a half century later, from the Caughnawaga reserve near Montreal. Probably the Orkneymen who later handled the York boats

A typical voyageur, drawn by the Canadian artist of the western frontier, Paul Kane.

in the western interior also worked as hard, although their labours have not been romanticized like those of the voyageurs, and John Jacob Astor's statement that he would prefer to have one voyageur than three of any other kind has been quoted more often than it deserves.

The achievements of the fur trade canoeists are so extraordinary compared with those of modern man that I have often wondered what forces impelled them. Pride was a first factor. They were not driven like slaves by their masters, but delighted in their physical prowess. Voyageurs were known to paddle for forty-eight hours without stopping simply to beat another canoe in an informal race. A bowman would sulk for days in shame after his canoe hit a rock. Second, the fur trade to be profitable demanded all-out speed because the distances in the fur country were so great, the season so short, and the canoe such a costly way of transporting goods. Third, canoeing, in spite of its hazards, was healthy, varied and interesting outdoor work. Fourth, people worked harder in those days, and the comparison between canoeing in the fur trade and other jobs like farming, mining or a factory, where the work week was then often seventy hours, was not as marked as it is with modern forty-hour weeks. Finally, the canoeists of the fur trade regarded themselves as an élite. Their horizons were narrow. They spent their working lives in the brigades, advancing from *milieu* to *avant* and perhaps even *guide* before old age or accident caught up with them. Within their closed system physical prowess graded men. Probably the linguistic and religious gaps between the English-Protestant company officers and the French-Catholic voyageurs accentuated the latter's sense of pride and identity.

The risks and hardships of the work moulded the character of the voyageur, whom Grace Lee Nute described as 'class conscious; he considered himself favoured by fortune to belong to his group; he took a happy pride in doing his work in such a way as to bring credit to his fellow workers; and he considered the toil and hardships of his chosen work incidental to the profession and was seldom known to pity himself.'[3] This is slightly rosy-tinted. Sometimes voyageurs rebelled against hard labour and bad food, and Grand Portage and other large posts had jail cells for the rebels. Daniel Harmon, a fur trader from New England, described them in less favourable terms:

they are too volatile ever to admit anything either good or bad to lay hold on their hearts or affections – and although they make Gods of their bellies, yet when necessity obliges them, even when destitute of every kind of nourishment, they will endure all the fatigue and misery of hard labour and cold weather etc. for several days following without much complaining ... They are great talkers but in the utmost sense of the word, thoughtless ... make many resolutions which are as soon broke as formed ... never think to provide themselves to Day with what they may want for the morrow, but allow each Day to provide for itself ... and they, like Sailors, seldom lay up any part of their earnings to serve them in the decline of life, and they also resemble them in being shocking blasphemers ... They are not brave, however when they think there is little or no danger then they will, as they say, *faire l'Homme*, that is make the Man – and while before a person they are as bare-faced flatterers, as they are base detracters, when behind his back ... in short (they like other People) are a compound of what is good & bad but the latter qualities far out balance those of the former.[4]

Still, without this childish boasting, competitiveness, and willingness to live for the present and ignore the future, the voyageurs would not have tolerated, let alone survived and even enjoyed, the risks, rigours and difficulties of the fur trade. And without the prodigious labours of the voyageurs, the vast territories of Canada could not have been tied together.

Today, paddling a canoe at a rate of sixty strokes per minute for eighteen hours per day for weeks on end is beyond most people's physical capacity. Even persons who keep in good physical shape by regular exercise at endurance sports like running, cross-country skiing and distance swimming find it difficult to put more than ten hours per day into paddling and portaging, and the distances travelled are correspondingly reduced.

Six fit Americans in 1973 tried to retrace the route of Sir John Franklin's first expedition from Yellowknife to his winter post at Fort Enterprise near the headwaters of the Coppermine River. Although the U.S. crew had modern aluminum canoes, lightweight equipment and dried food, and although their workday was twelve to fourteen hours, they found that day-by-day they lagged behind the distances covered by the earlier heavier-burdened group. After twenty-one days they had covered 120 miles; Franklin had covered the same stretch in ten. The Americans decided to turn back. They concluded: 'We are killing ourselves.' The main differences between them and Franklin's crew, they decided, 'was not so much that our bodies and minds had degenerated significantly. It was that during the intervening 150 years the level of comfort and human expectations had changed. Too many soft sheets lay between Sam [one of the American party] and Akaitcho [Franklin's Indian guide].'[5] Other groups in recent years have succeeded, however, in reaching the Arctic Ocean via the Coppermine in a single season.

On one mid-October trip four healthy fit men from CORTS completed in forty-eight hours the loop in Algonquin Park from the dock in Lake Opeongo at Sproule Bay, to the Crow River, to Lake Lavieille and Dickson Lake, and back to the dock at Lake Opeongo. The distance is about fifty miles, of which more than forty miles are flat water, and seven miles are portages, including one three miles in length. About twenty hours were spent in active canoeing, which filled the hours from dawn to dusk at that late season. This was hard work. It left no time for resting during the day, for looking at animals and scenery, fishing, or any of the other activities that should accompany wilderness leisure travel. This trip has now been hallowed in CORTS' lore as the 'route march.' About every second year we do something similar. Most of the time we go more slowly, and do more than just canoe. However, there is a peculiar masochistic satisfaction in the occasional route march, much as there is in competing in Canada's two-day hundred-mile cross-country ski marathon.

Downriver canoeists on large rivers with a fast current and no portages, like the lower Albany River in northern Ontario, the North and South Saskatchewan Rivers, or the Mackenzie River, can easily complete more than fifty miles in a day. Smaller rivers which are obstructed by many rapids and falls are slower going, and on them a party putting in eight hours of actual canoeing may make only ten or fewer miles in a day. Headwinds slow canoes down, and can even prevent them from moving on a large river or lake. Upstream work is slower than downstream. The crew from the Geological

Sailing is a change from paddling over flat water, and can be just as fast.

Survey of Canada which first officially viewed Virginia Falls on the Nahanni took twenty-one days to make the slightly more than one hundred miles upstream to the falls, but only thirteen hours to descend the same distance. If the maps are poor, or if portages have grown over and have to be cleared, or cannot be found, a long day of canoeing can produce little progress. It once took us from 8 am to 8 pm to discover, blaze and clear, and carry gear over a three-mile portage with a 500-foot climb. This sort of wandering in the wilderness we call a 'bush thrash,' and a few thrashes are inevitable in little-travelled country.

A rough guide for an average modern party is three miles per hour on the flat, one mile per hour on portages, multiplied by the number of hours per day spent in actual canoeing. The hours per day, once lunch breaks, fishing breaks, and other delays are taken into account, will not often be more than ten, and are more likely to be fewer than eight. Considering all these factors, the distance an average crew can cover in a day of moderately difficult canoeing is rarely more than twenty miles. If the party includes unfit people and children, or if there are stops to play in rapids, to fish, to photograph or to take side trips, distances are correspondingly reduced. This is not impressive in comparison with the voyageurs, but the voyageurs' goal was to transport trade goods and furs as quickly as possible between two points, regardless of the scenery or hardship; the goal of modern canoeists is to enjoy an unfamiliar feast of wilderness and physical exercise.

Food: Past and Present

Indians, fur traders, explorers and leisure canoeists have, in feeding themselves, varied between the extremes of living off the land and bringing their food with them. The Indians and explorers were close to the first extreme, the voyageurs and modern canoeists close to the second. In nomadic Indian bands, hunting consisted of brief periods of intense, arduous work followed by longer periods when the hunters rested while the fruits of the hunt were eaten, preserved or made into clothing and shelter. It was a precarious, subsistence style of existence. Indians of those days were not regular workers, and probably on an average put fewer hours into the hunt than modern salaried workers put in at their jobs. They certainly worked shorter hours than the voyageurs or the average nineteenth century farmer. They feasted when the hunt was successful, but also often suffered in semi-starvation. They developed great endurance and resistance to hardship in surviving the lean periods. Daniel Harmon observed that 'the Indians are not regular in their meals; and they will eat a little, half a dozen times in a day, if they have food at hand. But they are not great eaters; and they often subsist for a great length of time upon a very little food. When they choose, however, and in a particular manner, sometimes at feasts, they will gorge down an incredible quantity.'[6] Indians probably ate little more than modern canoeists.

The voyageurs by comparison were consistently prodigious eaters while on the trail. Their daily food ration was ten pounds of salmon, or fifteen pounds of whitefish, or three pounds of pemmican.[7] Assuming that these figures refer to the whole fish, and that one-third of the fish was waste, the value in food calories per day for this consumption is 6,900 Cal/day for salmon, and 7,200 Cal/day for whitefish.[8] Assuming an average value of 150 Cal/oz. for the pemmican (see below) the food value of the pemmican was similar, at 7,200 Cal/day. These calorie values are extraordinarily high. The Sierra Club has concluded that on backpacking trips, 3,500 Cal/day is the average maximum needed. Many grown males, to keep their weight down, now consume only 2,500 Cal/day or less. Few athletes consume more than 4,000 to 5,000 Cal/day.

The voyageurs consumed so many calories because they expended that much energy. The following table gives an estimate of the energy output of a voyageur on a typical workday, including the energy required simply to maintain his body's existence (the basal metabolism). The assumptions are: that the average voyageur weighed 155 pounds; that the level of energy expenditure in canoeing and portaging averaged 200 Cal/per hour for each hundred pounds a voyageur weighed; and that fifteen hours per day were spent canoeing. No allowance has been made for time spent doing camp chores. The average weight for a voyageur was suggested by Eric Morse. The 200 Cal/100 lbs/hour figure for canoeing is a reasonable level for prolonged vigorous exercise. In comparison, sawing wood consumes 260 Cal/100 lbs/hour, running 320, and walking at four miles per hour 160. If anything, the 200 figure is low.[9] Using these cautious assumptions, the energy output in a day for a voyageur was:

Basal metabolism: 155 lbs x 1100 Cal/100 lbs	= 1705 Cal
Canoeing: 15 hrs x 200 Cal/100 lbs/hour x 155 lbs	= 4650
Total	6355
Add 10% for 'specific dynamic action' (the energy consumed and wasted in metabolising the food)	635
Grand total, one day's energy output	6990 Cal

The historical records of food consumption, and calculations for energy requirements on the basis of modern nutritional science, thus produce almost identical calorie figures.

Even with their gargantuan diets, the voyageurs lost weight. Paul Kane remarked that at a three-day pause at a fort, 'the men did little but eat and sleep. The rapidity with which they changed their appearance was astonishing. Some of them became so much improved in looks, that it was with difficulty we could recognize our voyageurs.'[10]

Providing food was an important logistical problem for the fur trade. It could not be done by hunting. The voyageurs had to move furs and trade goods to a rigorous schedule during the season that the rivers were open, and could hunt only when the weather prevented travel. They gathered any game they discovered – bears, moose, deer, beaver (beaver tails were a special delicacy, permitted during Lent), ducks, turtles, duck eggs, fish, turtle eggs and anything else they could catch, shoot, trap or get from the Indians – but on the major routes provisions had to be carried. In any case, the frequent passage of fur trade canoes soon exterminated nearby game. Sir George Simpson in 1824 found that in the well-travelled six hundred miles from Fort York to Frog Portage between the Churchill and Sturgeon-Weir rivers in Saskatchewan, 'the Country ... is much exhausted, indeed we did not see a single animal on the whole route exceeding the size of a Musk Rat.'[11]

The favoured food of the interior fur trade was pemmican, a fifty-fifty mixture of dried lean meat and fat, made on the Great Plains from buffalo. The meat was cut into lean strips, dried in the sun, and pounded into flakes before being placed in bags made of buffalo hide (hair out) and mixed with an equal amount of melted buffalo fat. Saskatoon or service berries, or wild cherries, and sometimes sugar were added to the best pemmican. A standard bag of this mix weighed ninety pounds, and took one buffalo to make. As long as it did not get wet pemmican would keep for several years. It was the major trade good of the Hudson's Bay Company with the Métis of the prairies, and it was the only good for which the Company bartered liquor. It was an extremely concentrated food. Its calorie value, on the calculations that dried lean beef has 100 Cal/oz and tallow 200 Cal/oz, is 150 Cal/oz – far better than other preserved foods then available, and with an excellent balance of fat and protein, large quantities of both of which are necessary for regular hard labour in cold climates. In comparison, biscuits, dried peas, sugar, rice and flour contain about 100 Cal/oz and lack fat and protein. Pemmican also contained all necessary vitamins except c, which however was present when berries were added. It was eaten raw, mixed with flour and fried, or combined with whatever else was available in a thick soup called 'rubaboo.' Such a compact, well-balanced food enabled the voyageurs to perform long hours of heavy work. But often it was not of good quality:

take the scrapings from the driest outside corner of a very stale piece of cold roast-beef, add to it lumps of tallowy, rancid fat, then garnish all with long human hairs, on which string pieces, like beads upon a necklace, and short hairs of dogs or oxen, or both, and you have a fair imitation of common pemmican. Indeed, the presence of hair in the food has suggested the inquiry whether the hair on the buffaloes from which the pemmican is made does not grow on the inside of the skin. The abundance of small stones or pebbles in pemmican also indicates the discovery of a new buffalo diet heretofore unknown to naturalists.[12]

Only close to the Great Plains was pemmican the dominant food. Farther north it was supplemented by whitefish, to the west by salmon. In the east, pork, beans, peas and flour were staples. The men who wintered in the western interior contemptuously referred to the men of the east as *mangeurs de lard*, or pork-eaters. After his winter in the west Frances Hopkins's husband was described to Sir George Simpson as 'no more a porkeater,' but 'a regular voyageur' eating 'horseflesh, dog and everything like one who has been travelling all his life.'[13]

As they passed into less well-travelled country, travellers depended more on the land and less on food brought with them. The explorations of Mackenzie, Thompson, Franklin and others would not have been possible without hunting. Even Sir George Simpson's party took time off to hunt after they left the established routes. They had full bellies for once when:

We killed a fine large fat Buck Moose, and as ourselves and people were a good deal harrassed by continual marching since we left York and but indifferently fed I thought the present a good opportunity of indulging both them and us with a half holyday it being now about 3 O'Clock p.m. Preparations were forthwith on foot, the Moose was soon relieved of his Skin, a rousing Fire made and all hands employed to the utmost of their skill in the art of Cookery; a haunch the Nose and Tongue Mr. McMillan laid aside for ourselves and the rest of the Animal made over to the people, who were occupied from the time of putting ashore until the sound of leve-leve-leve the following morning in a continued succession of Eating roasting and boiling.[14]

Some explorers, like Samuel Hearne, David Thompson, and in this century Stefansson, depended on hunting for most of their sustenance. Hearne joined with Indians and adopted their lifestyle.

Franklin took some provisions with him on his first expedition, but also engaged some Indian hunters who, however, did not shoot enough game to

The Tyrrells could not have made their tremendous wilderness journeys without almost unlimited supplies of game. When they found caribou they stopped, hunted, and dried the meat in the sun – as on this day in 1893 at Carey Lake, NWT. Too many people travel in the wilderness now to enable canoeists to provision themselves in this manner, even if the game laws permitted it.

sustain his large party. The white officers did no hunting, and were a drain on the scarce food supplies. This was one of the causes of the tragic and unnecessary deaths of nine of Franklin's eleven voyageurs. A contributing factor was the inefficiency with which the party used the food. On their starvation-haunted return from the mouth of the Coppermine, his crew had the luck to find the skin and bones of caribou which had been killed and eaten by wolves. Skin is as nourishing as lean meat, and bones nearly as good if they are eaten raw or boiled. Instead, Franklin's party scorched both skin and bones letting 'most or all the food value go up in smoke and flames. Then they ate the charcoal.'[15] Good survival technique is to put all food together in a pot and boil.

On the Tyrrell expedition, in contrast, all men, including the Tyrrell brothers, took part in the hunting, and on their way to the Thelon they paused for several days after a successful caribou hunt to dry the meat. J. B. Tyrrell said he never missed a meal on his northern explorations, though sometimes a meal was delayed a day or so.

Explorers and prospectors often picked only the best cuts from the moose and caribou they shot and left the rest as waste. This profligate use of natural resources could be adopted only in little-travelled wilderness where unfamiliarity with rifles made big game easy prey.

Hunting and fishing to supplement brought-in provisions remained the norm for northern canoe journeys until well into the twentieth century. James Dickson, an Ontario land surveyor, in 1886 described a summer tour by canoe in what was to become Algonquin Park. His party brought bacon, flour, biscuits, tea, beans, dried apples, peas, raisins and sugar with them. In addition they shot at, wounded, but lost a moose and shot and killed two deer. They also caught quantities of lake and brook trout.

John D. Robins, a professor at the University of Toronto, and a companion in the late thirties brought the following provisions with them to Algonquin Park:[16]

Bacon, 7 lbs	Butter, 4 lbs
Chipped beef, 1/2 lb	Tea, 1 lb
Klim, 2 pound cans	G. Washington coffee, 1 can
Evaporated milk, 6 small cans	Prunes 3 lbs
Sugar 4 lbs	Beans, 2 lbs
Onions, 12 large Spanish	Jam, Strawberry, 1 lb
Cheese, 1 lb	Pancake flour, 4 packages
Oranges, 6	Chocolate bars, 7 ten-cent ones
Salt, 1 lb	Bread, 9 loaves
Rolled oats, 6 lbs	

The total cost of the food was $11.63, and it was to last sixteen days. It averaged 2,500 calories per man/day, and the weight including packaging was 2 lbs per man/day. This provided half as many calories per ounce as the voyageurs' pemmican. Robins and his friend caught vast quantities of fish to supplement the food, and with these were more than adequately fed, although they became heartily sick of the taste of trout.

Although many wilderness handbooks are filled with suggestions for living off the land, and modern back-to-nature enthusiasts long to do so, canoeists cannot now feed themselves by hunting and gathering. A fisherman in Algonquin Park is lucky to catch one fish per hour. The law does not permit big game hunting to the extent necessary for self-sufficiency, and without big game it is almost impossible to gather enough calories. Most vegetables and fruits contain ten to fifteen calories per ounce. It takes nearly thirteen pounds of fresh fruit and vegetables to provide 3,000 calories, and more than six pounds of fresh fish. Getting eight pounds of fish, or seventeen pounds of fruit and vegetables, or any equivalent combination of these, is in most of Canada a full-time occupation now as it was for the Indians, who knew more than modern outdoorsmen about wilderness foods, who lived when there was more game available, and who even so sometimes starved. Fresh trout, pickerel fillets, raspberries and blueberries, mushrooms and fiddle-heads are wonderful and tasty side dishes, but they cannot be relied on regularly for the main course. Usually the accompanying milk, sugar, butter and flour have as much food value as the wild-gathered provisions themselves.

The difficulty of living off the land affects the course of action after accidents. If a canoe is wrecked and provisions lost the odds are quite strong that if the party attempts to survive on wild-gathered food it will each day expend more energy than it gathers. If a party knows where it is, knows how to reach safety, and can make safety in a few days, it is better to go hungry and travel to safety than try to survive by fishing and gathering. If food is lost but the canoe is rescued, the odds favouring travel are increased. Only when the journey to rescue is measured in weeks of travel does staying put, scavenging, and waiting for rescue become the better alternative. Even then, unless the party shoots big game, each day is likely to see an excess of energy expended over energy gathered, and a corresponding loss of vitality and capacity to survive.

The modern canoeist, like the voyageur, must bring his food with him. There is little problem in provisioning short trips. Supermarkets have a vast array of dried, preserved and tinned foods covering the whole spectrum of gustatory persuasions. For a canoe trip of less than a week's duration, three pounds of food per person per day can be carried easily, and for this weight excellent variety and nutrition can be obtained. The normal calorie requirements for adult males on a vigorous canoe trip is about 3,000 calories for the first three or four days; then the appetite increases, and 4,000 to 4,500 calories can easily be consumed. Women generally eat less than men; teenage boys more. But there is little hardship in consumption below these levels: most adult North Americans are too fat, and a restricted diet plus healthy exercise can produce a beneficial loss of weight.

More care is needed in provisioning long trips in the northern wilderness where all supplies must be carried with the party. On these trips, although not to the same extent as in backpacking, every calorie and every ounce of weight is important. The pemmican of the voyageurs was the ideal food for this sort of work: rich in vitamins, fat and protein; concentrated in energy per unit weight; edible for years. It has no inexpensive modern substitute, and canoeists can only with great attention to detail achieve the 150 Cal/oz ratio of good pemmican. Some canoeists make their own.

The best guides to provisioning long northern expeditions can be found in books for backpackers, especially Colin Fletcher's *The Complete Walker*, and the Sierra Club Totebook by Hasse Bunnelle, *Food for Knapsackers*. Calvin Rutstrum's *The New Way of the Wilderness* is a good presentation of the culinary habits and rationale of traditional canoe travel.

With care food weight can be kept to two and a half pounds per man/day, providing a well-balanced 4,000 calories per day. Canoeists on trips of up to a month in duration do not need to worry about vitamins. Many good foods are prepared by the specialized makers of camp foods although they tend to be overweighted in carbohydrates and need additional fat and protein. The lightest protein sources are freeze-dried meats, but they are expensive. Canned meat is satisfactory, but adds weight. Some pre-packaged camp dinners require three or more cooking pots, and do not contain enough calories. The main meal on a long wilderness trip is often a one-dish modern *rubaboo*, with at least 1,000 calories per serving (equals 9 to 10 ounces of uncooked freeze-dried food). Appetizers, side-dishes and desserts are optional. At two or two and a half pounds per day, the food for a thirty-day trip will weigh sixty to seventy-five pounds per person which is not, except in kayaks, an unmanageable load.

A typical food day for CORTS begins with Tang, or some equivalent. I budget on at least one package of dried fruit juice per person for each whole day in hot weather. A package will do four people for breakfast. The main part of breakfast is usually oatmeal porridge, with milk (from dried skim milk) and sugar. Sometimes we have eggs and bacon, but I object to this because they take too long to cook. Bacon and dried eggs are excellent sources of protein and fat in cold weather and on longer trips when the fat from the bacon can be saved for other cooking. Sometimes in hot weather I substitute a nourishing ready-to-eat cereal like granola or Alpen for the oatmeal. I keep away from corn flakes and similar dry cereals: they have a lot of bulk and little nourishment. Sometimes we have cheese, another good source of fat and protein, with breakfast. Our normal daily ration of cheese is about three ounces per person. When we have fish, we often fry them for breakfast, and they, like the cheese, provide fat and protein. Bread, jam, and peanut butter complete breakfast. The most calorie-rich of these is the peanut butter. We also have coffee or tea, depending on the preferences of the cook.

During the day we have many short breaks and snacks, like the voyageurs' *pipes*. Our usual snack is a fifty-fifty mixture of raisins and nuts, rich in carbohydrates, proteins and fats. The ration of this mixture is four to five ounces per person per day and it all gets eaten, especially in cool weather.

Lunch is bread or biscuits (hard ship's biscuits or pumpernickel because they store and last well) with cheese, sardines, corned beef, salami, butter, jam, peanut butter, etc. Only on a very long trip will I cook the traditional bannock – simply my lazy preference. The calorie content of biscuits and pumpernickel is equivalent to that of flour. In cool weather we usually boil a soup to go along with lunch, but we omit it in the summer months. Tea for those who want it.

Supper is the largest meal. With the modern variety of dried foods nearly anything is possible: chili con carne, spaghetti with meat sauce, chicken with rice, stew, beef stroganoff, to name only a few. For fancy dinners we sometimes have two dishes, one of meat (tinned or freeze-dried) and one of potatoes. Sometimes we also have vegetables. For the first night out (the Saturday night on a weekend trip) we usually have a more elaborate meal of roast lamb or steak, potatoes and vegetables. One campfire meal treasured in memory was beef marinated in wine, grilled as shishkebab, and served on curried rice. In cool weather dinner is preceded by soup. In all weather it is preceded by toddies – rum mixed with various flavours of fruit juice in warm weather, or with a hot toddy mix of boiling water, sugar, butter and spices in cool weather. Sometimes we bring a bottle of wine to go with dinner. (The bottle, like all garbage, is carried out.) If fish have been caught, they are usually an appetizer before dinner. Or, if there are enough, the main dish. After dinner, those still hungry – the growing boys – munch on cheese, raisins and nuts, bread and jam. Then we gently subside around the campfire, sipping the later rounds of toddies, and discussing the state of the universe. We rarely bother to bring candles or flashlights, although a compact flashlight does sometimes come in handy. The whole procedure, from the end of canoeing until the end of dinner, is two hours or less. The campfire lasts as long as we choose. The voyageurs might have eaten more, but not better. CORTS culinary practices ebb and flow. Meals get more elaborate as each member, when he organizes a trip, tries to outdo the one before. Then someone rebels and there is a return to a spartan regime. Then a gradual build-up. Members constantly experiment with new foods and meals.

A type of provisioning which CORTS has not been able to try in Canada was named *le canotage gastronomique* by Arthur Koestler. 'The idea,' he wrote, 'is to travel, in a canoe, down one of the great rivers of France – the Dordogne or the Loire; to spend one's days on the water and one's nights at a comfortable hotel; to combine the virtuous satisfaction of a sporting achievement with a guilt-free guzzle in the evening.'[17] It is not that Canadian canoeists do not find good eating and copious drinking appealing – rum and vast amounts of food were as necessary for the voyageurs as toddy hour and good food is for modern canoeists – but that gastronomical facilities are lacking in Canada. Our canoeing rivers do not generally have hotels and restaurants along them where canoeists can stop for the night. Canoeing in Canada usually means getting away from civilization. A canoeist on the Bow River in Alberta might stop overnight at the Banff Springs Hotel; on the Credit River in Ontario he might have afternoon tea at the Terra Cotta Inn; or he might, after a spring day, have draft beer and pickled eggs in a local tavern; but these are not the same as the opportunities open to Koestler in Europe, such as comparing the differences between the vintage wines of a six-year period on as many successive nights, or a 'simple dinner on the terrace: river lobster in Pouilly; ham with cream sauce, Chavignol goat cheese. Wines: Pouilly Fumé 1956, Pouilly Fumé Loges 1952.' Not the same at all.

Campers in the United States now are debating whether a campfire or portable stove should be used for cooking. The arguments against campfires are largely ecological: with pressure of numbers on the American wilderness, many routes have become lined with unsightly black pock marks from firepits. Campfires can also cause forest fires. In Canada few canoe routes as yet are badly blemished by campfire scars, and there is usually enough small dead wood lying around so that firewood collecting does not damage the forest. Cooking by campfire in most of Canada is consequently still convenient and sensible. On some heavily travelled routes in Algonquin Park and in the settled south where firewood is not readily available a small porta-

A campfire is more sociable than a stove.

ble gas stove is useful. I carry a little stove which, with its gas, weighs less than two pounds, but can cook up a meal in wet weather or in crowded campsites in only a few minutes. The days of the Canadian campfire are perhaps numbered, however, as the American population at the urging of our governments takes advantage of our wilderness and brings their ecological problems across the border along with their canoes.

Clothing and Equipment

Modern gear has greatly reduced the discomfort of canoeing and camping, especially in cold and wet weather. Most sporting goods and department stores now stock camping clothes and equipment, but this comes from dozens of manufacturers, in a confusing abundance of different styles and materials, many of which are unfortunately not well designed or made. Keen canoeists tend to be fussy in choosing gear. They constantly experiment with new clothes and gadgets, and arguments over gear often fill the evening hours around the campfire. Not surprisingly, with so many options to choose from, so many different types of canoeing, and so many different personal preferences among canoeists, there is little agreement on what is best, and this section can do little more than highlight some of the important questions.

What the well-dressed voyageur wore in the 1820s –
these men paddled Sir John Franklin's canoe on his
second Arctic expedition. The one on the left has a hat
identical to that of the *avant* in John Halkett's
painting on page 21.

The voyageur did not have this problem. He wore an adaptation of Indian
and *habitant* clothing: a short woollen shirt, deer skin or woollen trousers,
moccasins made of smoked moose or deer hide, and the *Assomption* sash. He
had no tent, but slept under his canoe. He had one blanket for a bed. He had
no bug net or repellent: his years of bush life had made him partially immune
to insect bites, as they had to the cold, wet, and other discomforts which
bother less experienced wilderness travellers. By the end of the nineteenth
century, however, clothing for woodsmen was more elaborate:

a pair of strong kip or cowhide boots, with patch bottoms and Hungarian tacks in
the soles. The leg must not be long enough to interfere with the free use of the knee-
joint. A pair of light gaiters, or moccasins or leather slippers, to put on when round
camp; three or four pairs of light woollen socks, a couple of pairs of strong Guernsey
drawers and as many shirts of the same material, and two strong cotton ones, a pair
of brown duck and another pair of woollen pants, one coat and vest and a few coloured
cotton handkerchiefs, a hat and towel . . . [18]

Bedding was gray wool blankets, but two where the voyageurs had only one.
Even with these improvements canoeing was still unpleasant in wet weather,
sleeping uncomfortable and often cold, and insects a nuisance.

Our ancestors dressed more elegantly than we do for a canoe trip in Algonquin Park.

Modern clothing for canoeists is fancier. As for backpackers, it follows the 'layer' principle – several layers of adjustable garments which can be worn separately or in combination to fit different levels of exertion and weather conditions. Wool still remains a preferred material – it dries from within and drains and dries quickly, and as a result forms an insulating layer when the canoeist is wet, as he often is when lining and running rapids and on rainy days. In contrast, cotton and synthetics absorb and retain water and the wet layer thus created leaks heat from the body. Of all the common materials wool offers the best protection against hypothermia, but when the water is extremely cold, as in the spring and on rivers of the far north, a skin diver's wet suit, preferably of 3/16-inch foam, is the only reliable insulation. The main difficulty with wool clothing is that it is expensive and often hard to get. Members of CORTS in cool weather, usually wear a wool undershirt (some prefer cotton net), a shirt of light wool or viyella (a mixture of wool and cotton) and a heavier wool shirt on top. Below: woollen underwear, wool or twill trousers (not blue jeans – the dark colour attracts insects and jeans are dangerously slow to dry). Layers are removed as the weather warms. We bring along a second set of clothing, and put wet clothing on in the morning, saving the dry clothes for use in camp.

The greatest modern improvement to canoeing clothes has come in the outer shells for protection from wind and rain, where the choice is between completely waterproof materials like rubberized nylon or semi-waterproof outer layers which let in some rain but allow condensation to escape. During active canoeing, condensation can be as unpleasant as being exposed to the rain; I therefore use a semi-waterproof shell outer parka made of a mixture of sixty per cent cotton and forty per cent nylon. It has a hood attached, and many big pockets for storing matches, knives, fishing tackle, and other personal gear. The nylon adds strength and durability, while the cotton fibres expand when wet and improve water resistance. The fabric breathes enough to eliminate most condensation. Polyester-cotton is also a good mix.

My parka weighs under two pounds, and I use it year around. I use a completely waterproof cagoule (a thigh-length hooded mountaineer's garment) around camp. Others use a poncho. A souwester hat keeps the head and neck dry. Rain clothes made of plastic rarely last more than a few days in the bush, and as a result we prefer the more expensive but more durable waterproofed nylon.

For additional warmth canoeists often bring along down-filled sweaters or vests. These garments, made of a light nylon covering with good quality goose-down stuffing, pack into very small stuff bags, are of negligible weight, and can keep a camper warm and comfortable in below-freezing temperatures. The additional layer of a cagoule or parka on top adds more protection from wind, rain, snow and cold. In very cold weather as much as fifty per cent of the body's heat loss can come from the unprotected head, and a hat such as a woollen toque is useful.

There is little agreement on footwear. Many canoeists swear by the traditional shoepacks with rubber bottoms and leather tops, but in much of the North these have been replaced by ten-inch-high all-leather Grebs with a composition sole. Some canoeists use ankle-high hiking boots. For the kind of canoeing I do I prefer canvas sneakers. Wet-suit socks inside extra-large sneakers are warm and comfortable in spring canoeing. A pair of moccasins or other light footwear are good for camp use. In cold weather I bring along 'down booties' for a touch of luxury in camp.

From the stimulus of backpacking and mountaineering, sleeping bags have become lighter, warmer and more durable. The best for backpacking are, like down sweaters, covered with nylon and filled with goose down. They keep a camper comfortable from –10°C to over 20°C yet weigh less than four pounds. Good down bags are extremely expensive, however, and manufacturers have developed much cheaper alternative synthetic fillings like fibrefill. As yet

As a result of modern synthetic materials, camping is not only possible, but even can be enjoyable, in wet weather. These tents are two-layered. The outside layer is waterproof; the inside breathes, but keeps insects out. The campers wear waterproof cagoules and rain shirts. The camp was set up in the evening at the put-in point to ensure an early start next day. A camp stove in the back of a station wagon is useful on a day like this.

Canoe trips   155

these synthetics cannot be compressed into as small a volume, nor do they give as good insulation for the same weight as down. Backpackers prefer down, but canoeists are increasingly adopting the synthetics because down loses its insulating ability when it gets wet and it is slow to dry, while the water drains quickly out of synthetics and even when wet they still retain some insulating ability. My present bag, which I also use for backpacking, is one of the expensive ones filled with goose down, but the next I buy will almost certainly be synthetic-filled.

There is a growing tendency to use foam pads rather than inflatable mattresses because they do not develop leaks. Open-cell foam provides better comfort than closed, but if it gets wet it does not insulate and it is slow in drying. Half-inch closed-cell ensolite or a similar material is a good choice for canoeing. Bough beds are frowned on because far too many people now travel in the wilderness to permit the destruction to trees caused by building them, and the cutting of live trees is in any case forbidden to canoeists in many areas.

Modern camping tents are made entirely of synthetics, usually nylon. They have an inner tent with a breathable, porous cover. On top of this, separated by an air space of several inches, is a waterproofed fly. The floor, also water-proofed, is of 'bathtub' design, joining the walls six to eight inches above ground level. These tents need no trenching because water runs around and under, not into, them. The tents have good ventilation through large windows covered with mosquito net. Some have a hooded entrance for cooking. Some can be pitched and struck in rain without the inside getting wet. They provide excellent weather and insect protection. A six-foot by eight-foot tent, complete with floor, fly, poles and pegs weighs under eight pounds yet is roomy enough for three canoeists. The best cost about $200, but a canoeist can do nearly as well for less than $50 with a cheap nylon tent and a home made fly of sheet plastic.

I have tried packsacks made of synthetics but still prefer canvas for canoeing. The aluminum frame and nylon pack of the backpacker is too awkward to stow and move, too small in volume, and most leave the sleeping bag out to get wet. They are an abomination in thick brush because the frame ends catch continually. Coated nylon is less abrasion-resistant and more liable to tear than heavy canvas. The best canoe packs are large, rectangular, single-compartment, frameless bags made of canvas, with leather shoulder straps and tumpline attached. They are easy to fill, easy to load into a canoe, and easy to carry on short portages. They have the advantage over packframes in that two can be carried at the same time, one on top of the other.

Ash strip carrying baskets, with tumpline and shoulder
straps, are still common in Maine and New Brunswick.
The paddles are tied in the canoe to form a carrying
yoke.

Canoe trips   157

Food, clothing and sleeping bags can be kept dry in green plastic garbage bags inside the canvas packs. All gear should be tied to the thwarts to avoid loss if the canoe upsets. Running shoes are proper for white water canoeing.

There are many ways of keeping gear waterproof, including the use of heavy gauge plastic sacks, but the one CORTS has adopted is the green garbage bag. We place the garbage bags in nylon stuff sacks, and put any gear which must be kept dry in these double containers, tying the bags after expelling the air. Each packsack takes its share of the waterproof packages. Gear stays dry through days of rain and through heavy rapids which may swamp the canoe. On one of our trips an aluminum canoe filled with water and overturned. The rivets holding a thwart broke, and the bags, which had been strapped to the thwart, floated nearly a mile downstream through several rapids and a fifty-foot waterfall before they were rescued. Nothing within them was seriously wet. A green garbage bag with holes for head and arms also makes a satisfactory emergency rain garment. I never go on an extended canoe trip without a dozen spare green garbage bags.

These contributions of technology to outer clothing, tents and packaging have dramatically increased the comfort of canoeing and have reduced weight of gear. Increased comfort is not a small factor in encouraging many people, who previously were not willing to put up with the hardships, to travel into the wilderness. And equipment is constantly improving. Ten years ago we used fine cotton parkas and tents. Ten years from now there will be many

In insect-free weather a century ago, a simple lean-to made a good shelter. It still does, although today the tarpaulin is apt to be plastic.

other new materials and designs, and canoeists will still be experimenting, arguing and refining their gear. Good clothing and gear is usually expensive, but it pays to buy quality.

Canada still does not have enough suppliers of high quality gear. One of the best ways of economizing is to make your own, and this is done most easily by purchasing pre-cut kits which include all materials and need only to be sewn and assembled. The saving can be up to fifty per cent over normal retail prices in Canada. Parkas, down-filled clothing, ponchos, sleeping bags, tents, backpacks and many other types of gear now come in kit form. Two good suppliers are Frostline Kits (452 Burbank Street, Broomfield, Colo. 80020 usa) and The Happy Outdoorsman, 443 St Mary's Road, Winnipeg.

A check list I use for ensuring I have remembered everything for a canoe trip is included as Appendix C.

SIX

The river

Because of its sparse population and the remoteness of much of its vast territory many of Canada's rivers are seldom canoed and for only a small fraction do published guides or descriptions exist. Part of the pleasure for a proficient canoeist is to venture into the unknown and explore new rivers. But before starting out he wants to have a good idea of what white water difficulties he will face, what water flow he can expect, and what sort of terrain he will find for camping or portaging. Even the river guides that are published sometimes omit important information like river flow. Fortunately there are other ways of learning. This chapter introduces some basic aspects of river geology, climate, and the use of maps and other sources of information.

Rivers

The science of geomorphology, the study of landforms, offers some guidance towards predicting the character of a river. But the more geologists study rivers and river systems, the more they have been forced to realize how rich, varied and complicated are the factors which create the shape of the earth.

Eighty years ago, in the flush of nineteenth century optimism, the problem seemed to be much simpler. Then W.M. Davis, who almost singlehandedly created the science of geomorphology, claimed that over the span of geologic time rivers gradually progressed from a 'youthful' to a 'mature' stage before finally reaching 'old age.' According to Davis, youthful rivers were characterized by valleys with V-shaped cross-profiles, contained waterfalls and rapids, and were separated by extensive areas with poorly defined and ineffective drainage networks. In maturity, valleys became much broader and extended themselves so that the surrounding regions had well-integrated drainage systems. The lakes, rapids and waterfalls which existed in youth disappeared. In old age, rivers became placid and slow, the valleys broad and gently sloping; swamps were to be found on the flood plains rather than between rivers as in youth. Underlying Davis's classification of rivers by age was his belief that in geologic time land masses rise out of the oceans and then are eroded and dissected by rivers, until ultimately the debris of the continental mass returns to the sea and reforms into layers of sediment. He thought that the time when the seas last withdrew from a continental mass could be determined from the shape of its river valleys. In his terminology, the rivers interesting to white water canoeists would have youthful features.

Modern geomorphologists have retained Davis's classification of river valley features, but they no longer believe that the possession of so-called youthful, mature, or old features accurately establishes the age of a river. They believe that a landscape is formed, not so much by river erosion on a continent-sized mass of rock that has emerged from beneath the sea, as by the action on the primary geological structures of several complex processes. Among these are the raising and lowering of terrain and sea level, volcanic action and earthquakes, chemical weathering, biological action, glaciers, wind, and water. Depending on the structures of hard and soft rocks over which rivers flow, the processes to which they have been subjected, climate and vegetation, and the time over which these processes have worked, a river might have youthful, mature or old features anywhere along its course, regardless of whether it is flowing over ancient or recent rock formations, and regardless of whether the drainage system itself is recent or ancient.

The difficulties in determining the age of features are especially obvious in the Precambrian Shield of Canada, where on a single river stretches of gentle meandering, the features of old age, are often preceded and followed by rapids and even waterfalls. The Shield, in which so many of the good canoeing rivers of Canada are found, is in fact a first-class example of the complexity of geomorphology. Some of its rocks are amongst the oldest in the world – formed more than two billion years ago. Hard granites and softer metamorphic rocks form complex, twisted and convoluted patterns in the bedrock structure. In the earth's early geological periods, the Shield acquired its present hummocky topography, and a drainage pattern was established adjusted to the complicated underlying structure of the bedrock, with the river valleys in the softer bedrock formations. Later, but still hundreds of millions of years ago, the Shield was submerged under the oceans and blanketed with deposits of sedimentary rock. Still later the Shield again rose above sea level, and the new sediments subjected to erosion. A different drainage system formed on these rocks, but as the younger levels eroded over the vast expanse of geological time, the previous Precambrian topography and drainage patterns were exposed and the rivers returned to the ancient locations. The glaciers of the recent Pleistocene Epoch, which melted away

The small rivers of the Precambrian Shield are often
excellent for canoeing, even though their flow is small.
The rounded, smooth, bare rock of the shoreline, the
tranquil pool and the abrupt drop on this piece of the
Moon River in Muskoka are typical.

only ten thousand years ago, contributed further to the erosion of the sedimentary blanket and the harder Precambrian rocks; they buried some of the
features of the old Precambrian topography, but in effect only put the
finishing touches on a landscape that was already hundreds of millions of
years old, and had now been buried and resurrected at least twice. Half of
Canada as a result is an ancient, exhumed 'fossil' landscape. Its age appears
in its eroded roots of old mountains, time-worn rolling surface and ancient
pattern of rivers. Yet the landscape is young as well, in its irregular surface,
cliffs and valleys, unweathered rocks and swampy terrains. The paradoxically
youthful features of this old landscape are the reason it has such superb white
water.

There is no simple way from the age of rock formation or landscape to tell
which rivers will interest white water canoeists. Good canoeing rivers exist
in most parts of Canada, but even within a region there can be enormous
variety. No two rivers are alike, and neighbouring rivers with comparable
gradients can have quite different canoeing appeal. One will have all the drop
concentrated in an unmanageable waterfall, while another will have many
short and challenging drops with safe pools for recovery below each. One river
will have many fat, healthy fish, the next only a few underfed runts. One will

Many of the rivers in the softer sedimentary rocks of
Canada are like this stretch of the Abitibi in northern
Ontario – wide, shallow and fast. They often have mile
after mile of Grade II, with occasional pieces of III.

be dry from early summer to winter, the other have good canoeing from
spring to fall.

Other things being equal, white water rivers in soft sedimentary rocks tend
to have gentle gradients and continuous fast runs, while in hard granitic
rocks they tend to drop suddenly and often form twisted rapids with complicated cross-currents. But a river's character is the result of many mixtures
of processes on widely differing structures at variable rates for different
lengths of time, and the other things are rarely equal. The features of a river
are as complicated as the bone structure, lines and expression, the consequences of heredity, character and a lifetime of experiences, that create the
individuality of a human face. Some rivers in hard granitic rocks are gentle
meandering streams, and others in soft sediment are confused raging
torrents. Part of the delight of canoeing is to explore a new river and learn
its character. Although the study of geology gives no easy way of predicting
this character, it does help in understanding and appreciating it.

The important conclusions for canoeists are: first, that good and bad
canoeing rivers can be found in most parts of Canada; second, that upper,
middle or lower reaches of rivers can vary dramatically, and be good or bad;
third, that detailed river guides and first-hand experience rather than

The Moira River passes from the Precambrian to softer limestone on its way to Lake Ontario. In early spring it reaches grade IV, but by late May when this picture was taken it is easy grade II, and warm enough for swimming.

geological maps are needed to learn conclusively what a river is like; and fourth, that even so, rivers are full of surprises.

The volume of water flow necessary for good canoeing depends on the size of the river's bed. In rivers with small beds, good canoeing can be had with as little as 150 cubic feet per second of flow, while on the broad lower reaches of rivers like those in the Hudson Bay lowlands, such as the Albany, even a hundred times this flow is inadequate to float a canoe. Rivers still usually offer good canoeing at a fifth of normal peak flood flow, but not at a fiftieth. Thus if the usual peak floods are at 1,500 cubic feet per second, there can still be good canoeing at 300 cubic feet per second, and a river whose usual peak is 100,000 cubic feet per second might offer good canoeing at 20,000 cubic feet per second but probably not at 2,000. Below about 150 cubic feet per second, even small rivers are usually too obstructed to interest white water canoeists.

Some rivers have a seasonal pattern of flow which is much the same from one year to the next; these are 'reliable' to canoeists. Other, 'unreliable' rivers vary dramatically from one year to the next, or even from one day to the next. The pattern of flow of a river over the year is called its 'regime.' Graphs of river regimes usually show the average flow for each month; canoeists are

By August, the Moira has too little water for canoeing.
This is the same old dam as is shown on page 98. That
photo was taken in early May about two weeks after
the Moira reached its peak. The stretch of rocks in this
picture creates an excellent grade III rapids in spring.

also interested in the maximum and minimum experienced over the years in
each month, and whether the regime is reliable. Information about river
regimes tells canoeists when a river is likely to be so much in flood that it
is dangerous, when it is likely to be good for canoeing, and when it will be
too dry. Canada is so huge and sparsely populated that the regimes of many
rivers have not been measured, even though the federal and provincial
governments operate many thousands of gauging stations.

A canoeist looking for adventure beyond familiar large rivers to their
smaller and less well-known tributaries should, to assess the latters' canoeing
potential, have some understanding of factors affecting river flow. River
regimes are affected by climate, vegetation, soils, glaciation, rock structure,
and the shape and size of drainage basins. In Canada, important factors of
climate are not only the amounts and timing of precipitation, but also the
times of freeze-up and thaw. Rain is immediately available for runoff or
absorption into the ground, but snow stays on the ground until it melts. Snow
melting in spring may create large and sudden runoffs. As a result, northern
regions generally have a low winter runoff but a high spring runoff, but the
south and maritime regions which undergo many successive freezings and
thawings have high late fall and winter runoffs as well. Runoff is much faster

from deforested regions than from forested ones, and where agricultural practices leave the soil bare runoff is faster still. The summer flow of many rivers of southern Ontario has been reduced to a trickle by the cutting of the forests and bad agricultural practices. For the same reasons these rivers are prone to flash floods. Where there are porous rocks, water is absorbed in the springtime and during periods of heavy rains, and then 'released' in periods of drought to maintain flow. Hard, impervious rocks on the other hand facilitate rapid runoff, as does the permafrost (permanently frozen subsoil) found over much of the north. The steeper the average gradient of a river basin the faster the runoff and the more responsive the river is to precipitation. The smaller the river, the more responsive it is as well. Swamps and large lakes act as reservoirs and even out runoff: in times of heavy precipitation their level rises since the maximum outflow is usually restricted, and water is thus stored for gradual release, maintaining the river flow. Large rivers tend to be more consistent than small ones.

With all these geological, climatological, biological and other factors contributing to the infinite variety of detail, feature and flow, it is not surprising that each river has an individual personality. But, accepting that in the study of rivers there are nearly as many exceptions as there are rules, this variety can be simplified into general character types dependent on region. The main river regions are: the Western Cordillera; the Western Interior Basin; the Precambrian Shield; the North; the St Lawrence and Great Lakes Lowlands; and the Maritimes.

The Western Cordillera is a belt 450 to 700 miles wide of rugged mountains and dissected plateaus which extends from the U.S. border nearly to the Arctic Ocean. The ranges of sedimentary rock on the eastern side have been folded, faulted, upthrust and glaciated to form castle-like peaks, sharp ridges and crestlines. The coastal range comprises richly mineralized, intrusive rock. Between these ranges are wide, rolling tablelands and low mountains, cut by long narrow trenches paralleling the mountain ranges, north-northwest to south-southeast. The greatest of these is the Rocky Mountain Trench, through which flows the west's great rivers – the Columbia, the Fraser and the Peace. The landscape varies from extreme youthfulness to maturity. The large rivers are long, with steep gradients and many fast and dangerous rapids. The smaller ones are frequently interrupted by waterfalls. The rivers of the mountains usually carry a high level of silt, a product of glacial erosion. The ruggedness of the landscape often makes portaging difficult. The rivers of the interior, fed by melting snow from the mountains, have a flood season in the early summer months, but canoeing can be as difficult at low water

The great western rivers like the Peace are long, with steep gradients and many fast and dangerous rapids. The portages, as at Vermillion Chutes, can also be long and steep. The photo was taken in 1933.

levels as at high. Levels can rise quickly with high rains, or in late afternoons on hot days which melt the snow. The coastal rivers are fed by extremely high rainfall, and can as easily flood in winter as in summer. The recreational use of rivers of the Western Cordillera has just begun. They offer some of the most interesting but most difficult canoeing in North America.

The Western Interior Plains are underlain by thick layers of sedimentary rocks which exceed 10,000 feet in thickness in the Calgary-Edmonton region. Rolling areas of hummocky glacial deposits occur between large flat expanses of glacial lake sediments. The prairies are cut by long, wide, flat-bottomed, steep-banked channels which were once spillways for the melting waters from the glaciers. Many of the rivers of the prairies are grossly 'underfit' (too small for their valleys) like the Qu'Appelle of southern Saskatchewan which meanders with the slowness of old age across the bottom of a huge valley left by some melt water channel. Because the climate of the interior plains is arid, these rivers have little water. The North and South Saskatchewan Rivers and their tributaries which rise in the western mountains are, however, good for canoeing, with peak flows in mid-summer. They are quite silty, and in places polluted as well. Until the Canadian Pacific Railway was built they were the means of communication across central Canada. North of the prairies is a forested zone in which are many good canoeing rivers, marked by frequent sections of rapids and waterfalls which are normally easily portaged.

The landscape of the Precambrian Shield is spattered with innumerable swamps and lakes. The rivers are full of rapids and falls. The drainage pattern is a crazy quilt of rivers, lakes and tributaries. This area, the birth-place of the canoe, is the best region in the world for long wilderness canoe trips – a landscape of striated, grooved and polished surfaces, rock basins and rounded rock knobs, interspersed with patches of glacial drift. The marks of glacial erosion dominate the parts of the Shield that were under the edges of the glacier, but not the vast central region which may appear much as it was before the Pleistocene Epoch. Since glaciation the climate has remained too cold for chemical and biological activity to create deeply weathered soil. Rivers in the Shield are normally very clear and carry little debris either in summer or spring floods. Many are as pure as rainwater; their purity indicates how slight is the erosion of the streambed. The rivers of the Shield are largely of the pool-and-drop type. They have long stretches of placid lake and near-lake water followed by short, sharp drops. Often these drops are uncanoeable, but generally there are portages which have been used for centuries around difficult parts. In recent years, through lack of use, some portages have become overgrown. Most of the Shield in southern and mid-

Although deep in the wilderness, the Ross and many
other rivers of the Yukon have mile after mile of fast
smooth water that scarcely ever reaches grade II in
difficulty. The men, part of the Keele survey crew, are
skinning a moose.

Canada has moderate precipitation spread evenly through the year. The
spring runoff of melting snow creates a high water season, but on many
rivers this high water, and the later low water of the summer, are markedly
modified by the reservoir effects of large lakes. As a result, the regimes of
otherwise similar rivers can vary tremendously: some are canoeable in the
summer, others not. The very large rivers tend to have even, reliable flows
throughout the year, little affected by flash floods and dry summers.

The North, as used here, comprises the Yukon, Northwest Territories, and
Quebec north of the 60th parallel of latitude. This includes more than a third
of Canada and many different climates and landscapes, and the only justification for considering it as one region is that collectively it forms the northern frontier of the country. The three main canoeing areas of the North are
the Yukon Territory, the part of the Northwest Territories west of the
Mackenzie River, and the Territories and Quebec east of the Mackenzie. The
Yukon is essentially mountainous, an extension of the Western Cordillera,
and its rivers are like those of the Cordillera. Although the canoeing season
is short – hardly more than ten weeks from break-up in late June until
freeze-over in September or October – they are excellent for wilderness
canoeing, with long stretches of low-difficulty water. They normally have

mature rather than youthful features. The second northern region, the area to the west of the Mackenzie River in the Northwest Territories, is mountainous, with high precipitation. Most rivers there have steep gradients with many rapids and waterfalls. Because of the underlying permafrost the rain cannot penetrate the ground but runs directly off, and this often creates flash floods. Large rivers can rise or fall more than ten feet in a day. The Nahanni River is the best known, but there are many other potentially outstanding canoeing rivers. The third region is bisected by the treeline, which extends roughly from the mouth of the Mackenzie southeasterly towards the border of the Northwest Territories with Manitoba. The rock in this region is mostly Precambrian, and canoeing is comparable to that in the southerly Precambrian region except that the season is extremely short in the tundra zones – as little as six weeks – and all of it is remote from civilization. The Coppermine, the Thelon, and many other famous canoeing rivers are in the barrens. The North is one of the last great canoeing frontiers of the world. The rivers are largely untouched by man. But canoeing there, because of remoteness and climate, is hazardous, requiring expedition-type planning and equipment.

Of all the rivers in Canada, those of the Great Lakes and St Lawrence

The Koksoak River runs into Ungava Bay in northern
Quebec. Like many other rivers in the same area, it is
excellent for challenging wilderness river canoeing.
This photo of an HBC crew was taken in the 1930s, but
the Koksoak was used as a freight route until after the
second world war.

In the barren lands between Great Slave Lake and
Hudson Bay, lakes can retain some ice year-round,
presenting severe problems to canoeists. J. W. Tyrrell
is crossing Artillery Lake, NWT, in 1900.

Lowlands have been most affected by man. They have been dammed,
diverted, drained, canalized, deforested, polluted, filled with sediment, and
a few have even been restored and improved. The landscape is largely dominated by glacial deposition: terminal moraines, ancient lake beds and
beaches, drumlins, dunes, deltas and sharp bluffs. Many of the river valleys,
however, are preglacial in origin. The rivers are small, except for those which
descend from the Precambrian Shield and pass through the Lowlands on their
way to the Great Lakes and the St Lawrence. The climate is temperate, with
precipitation spread evenly through the year, but the river regimes are
marked by sharp peaks in early spring, followed by negligible flow during
the summer. Most are fit only for spring canoeing, when they can be exciting
challenges of grade II level and up.

The Maritimes are more mountainous than the Great Lakes and St
Lawrence Lowlands. Their rivers are short, with steep gradients, many
rapids, but few waterfalls. Precipitation is heavier than in central Canada.
River regimes are marked by a high spring runoff, followed by a reduced
summer flow which, however, is often ample for canoeing. There are few
large lakes to stabilize flow. Their water is usually pure, except in areas of
lumbering and pulp and paper industry. The rivers make good canoeing

although few of them offer runs of longer than a few days' duration.

No other country can equal the number, variety and quality of canoeing rivers Canada enjoys. The problem for the Canadian canoeist is to find and choose, from this huge potential, a river which fits his interest and matches his skills. Here river guides and experience are the best teachers. Appendix A contains a list of sources of information, including river guides. The next section examines maps and other information and their use.

Maps and Other Information
The most important maps for canoeists in Canada are the 1:250,000 scale series and the 1:50,000 series produced by the Surveys and Mapping Branch of the federal Department of Energy, Mines and Resources. The 1:250,000 scale is approximately one inch to four miles, and the 1:50,000 scale approximately an inch-and-a-quarter to the mile. Canada has been completely covered in the 1:250,000 series; the 1:50,000 series covers most of settled Canada and much of the near north. As mining, hydro-electric and petroleum development advances into the far north, the Surveys and Mapping Branch is extending coverage on the 1:50,000 scale. The Branch prints status maps which show the extent of present coverage, maps in compilation and proposed new mapping. Some of mid-Canada is covered also by a 1:125,000 series, but this is in abeyance because of the demand for 1:50,000 maps, and the information on them might be out of date.

The most useful maps for canoeists on short trips are those on the 1:50,000 scale. Both these and the 1:250,000 scale include indications of falls, portages and rapids, but the larger-scale 1:50,000 gives a much more precise indication of the details of the channel shape and size, small islands and buildings, roads, small dams and other man-made features. In mountain regions where the landscape is on a large scale, the 1:250,000 series is useful because maps can encompass the distances and landscape features that the traveller sees. On long trips in the north this scale also reduces the number of maps to a manageable load. Some of the settled south is also covered by a 1:25,000 scale which is about two and a half inches to the mile. I have not found these maps as good for canoeing as the 1:50,000 series: they contain little more information, and do not cover enough river length.

In the old days topographical maps were drawn from information recorded by ground crews. These crews often travelled by canoe and their reports included details important to canoeists, such as the precise location of portages, rapids and waterfalls. Many used to give the length of portages in the old surveyors' measure of chains (one chain equals sixty-six feet). The timber crews and prospectors who used the maps also travelled by canoe and they needed this information. Now, however, maps are compiled from aerial photographs taken at altitudes of 30,000 feet. Sometimes the photographs are taken at periods of high water when rapids are concealed, and some river channels have been missed or misrepresented. Portages are not apparent in aerial photographs and have often been omitted. The Surveys and Mapping Branch is now undertaking to correct these deficiencies and has engaged Eric Morse, the experienced and knowledgeable wilderness canoeist, to serve as a consultant on this task. The revisions will first be made to the 1:250,000 series. The Surveys and Mapping Branch corresponds with provincial governments and other agencies familiar with canoe routes in order to get rapids, portages and falls correctly placed. Canoeists who find errors and omissions also are invited to send corrections to the Branch in Ottawa. Canoeists should understand, and be warned, that topographic maps attempt to show an *average* condition which is neither high nor low water. The actual canoeing features encountered by a paddler can be quite different from those indicated on a map.

The revision cycle for both series is: urban and suburban sheets every eight years; rural and recreation sheets every fifteen years; wilderness sheets every twenty-five years. Recent energy development in the north has put heavy demands for new mapping on the Branch and there has been about one year's slippage in each cycle. With the rapidly intensifying development of Canada's wilderness, and changes caused by roads, developments, dams and settlements, the information on wilderness maps is often out of date and needs to be treated with caution. The date of most recent revision can be found on the credit note in the lower left hand corner of each map.

The contour intervals of the 1:250,000 series are 100 feet on relatively flat terrain (new recompilation - 25 metres), 200 feet on foothills and rolling terrain (new recompilation - 50 metres) and 500 feet in mountainous areas (new recompilation - 100 metres). For the 1:50,000 series, the contour intervals are: for very flat terrain 25 feet or 5 metres; for relatively flat terrain 25 feet or 10 metres; for foothills or rolling terrain 50 feet or 20 metres; and for mountainous areas 100 feet or 40 metres. The conversion to metric contours will take many years to complete and, in the meantime, it is necessary to check which system is employed on the maps being studied. There is enough difference between the scales to make this important.

The National Air Photo Library in Ottawa has complete coverage of Canada by aerial photographs, of which prints can be obtained. These are useful in unfamiliar terrain, especially in showing details of rapids and waterfalls. But an aerial photograph depicts conditions only for the day it was taken which, on request, will also be supplied by the National Air Photo Library.

Provincial governments have mapping services whose work is generally directed towards specialized scientific, resource and administrative mapping. They include, for example, maps showing geological features which are of interest to prospectors and mining companies. Some provinces have also produced maps specifically for canoeists describing routes in detail. But the other series can also be useful in planning trips. For instance, the province of Ontario is covered by seven large sheets, at the scale of one inch to eight miles, which show the administrative divisions of the province and also include the drainage patterns of rivers. These give a good overview of a large area, suggest the size of a river by the size of its drainage basin, and show road and rail access together with other detail. Another Ontario series, at the scale of one inch to two miles, does not have contours but indicates natural and human landmarks. Markings of portages on these maps is excellent, detailed and normally accurate. These maps cover the areas between 46 and 50 degrees of latitude in Ontario. They show Crown land in colour, which helps in choosing campsites. They are revised every three to five years. The other provinces produce comparable maps. A canoeist should get in touch with the appropriate government department to discover what is available about the province which interests him.

Information on river regimes is hard to get. Some published guides to rivers include water flow data, but most do not. Both the federal and provincial governments publish tables showing measured stream flow for selected rivers. The most detailed of these have stream flow each day, and show when ice cover first appeared and when it broke up; but only the libraries of very large cities or of good universities are likely to have these volumes. Many rivers are not measured, and for them the canoeist must estimate by comparing basin size and characteristics with those of nearby rivers for which stream flow measurements have been made.

The Meteorological Service of the federal Department of the Environment publishes many records of climate and, for some regions of Canada, detailed studies. These are good guides for choosing the best canoeing season; they also indicate what rain, temperature and wind the canoeist will likely encounter.

The geographical features of greatest importance to canoeists are the drainage patterns and contour intervals shown on the standard topographical maps. Contour intervals of even 25 feet, however, do not reveal enough. A smooth, steady drop of 25 feet per mile in some river beds produces grade II water. Another river which drops only half as fast – a 25-foot contour interval every two miles – can be obstructed by impassable falls, and can be in a narrow steep-sided gorge which makes lining or portaging difficult or even impossible. The 100-foot contours of the 1:250,000 scale hide correspondingly more. Short of finding a good river guide, the best way of predicting what an unfamiliar river will be like is to examine the maps of the district, study climate and river regime, and seek out information on geology. The books, pamphlets, articles and maps describing the geology of Canada are innumerable, and most decent libraries have a good collection.

The best single survey volume covering all regions of Canada, and including history, topography, climate, drainage basins, river flow, settlement and the works of man, is the *National Atlas of Canada*. It costs more than fifty dollars, but as a starting place for dreaming about and planning a canoe trip on a long winter evening, or as a mind-expanding feast of new possibilities for canoeing, it has no comparison. Every library worthy of the name has a copy.

Using Information
First I choose a river. For the southern Ontario region I begin with the eight-inches-to-a-mile map prepared by the Ontario government. After I have canoed a new stretch of river I mark it on this map with a yellow felt pen. Then it is easy to pick out the pieces I have not done, and to plan my spring canoeing schedule to take in some interesting-looking new stretches. The network of yellow lines is gradually covering the map, but there are still many years of interesting canoeing left. I take more care in choosing a northern river, because the trip, which will probably last at least five days, involves more time and effort than the day or weekend trips of the south. Often the choice is not mine because someone else is organizing the trip. Usually I have thought about a northern river for several years before I canoe it, and make my choice by comparing rivers on the basis of historical interest, canoeing challenges, opportunity to see new territory, popularity (generally the more popular it is, the more I avoid it) and the cost and time required. Arranging a time, and companions, is part of this process of selection. I use 1:250,000 maps, any river guides and reports of previous trips, and all other information I can find in making the choice. I usually determine the start and finish of the trip at this stage, and work out length of trip and days of canoeing.

Once the river is chosen, I get topographical maps of the regions, usually the 1:50,000 series in the south. The 1:250,000 series is best for the north. Next I mark on the maps where the contour lines cross the river. I reckon that ten to twenty feet of drop per mile of river makes a good, hard river. Anything much above twenty feet per mile will be difficult and demand extreme caution, while below ten feet the river is likely to be slow. I mark off also the points of access, the points of interest, and possible danger spots. Once this is done it is possible to make a first assessment of how hard the canoeing is likely to be, and whether the first calculations of time and distance are reasonable. I get copies of guides to the river if these are available. Sometimes the route plan gets changed at this stage. If I have doubts, I look for other sources of detailed information, including aerial photos, reports and river guides. On many northern rivers the reports of old explorers, like Franklin for the Great Slave Lake-Coppermine, Back for the river named after him, Tyrrell for the Dubawnt, and party leaders of the Geological Survey, are still the best published guides. On the topographical maps I write the pertinent information on rapids and falls, whether they were run, lined or portaged, where to find portage trails (especially which side), how long the portages were, as well as good campsites and fishing, access points and danger spots. I also put this information in my canoeing diary, which I keep in a surveyor's field book. (The paper, ink and cover of these field books are waterproof, although the glue on the bindings sometimes is not.) This completes the planning. In the familiar country of southern Ontario many of the steps often can be skipped. A useful brochure which outlines and explains parts of this process is *Maps and Wilderness Canoeing*, available without charge from the Canada Map Office, 615 Booth Street, Ottawa K1A 0E9 (specify map MCR 107).

One of the problems on any trip is to keep maps and other information dry and usable. When they get wet, as they often do in river running, maps and guides become soggy masses of wet pulp. Maps can be sprayed with an art fixative which waterproofs them. Some canoeists instead attach their maps to clear adhesive plastic sheets. I keep maps, waterproofed or not, in soft flat plastic containers. The ones I like best are clear, unlined plastic and are nearly waterproof; they are made for schoolchildren to hold pens and pencils, and cost only a few cents.

Before we start on any trip, I make sure that each canoe has a set of maps and river guides, and a copy of the summary we have prepared of route information. On the river each canoe keeps this data readily available but safe in case of an upset. A good place is in the pocket of a jacket, or in the top of a packsack. As we go down the river I mark on the map the time when we meet important features like rapids, waterfalls, other notable topographical features like tributaries and islands, and man-made features such as bridges, hydro lines and roads. On long smooth stretches I make an estimate of where we are, and check this from landmarks. When I'm feeling energetic, or we're in the wilderness and want a careful record – for locating scenes in photographs or writing a description – I supplement the information on the maps by keeping up a diary. Sometimes when it's an easy river and the sun is warm, I pack map and diary away and forget about knowing where I am. It is harder to get lost in downriver canoeing than in any other form of wilderness travel.

On Over-use of Information

Some canoeists think too much. They bury their trip with historical knowledge, geological knowledge, map knowledge, technical canoeing knowledge, nutritional knowledge, equipment knowledge, and so on. To them, canoeing is not of value 'in itself' but 'because of.' Route knowledge is of value because of the need for safety and planning, historical knowledge because of the importance of the past, geological knowledge because of its scientific content, and so on. Canoeing to them is a collection of means to many different ends, some articulated, some not, each of which has little to do with actual canoeing, and each of which is, when it is examined further, a means to another, more abstract end. Modern man often feels this way; as Hannah Arendt has commented

it was as though meaning itself had departed from the world of men, and men were left with nothing but an unending chain of purposes in whose progress the meaningfullness of all past achievements was constantly cancelled out by future goals and intentions.[1]

At the other extreme some canoeists think too little. They don't expand their skills or their understanding. Their canoeing is an immediate feeling, an action, an ecstatic form of self-expression without depth of understanding. These canoeists do not pioneer new routes, or improve their techniques. The trips of canoeists at both extremes tend to be filled with rigid rituals, and the experiences on one trip very much like a rerun of a movie of a previous trip. Both extremes are ways of escaping reality.

But some canoeists put knowing and feeling together as part of an integrated whole. As Lao Tzu said about the uses of knowledge, 'What we gain is Something, yet it is by virtue of Nothing that this can be put to use.'[2]

There is a mystical but important entity in canoeing which CORTS calls for want of a better term the drinking-to-canoeing ratio, although alcohol is not essential or even important to it. Many more factors go into it than amounts of canoeing and toddy – among them the quality of the canoeing and the qualiy of the companionship. At one extreme are the canoeists who drink or play too much and miss the rewards of hard work and thoughtful under-standing. At the other extreme are the canoeists to whom canoeing is always work, not play, and do not experience the canoeing itself as a pleasure. In between is the point where work and play, thought and feeling are in balance. Sometimes the right ratio is fourteen hours of backbreaking labour and no drinking. Other times it is six hours of floating and swapping yarns followed by an elaborate relaxed dinner of fried trout, steak and fresh fiddleheads, with cocktails before, wine during, and toddies afterwards. To seek the criti-cal balance of thinking and feeling, or planning and doing, of paddling and drinking is meritorious; to achieve it is to achieve good canoeing.

Five Canoeing Rivers
This section describes five rivers. The first is typical of the small rivers of the St Lawrence Lowlands, the next two of the Precambrian Shield of mid-Canada. These three give some idea of the opportunities that exist within easy reach of Canada's main centres of population. Many people do most of their canoeing on rivers like these. The first river can be canoed in an after-noon, the second in a weekend, and the third in a week. None of the three requires expedition-type preparation. Canoeists should be proficient in running rivers like these and in organizing trips on them before they advance to long trips on remote northern rivers.

The other two are longer trips in the more remote wilderness. One was a highway for the fur trade, the other has not yet been completely explored by canoeists. With care, intermediate canoeists can paddle the first. The second is only for experienced and expert white water travellers.

Example 1: The Salmon River, Ontario
The Salmon is a good canoeing river from late March to May, offering long stretches of grade II water. It can be canoed from north of Highway 7 to Lake Ontario, a distance of more than 60 miles. Old Indian paths once joined its headwaters at Hungry Lake to Clarendon Lake on the Mississippi River system to the north, and to the Moira River system to the west. The most interesting stretch begins at Roblin, eight miles north of Highway 401 near Napanee. In April this offers some of the best and most consistent beginner's

The Salmon is an excellent spring canoeing river. By late summer you can walk up this stretch without getting your feet wet.

water (for open boats especially, but also for covered) in southern Ontario. This stretch of the Salmon has a regular, steep gradient. It flows in a narrow valley with steep sides up to 100 feet high. It is quite wild and untouched considering that it flows through populated farmland. The Salmon rises in the Precambrian Shield, but leaves it just below Tamworth, and from there to Lake Ontario runs through flat-lying limestone.

Put in where Highway 41 crosses the Salmon River at Roblin. Take-out can be at any crossing below there from Kingsford (seven miles) to Shannonville (twenty miles). The fast water ends one mile below Lonsdale. For canoeists coming from Toronto, a good take-out is where the Salmon River crosses Highway 401, giving a run of fifteen miles, of which all but the last three have fast water.

Two hundred yards below Roblin there is a dam which can be portaged on the right. From here to Forest Mills are five miles of uninterrupted fast water, all easily canoeable in open boats. One gut, a mile below the Roblin dam, should be inspected before running. Portage around the two dams and waterfall at Forest Mills along the road on the right until it meets the river. Stop for a snack at the Old Mill Store.

Look for spectacular Buttermilk Falls on a tributary to the right, a quarter

The river   179

of a mile below Forest Mills. The Salmon here runs through a narrow valley with a steep cliff on the right.

Fast grade II water runs from Forest Mills to the headpond for the mill at Lonsdale, seven miles further on. The left-hand chute under the bridge at Lonsdale has been run by open canoes, but only after careful scouting, and only by experienced crews. It can be easily portaged.

A further mile of Grade II-III.

The river then becomes flat and placid, going through quiet eastern Ontario farmland. Above and in Shannonville there are dams. There is a take-out at Highway 2 in Shannonville.

On a sunny April day, the Salmon offers the ultimate in relaxed spring canoeing. Its peak flow normally occurs in April at about 1,200 cfs (cubic feet per second) although it can reach more than 2,000 any time between early March and late May. By late July it usually cannot be canoed, and can drop to less than 5 cfs by October.

A hundred years ago the Salmon must have had a more regular regime in order to be named after the now extinct Ontario Salmon which ascended it to spawn. There are still trout in some of its source streams.

River rating I - II

Rapids rating II - III

Topographical map 1:50,000: 31C/6 – Tweed (for the Roblin to Lonsdale stretch)

Example 2: The Madawaska River, Ontario

The Madawaska is one of the finest canoeing rivers in Ontario. It runs 140 miles from within Algonquin Park to the Ottawa River, and can be canoed for its entire length. For the most part it travels through the Precambrian Shield, although it enters the Great Lakes Lowlands as it nears the Ottawa. Most of the rapids on the Madawaska are of the pool-and-drop variety, and there are well-marked portages around them. Where there are no portages, the river can be lined. Most of the banks of the river and the shores of many of its lakes are still Crown land, with many good campsites.

The Madawaska River has been dammed in many places for hydro-electric power and its flow is largely controlled during the summer months. There are three stretches which are still of interest to white water canoeists. These are called the upper, middle, and lower sections.

The upper section begins at Whitney, just outside the west gate of Algonquin Park on Highway 62, and extends seventeen miles to Madawaska on the same highway. The rapids on this stretch are most challenging in April and

May, when they can reach grade v. Many are grade iv. If the water level permits, however, it can be canoed at any season. Experienced paddlers exercising extreme caution can canoe it in open boats. This stretch can be run in one day or, more often, in two. This section of the Madawaska has been proposed as a wild river park by the government of Ontario.

The middle Madawaska is the two-mile stretch between the outlet of Bark Lake and Lake Kaminiskeg. There is a dam at the outlet of Bark Lake. When the dam is open and the water is running, this is an excellent set of grade ii-iv rapids. When it is closed, this stretch cannot be canoed. Here Hermann and Christa Kerckhoff run their Madawaska Kanu Camp, a training school for paddlers in closed boats, and the river is festooned with wires and suspended gates for their slalom training courses. Many championship races are held on these courses as well. Canoeists from Toronto can drive up for a day or weekend and run the rapids several times each day. During the week there is usually a flow of 1,000 cfs, but over the weekend it is often down to 150 cfs. This section of the Madawaska, it is hoped, will also become a wild river park.

The lower section of the Madawaska extends from Palmer Rapids on Highway 515 to Griffith on Highway 41. This seventeen-mile stretch can be run at any time it is free of ice, from early spring to late November. The rapids range from grade ii to grade iv. Slate Falls, which has a rating of iv to vi, can be portaged on the right. All the rest of the rapids can be run by open canoes, although some involve a strong risk of swamping. The river is forgiving, however, because each stretch of rapids is followed by a large pool from which recovery is easy. As many as twenty or thirty parties will sometimes canoe this stretch on a summer weekend, and the river is big enough, with enough campsites, that there is no sense of crowding. Canoeists can leave a car at each end of this stretch or, once they reach Griffith, can arrange a lift back to the starting point with the storekeeper or another resident. The water flow rarely drops below 600 cfs during the summer, and is often above 2,000 cfs. It is good canoeing at both levels. Canoeists can thank Ontario Hydro for controlling the flow and making it worthwhile white water during the summer.

There are relics of the lumber trade all along the Madawaska – old channels, pieces of chain, embankments, and names carved in the rock. But the lower Madawaska is threatened. Ontario Hydro has considered putting a small dam and station for peaking power below Slate Falls, although the plans are (as this is written) in no way definite or confirmed. Many canoeists and others who value variety in recreation in southern Ontario are opposed to the dam.

If any stretch of water in southern Ontario deserves to become a wild river park it is this one, which is unique in its easy access and fine canoeing qualities of safe, interesting rapids and steady unpolluted flow.

Below Griffith the Madawaska has been made into a series of large lakes by Ontario Hydro.

River rating II - III

Rapids rating II - VI

Topographical maps 1:50,000: Upper Madawaska 31E/9, Opeongo; 31E/8, Whitney; 31F/12, Round Lake. Middle Madawaska 31F/5, Barry's Bay. Lower Madawaska 31F/5, Barry's Bay; 31F/6, Brudnell; 31F/3, Denbigh.

Example 3: The Pukaskwa River

The Pukaskwa River is one of the delightful small rivers that run into Lake Superior along its north shore. It descends very rapidly, falling more than seven hundred feet in less than forty miles. There is no access to any part of the river by road or rail. Local air services fly canoeing parties into Widgeon Lake, from which the river can be reached by a short portage or by paddling down the Fox River to meet the Pukaskwa.

The Pukaskwa is primarily a spring river, although because it is of the pool-and-drop variety it can be canoed during the summer as well. It is only canoed by a few parties each year, and the fishing for speckled trout is superb. Much of the river is soon to become part of a large new national park, and will then doubtless be better known and more used.

The river is difficult with many unrunnable rapids and waterfalls which must be portaged. The portages are not well marked. Some of them follow old lumber roads, since the region was lumbered in the 1920s by Abitibi Pulp and Paper. Canoeists should allow six days at least for the forty miles from Widgeon Lake to Lake Superior.

There is a two-mile-long gorge about ten miles above Lake Superior, with a portage on the right. Sometimes the gorge is lined, although this is extremely difficult and dangerous in high water.

Canoeists can arrange for a fishing boat from Marathon to pick them up at the mouth of the Pukaskwa. The District Office of the Ontario Ministry of Natural Resources at White River will help make contact. Or they can hope to be picked up by the air service, but the high winds and bad weather of Lake Superior can mean a delay of many days. An alternative involves a three-mile portage to Loon Lake, which climbs more than 500 feet. Even here the winds can be strong enough to delay air service.

There is no flow data for the Pukaskwa, but an estimate of high water in late May would be about 2,000 cfs at its mouth.

The Pukaskwa is a hard river, but the high rugged hills, which reach one thousand feet above lake level, the wild animals – moose, bear and wolves – and the excellent trout fishing make it an outstanding trip.

River rating III

Rapids rating II - VI

Topographical maps 1:50,000: 42C/4, Pukaskwa River; 42C/5, Lurch Lake. Ontario 1 inch to 2 miles map: Pukaskwa River

Example 4: The Churchill River

The Churchill River rises in the interior plains of Saskatchewan and Alberta, but just below Ile-à-la-Crosse in Saskatchewan it enters the Precambrian Shield, where it remains until it enters the Hudson Bay Lowlands. For most of this length it is of the pool-and-drop nature, a series of lakes with short rapids and falls linking one lake with the next. The most popular stretch for canoeing runs in Saskatchewan from the old fur trading post of Ile-à-la-Crosse to Sandy Bay. Many canoeists, however, like the fur traders, leave the river and get back to civilization by moving over an easy 300-yard portage at Frog Portage to the Sturgeon-Weir River which drains south into the Saskatchewan River. The Churchill has one of the most stable regimes of any river in Canada. At Ile-à-la-Crosse its flow is about 6,000 cfs, at La Ronge about 10,000 cfs and, at its mouth at Hudson Bay, about 60,000 cfs. The weather is superb for canoeing from July until late September.

Many of the rapids are runnable, and those that are not have good portages. Sigurd Olson's *The Lonely Land* describes a canoe trip down the Churchill and Sturgeon-Weir two decades ago when wilderness canoeing was still unusual. The government of Saskatchewan is now making a minor industry out of canoeing in the Churchill basin, and has prepared descriptions of fifty canoe routes in the area, including the historic fur trade routes on the river itself.

The Churchill is not yet crowded, however, and offers an acceptable wilderness experience. Wildlife is numerous, and some of the Indians of the region still pursue their traditional life of hunting, trapping and fishing. The scenery is that of the Shield at its best: clear water, rugged rocks, fine stands of virgin forest, many islands, boiling rapids. The fishing is good.

Access to the Churchill can be by road or air. Highway access points are at Ile-à-la-Crosse, at Missinipe on Otter Lake, and at Pelican Narrows on the Sturgeon-Weir in the east. There are airports and seaplane bases at Ile-à-la-Crosse and at Sandy Bay. Outfitting at Otter Lake can provide partial or complete gear for canoeists, and guides if they are desired.

Trips on the Churchill River can be longer than the five hundred miles from Ile-à-la-Crosse to Cumberland House at the mouth of the Sturgeon-Weir, or as short as the hundred miles between Otter Lake and Pelican Narrows.

The Churchill River is not dangerous or difficult although many of the rapids are not runnable in open canoes. The water volume suggests that some of these rapids are heavy water in the grades IV to V range, and would be challenges for experts in covered canoes and kayaks. The part of the Churchill below Sandy Bay in Manitoba, which is seldom canoed, has even heavier flow and less rugged drops than the more popular sections in Saskatchewan to the west.

River rating II
Rapid rating II - VI
Topographical maps 1:250,000: 730, Ile-à-la-Crosse; 73P, Lac La Ronge; 63M, Pelican Narrows. 1:50,000: 73P/10, Otter Lake; 73P/7, Stavly; 73P/8, Nistowiak Lake, 73P/9, Guncoat Bay.

Example 5: The Firth River
The Firth, one of the most northerly rivers in continental Canada, runs ninety miles from Alaska across the northwest corner of the Yukon Territory to the Beaufort Sea near Herschel Island. It rises in steep mountains and follows a tumultuous course on its way to the sea. In its upper reaches it is in a braided channel, while most of its lower stretches are incised into a canyon with sheer walls several hundred feet high. Its gradient exceeds twenty-five feet per mile for long stretches.

The Firth has not been completely canoed. In August 1972, a crew from the Wild Rivers Survey of the Parks Branch of the federal Department of Indian and Northern Affairs ran thirty miles of it from an access point at Marguerite Lake, twenty miles downstream from the Alaska border, to the beginning of a canyon above Sheep Creek, forty miles above its mouth. They encountered difficult rapids, and examined but did not run a canyon, about which they concluded:

In running this section of river many portages may be necessary and situations will arise where a portage cannot take place. The choice of attempting to climb the vertical walls (all but impossible) or attempting to safely run the rapids, is all that would be available. Many of the rapids in the canyon are navigable. It is only five or six that cannot be run by an open canoe. Kayaks or large rubber rafts with experienced people aboard, may be able to handle the water.

The flow of the Firth, like other rivers in mountainous permafrost regions, is extremely unreliable. The river is subject to flash floods. The climate is cool and frequently wet as well. Access is only by seaplane or helicopter.

Someday the Firth will be run. When it is, the crew will use covered canoes and kayaks. They will be experienced in difficult grade v water, and will be the sort of wildwater canoeists who, in the Grand Canyon, deliberately seek out the worst turbulence for fun. Their Eskimo roll will be infallible. They will first scout the river by plane or helicopter. The Canadian north has hundreds of unexplored rivers like this, some suitable for open canoes, some only for covered.

River rating v

Rapids rating II - VI

Topographical maps 1:250,000: 117B, Davidson Mountains; 117C, Demarcation Point; 117D, Herschel Island.

SEVEN

The canoeist and
the river

The canoeist competes with many other human beings for the use of the river. Some of the other uses are consumptive and reduce the river's flow; some pollute the river so it is unpleasant to canoe; some destroy the rapids and wilderness that canoeists value; and still others prevent the canoeist from using even the most perfect river. Sometimes it seems as though all good canoeing rivers are being destroyed one by one in the inexorable march of progress. Most canoeists are concerned with ecology and the quality of the environment. This chapter looks at two aspects of these problems: first the canoeist's legal rights, and second the ecological problems of rivers.

The Law and the Canoeist

Most canoeists have encountered fences across rivers, have found signs saying NO TRESPASSING, have been told by a farmer to get off his land, or have been forbidden by a cottager to camp. Sometimes a canoeing party reaches a river only to find its flow blocked by a dam, or the water so polluted by a factory or town that travel along it is unpleasant. In these circumstances canoeists begin to wonder what rights they have. They have heard vaguely of navigable rivers, and perhaps even of riparian rights, but aren't too sure what these mean – in law or practice.

Rivers in themselves have no rights. The rights belong to humans, not to nature. Human rights to rivers can be classified as either public rights or private rights. Public rights are not owned by governments, whether federal, provincial or municipal. They are vested in all members of the public and can be enjoyed by any member of that public. They are grounded in common law, and can be taken away only by statute. The right of navigation is a public right. Private rights belong to owners of land, whether they are governments or private persons. Governments often permit members of the public to use the private rights they possess. There are two kinds of private rights: riparian (riverbank) rights, which belong to the owner of the bank of a river or lake, whether he owns the river and lake bed or not; and rights associated with ownership of the bed. The body of statutes, common law principles, regulations and legal interpretations relating to the water rights is among the most complex parts of modern law.

So far the law has not done much to consider the special requirements of the leisure canoeist. The factors that affect him are diffused throughout rights belonging to the public, to riparian and river bed owners, and to governments and private persons by statute. The canoeist's concerns are, first, that he have access to the water and the right to canoe on it; second, that he have the right to camp along the river's edge; and third, that the river be satisfactory, in water flow and absence of pollution, so that he can have a pleasant trip. The unique feature of the canoeist's concerns, as opposed to the interests of other groups, is that he for the most part wants the river to be left alone, undammed, undiminished in flow, unpolluted, and unaltered in channel form. He does not want to consume and change the river, but to enjoy it. The law has not been strong to recognize these sorts of interests, and the general result is that canoeists, much like the rivers themselves, have few rights. Those they do have belong to them because they are part of a larger class, such as members of the public, property owners, or benefactors of a government service.

The three public rights to rivers in Canada are: first, the right of navigation; second, the right of floatability; and third, the right of fishing. The most important of these to the public generally, and to canoeists, is the right of navigation. This right is derived from English common law, although some English rivers have also been declared navigable by statute law through an act of Parliament. There is a common viewpoint amongst lawyers including G.V. La Forest who has written extensively on the subject, that the right of navigation in England applies only to tidal streams and rivers.[1] But the Magna Carta has in it a clause about the removal of kiddles and fish weirs from the River Thames, presumably because these traps blocked the river and interfered with navigation, and a right of navigation exists on some non-tidal British rivers, even when they run through private property and their beds are privately owned. Professor Stuart Ryan of Queen's University has argued that the common viewpoint is wrong, and that in both Canada and England, if rivers are *de facto* navigable, the public rights of navigation exist, whether the waters are tidal or not.[2] The two important questions about this right are: first, which waters are considered navigable; and second, what rights classification as navigable confers.

Navigability has a limited meaning in Canadian law. It is a question of fact (a legal expression meaning that it is a question of how the judges choose to decide). On big rivers like the Ottawa and St Lawrence there is no serious problem, but in marginal cases, and these include the small turbulent rivers of interest to canoeists, the criteria for navigability are less obvious. In *Reg.* v *Meyers*,[3] Macauley, CJ said that the adaptability of a stream for purposes of navigation, and not whether it is actually used for navigation, determines whether a river is navigable. But in *Attorney-General of Quebec* v *Fraser*,[4] Girouard, J doubted whether the size of boats capable of navigating in the waters had much to do with the question, and left the impression that so long as a river was actually navigated by boats, even very small ones, for commercial purposes, this was enough to establish its navigability. Anglin, J again emphasized commercial purposes in *Keewatin Power Co.* v *Kenora*.[5] He held that it is not every small creek in which a fishing skiff or gunning canoe can be made to float that is navigable. It must be generally useful for some purpose of trade or agriculture, either in fact or potentially. However, there are many other cases which suggest that Anglin, J and Girouard, J overemphasized the importance of commercial use. The end result of this is that there is no certainty whether many interesting canoeing rivers of settled Canada are considered navigable. The arguments of one school of lawyers, to which La Forest belongs, lead to the conclusion that simply because canoes can use rivers during spring freshets, or even all year round, does not mean that they are navigable waterways – that leisure canoeing is not a commercial purpose of trade or agriculture; the river has to be used for earning money for it to be considered navigable. A second school, to which Ryan belongs, argues that use by small pleasure craft such as canoes makes a river navigable. Canoeists, naturally, hope that the second school and Professor Ryan are correct. They are supported by some court cases which have held that rivers can be considered navigable even if they are suitable for travel only in times of flood.

There is no list of what rivers in Canada are, legally, navigable waters. The most cautious approach for canoeists is to treat rivers of the south – unless they are obviously used for commercial motor boat traffic – as non-navigable waterways. In the north, where Crown lands predominate, the question is not so important. Clarification of which rivers are navigable would be useful, because the right of navigation is valuable to canoeists. It confers other rights similar to the public rights on a highway. These include all rights necessary for the full enjoyment of rights of passage, such as the right to pass, to anchor and moor, and to stop for loading and unloading. (They do not however include the right to moor at a private dock without the owner's consent.) More important than these rights is the fact that the right of navigation is paramount. It cannot be interfered with by provincial governments or by private owners without the permission of the federal government, which controls navigation. (The federal government has shown no interest to date in asserting this right simply to preserve rivers in their natural state.) In contrast, on non-navigable rivers, the canoeist has no right of passage. He is only there on the sufferance of the owners.

The rights of floatability and of fishing are of little importance to canoeing. Floatability refers mainly to the right to use rivers for log drives. If log drives interfere with navigation, then navigation takes precedence. Whether the river is considered navigable or not, in actual practice the canoeist must protect himself against logs in the river. The public right of fishing exists only in tidal and sea waters, and is not consequently important to river canoeists. However, when the Crown owns the bed of a river, it usually gives the public the rights to fishing.

Riparian rights belong to the owner of land adjoining a river, stream or lake, whether he owns the bed or not. He owns the use of the water as it passes his property, not the water itself. The most important riparian right is that the owner is entitled to the full natural flow past his land of the water of the stream in its pure natural state – as it has been accustomed to flow, substantially undiminished in quality and quantity. If this were an absolute right, pollution and damaging of the flow by damming, diversion or channelization could be prevented by a downstream owner. A pro-ecology or canoeing group could buy small tracts of land with frontage on the lower stretches of a river and prevent pollution or reduction in its flow. But unfortunately the right is not absolute. It is subject to equal riparian rights of other owners to use the water as it flows past them. These uses can affect both flow and water quality, as long as the use is 'reasonable.' Upstream and downstream owners have an equal right to use water. As a result of upstream uses a downstream owner can suffer injury, and he then has no redress for this injury unless he can prove first that he suffers actual harm because of the change in flow, and second that the upstream use is not 'reasonable.' Both of these are difficult to prove, the term 'unreasonable' especially so. Substantial pollution, and great damage to flow, have sometimes been accepted as reasonable by law courts. Only an owner of riparian rights on non-navigable rivers can sue for redress on the basis of harm to stream flow, not members of the public at large.

The common law doctrine of riparian rights was suited to simpler times when the harm to rivers came from the needs for power of small saw and grist mills, or from the pollution of small factories. Now engineers can, and do, make plans for damming and diverting the large rivers of the world. Large cities and factories can destroy the biological balance of a river for hundreds of miles downstream. Flow can be reduced to a polluted trickle by irrigation. This harm can cross provincial and international borders. Usually the builders of large-scale projects acquire permission by passage of statutes to alter and harm downstream flow. This exempts them from liability, but it also destroys the common law system of rights. A downstream owner who cannot sue a pulp mill or chemical factory for pollution is not likely to sue other polluters. As a result, other persons pollute and affect rate of flow. In the end, the total of damage to the river can be many times greater than that caused by the original agent who acquired the statutory right to pollute or alter flow.

The owner of the bed of a stream or river has rights in addition to riparian rights. These are similar to the rights of property and use which belong to any other landowner. Rights of ownership include the right to fence the river, to prevent access, and the exclusive right to fish and to erect wharves, dams, booms, piers, bridges or other structures. Who owns river beds, and because of this can prevent canoeing, is consequently important to canoeists. The issue is further confused because sometimes the bed of a navigable river is privately owned.

The traditional common law doctrine of river bed ownership is *ad medium filum aquae*. That is, that in the absence of any explicit contrary statement, the ownership of land which has a river as a property line extends to the middle line of the river. When an owner owns the banks on both sides there is, of course, no problem as the owner also owns the entire bed of the stream. In England this doctrine applies to all non-tidal rivers and streams. In Canada it has been construed differently. There is no question that the owner of the bank owns the bed on floatable rivers and small streams, and in the maritimes private ownership of the bed, as in England, applies to all non-tidal streams. In England, and probably in Canada as well, the beds of navigable rivers as well can be privately owned. But in Ontario a series of law cases over navigable waters finally resulted in the Beds of Navigable Waters Act of 1911 which states that in that province the Crown in right of Ontario owns the beds of most navigable waters. Where the legal question of navigability has not been resolved, quite possibly the ownership of the bed is also in doubt. The provinces to the west of Ontario have followed the pattern of Ontario rather than of the maritimes. The only right that provincial ownership of river beds gives to canoeists, apart from the public rights they already have because the rivers are navigable waterways, is the right to fish in non-tidal navigable waters. When the bed of a navigable river is privately owned, the public has the right to navigate, but not to hunt, shoot, fish or trap.

Canoeists need to be able to portage around rapids, waterfalls and other obstacles. On navigable rivers this is no problem, as the right to portage accompanies navigation, and even when dams are built there must be a path for portage. Further, section 67(4) of the Public Lands Act of Ontario says that when public land, over which a right of portage has existed, has been or is sold, any person travelling along the water still has the right to portage. Many canoeists have, however, found it better to use diplomacy rather than the law to persuade land owners to let them portage.

The problem of ownership and rights of access in Ontario is complicated because, from the mid-nineteenth century onwards, surveys and land grants reserved for the public a public road allowance sixty-six feet wide paralleling the shores of navigable lakes and rivers. In 1953, the government reserved a strip of land sixty-six feet wide between the water and the front boundaries of all land grants fronting on water where the original road allowances did not exist. The intention was to ensure public access to and from the shores, to place the ownership of beaches in the public domain, to permit the government to control structures attached to the bed and banks of waterways, and to permit some fluctuation in water levels.

Where these sixty-six-foot allowances exist, the canoeist has unquestioned rights of access, the right to stop briefly as for meals, and the right of passage to reconnoitre, to portage, to track or to line. He probably also has the rights to camp and to gather firewood. The government of Ontario has not been forceful in exercising its rights to control structures, and many cottages, boathouses, wharves and other structures have been built on the allowance reserved to the public. Many private owners are not aware that the province owns, and controls, the sixty-six feet back from the high water mark on their cottage lots. The canoeist doubtless has as much right to camp as the cottage owner to build. However, this is a hard right to claim from an irate cottage owner.

The problem facing canoeists is to know where these public reserves exist. Many land grants pre-date the mid-nineteenth century and do not have the sixty-six-foot reservation. The reservations have been made only along some rivers, not all. In some places the rights have been expunged.

I have tried to obtain from the government of Ontario a list of the rivers, or areas, or townships of the province where there is a sixty-six-foot reservation for the public. I was not successful. The information has not, apparently, been centrally compiled. The potential value of these rights to canoeists is great but, at present, it is hard to find out where they exist, what they are, or how to claim them. It is important to canoeists that a strong effort soon be made to clarify this issue, as well as the problem of which rivers are navigable.

Each of the western provinces has, like Ontario, its own unique history and pattern of water rights. The effective value of these rights to canoeists is about as great as in Ontario.

The rights of canoeists can be summed up as follows: They have rights of access, portaging and passage on navigable waters. On other waters, unless there is an explicit public reservation of the river bank, the canoeist has rights only by permission from the owners - he cannot trespass, canoe, fish or camp without the owner's permission. There is no clear rule to establish which canoeing rivers are navigable waterways, nor is it easy to find out which rivers have an explicit public reservation of the river bank. More rivers are probably legally navigable than has generally been recognized, but this is of only limited satisfaction at this time. The canoeist has no rights to water quality, and rights to flow only on navigable rivers.

On Crown lands canoeists have the rights which the governments - the owners - give them. These rights are generous and usually include access, camping and fishing. But canoeists even in Crown lands have no legal rights to demand water flow or to prevent pollution. In Quebec and New Brunswick, the rights to fishing have often been given to private groups and there, as in other provinces, the canoeist also often has to share the river with log drives. Nevertheless, the Canadian canoeist is well treated by the law, and has more access to rivers and rights than the canoeists of most other countries.

These traditional common law rights have been substantially altered by statutes passed by federal and provincial legislatures. In many places downstream rights have been expunged to permit construction of dams, water diversions and factories. The law has not proven an adequate instrument to guarantee the quality or flow of water, and human uses have competed with each other, damaged each other, and harmed the human and natural environment. To cope with questions of water usage and pollution, governments have established many special agencies. Some are concerned with specific exploitation of water resources, as for hydro development, fisheries, parks and canoe routes, municipal and agricultural uses. Others, like the Ontario Water Resources Commission, have general concern for research and quality. A third group, like the Conservation Authorities in Ontario, oversee water use, quality and pollution within a drainage basin. The agencies concerned with water in Ontario alone now number in the many dozens. As the demands on water resources increase, these agencies, like the law itself, face enormous problems of reconciling the claims of competing and conflicting uses. They, like the rest of the world, must play their part, to use the economist Kenneth Boulding's expression, in trying to fit a cowboy economy into a spaceship ecology. The welfare of the river and of leisure canoeing now depends on the political response of governments to the canoeist's expression of his concerns. Whether he likes it or not, the canoeist must try to influence politics if he wants to save his rivers.

Ecological Problems of Rivers
Pollution is a strange thing. Human beings like to keep their houses clean, their gardens well tended, their clothes and cars in good repair. Yet the most vital parts of the world around them – the air they breathe, the water they drink, the plants they eat, the earth they till – are being damaged and degraded by human activity until in some places the results of this damage actually harm human welfare. If we assume that human beings would like all aspects of their lives and the objects that affect them, man-made or not, to be of good quality, then it is logical to conclude that they will try to eliminate pollution and protect their natural environment. Yet the world, we are told, teeters on the brink of an ecological catastrophe. Many of the reports of ecological disasters are exaggerated, but there is enough obvious pollution in the world to make important the questions of why it arises, and how it can be avoided.

Pollution can arise from three different kinds of problems. First, it can come from what economists call externalities – undesirable consequences of an activity which do not bother the person doing the activity and hence are not a cost to him, but are a cost to somebody else. Many of the classical problems of river pollution are caused by externalities. For example, along the St Lawrence River there is a series of municipalities spaced ten or twenty miles apart. Each of these municipalities used to take its drinking water from the upstream side of town and put its sewage into the downstream side. As long as the towns were small this worked reasonably well, and although each town was drinking another's sewage it was diluted and made harmless by mixing and biological processes of the giant river over the intervening miles. But when the towns grew larger and became industrialized the river could no longer handle the wastes. The natural response of each town was to build a water purification plant so that it could purify the river water. This did little for the quality of the river itself. The river remained polluted, the fish scarce and inedible, the swimming unhealthy, and the boating unpleasant. But there was no advantage to a town in building a sewage disposal plant that would prevent pollution because other downstream towns, not the town which built the plant, would benefit from the cleansed water. The St Lawrence as a result had a series of water purification plants, even though the costs of sewage disposal facilities which would have protected the river would have been no greater. The advantages of downstream sewage control, like the problems caused by their sewage, were external to the decision-makers in each town council.

In order to solve the problem of the polluted St Lawrence, decisions needed to be made at a broader level at which the costs and benefits which were externalities at the local level became internal. This meant primarily the provincial government of Ontario, and to a lesser extent the federal government, the International Joint Commission, and the governments of New York State and the United States (because the St Lawrence is both a navigable waterway and an international boundary). These broader levels of government, unlike the municipalities, could evaluate the benefits of preventing pollution and not just of purifying water. They felt that an unpolluted St Lawrence was worthwhile, and by regulating municipalities and industries, by helping to pay the costs of sewage handling facilities, by informing people, and by persuasion of local governments and businesses, they have helped to restore the river. The governments needed first a very complicated administrative system to plan and direct the work, second an

This idealized drawing from the 1950s reflects the optimism of that decade that technology could harness nature to meet human needs. The experience of the past twenty-five years has shown that this sort of vision is not often achievable. In reality the shoreline of the reservoir is likely to be unsightly and ill-adapted to recreation because of fluctuations in water level for power generation; the various diversions and downstream dams are likely to create semi-stagnant and polluted pools; the irrigation and factories most probably are creating further pollution. Most of the 'improvements' to the river in this picture harm it for the white water canoeist.

The canoeist and the river   195

information-gathering system to analyze the pollution and to help plan the means of controlling it, and third a regulatory system compelling municipalities, industries, and individuals to abide by the pollution controls.

The efforts began in the nineteen fifties. Down to the Quebec border, the St Lawrence now is a fairly clean river, capable of providing hundreds of thousands of people with water for houses, industry and recreation. From Montreal downwards, however, it is still polluted, as are many other Quebec rivers. The provincial government of Quebec has just begun on the task which Ontario undertook twenty years ago.

The likelihood of problems of externalities being resolved depends very much on the quality and organization of governments. The Thames River in England is gradually being cleaned, as is the Potomac in the United States. But the Rhine River, which is squabbled over by Germany, France, Holland and Switzerland, is rapidly deteriorating. It is difficult often to organize pollution control on rivers which flow from one country to another, like the Rhine and the Colorado, although because of the International Joint Commission many Canadian-U.S. rivers are in very good condition. If the governments of two countries or provinces cannot agree on controls, it is unlikely that local decision-makers will agree. Corrupt governments, and governments that respond only to large-scale organized interests, are rarely active in controlling environmental degradation.

Governments generally intervene to control pollution caused by externalities only when there is clear evidence of harm to downstream users, and when political pressure is brought to bear. Harm to the quality of the river seems to have little political significance unless the polluted or altered river creates serious economic damage to organized downstream interests. In wilderness areas, or where the harmed people (like Indians or canoeists) are weak and unorganized, pollution controls are usually lax. In this way the welfare, culture and lifestyle of 5,000 James Bay Cree Indians were treated as externalities by Hydro Quebec in its planning for the James Bay power development, but the clout the Indians have been able to wield, partly because of financial help from the federal government, has enabled them to wage an effective political and legal battle with the government of Quebec and Hydro Quebec.

Overuse of a free resource creates a special kind of problem of externality, because each user wants to take fullest advantage of the resource but does not directly suffer the costs of over-exploitation. This is called the 'tragedy of the commons,' after an apocryphal story of a piece of common land on which each sheepherder added to his flock until the land itself was destroyed.

There are ten dead caribou in this picture, and they are only half those killed on the previous day by an expedition along the Yukon River in 1895. Animal populations cannot stand this sort of hunting pressure, and modern canoeists must bring their food with them.

In actual fact the use of the numerous common lands which still exist in England is regulated by custom and common law, and use has been adapted during the thousand and more years the commons have existed to preserve their qualities. The huge Port Meadow near Oxford is as good grazing now as it was in King Alfred's time. The real tragedy of the English commons has occurred when they have been steamrolled into the twentieth century, as was Winfrith Heath (Hardy's Egdon Heath), first to be a military tank range, and then to become an atomic energy research establishment. The problem in North America is that our use of common goods has no tradition or custom as a control, and is limited only by the greed which destroys the resource. This greed is the self-oriented interest that economists call rational behaviour. The value of common goods which have no cost, like clean air, unpolluted water, wildlife and the natural environment, does not enter into the calculations of the economist's rational man.

A second cause of pollution is conflict of values. One form of such conflict occurs when uses of a water resource compete, even though the users are agreed that all the uses are worthwhile. For example, the reservoir created by a dam can be controlled to produce electricity, which means that the water level will rise and fall as the demands for electricity change. Or it can be controlled for recreation like fishing and swimming, which means that the water level should be kept constant to avoid the ugly shoreline which comes with constantly changing water levels. Use of water for irrigation competes with both recreation and the generation of electricity. The agencies which allocate water between these sorts of competing uses try to maximize economic benefits, but the value of recreation and, to a lesser extent, of irrigation is not easy to measure and as a result is hard to compare with more easily measured hydro power.

A second type of conflict of values occurs when people disagree fundamentally on what *is* of value. For example, some people regard a long stretch of wild rapids, navigable only by skilled canoeists, as a treasure. To the average fisherman and motor boater the same stretch of wild water is dangerous and useless. Electricity utilities argue that the dams they build create opportunities for recreation – boating, fishing and swimming – in the lakes behind them. But to a canoeist, these opportunities are created by destroying his sport and drowning the rivers he loves. This conflict of values is irreconcilable as long as human beings want different things. It can disappear only if humanity becomes a statistical average instead of a confusing mosaic of varied individuals. Canoeists and other lovers of the wild must make it clear to governments that variety is needed in recreational resources. Some rivers must remain wild while others are tamed.

Conflicts of values are not well handled by either the science of economics or the science of politics. The practice of politics, irrational and messy though it often is, handles them better. In fact what appears at first to be irrational and messy in politics is often the effective working process by which conflicts of values are resolved, and a confused policy is sometimes in reality a sensible accommodation of conflicting values. Consistency and uniformity can be very foolish objectives. This makes it all the more important for minority interests like canoeists and environmentalists generally to get involved in politics and make their voices heard.

The third cause of pollution is ignorance. Most human actions have a good portion of blindness in them. Dams and factories are built, rivers controlled and biological systems altered on the basis of If/Then logic. The assumption is that if A is done, then B will result. A can be building a dam, diverting a

A responsible canoeist puts out his campfire –
thoroughly.

river, reforestation, or any other proposal. After the ratio of benefits and
costs of various A's and B's are compared, the choices which appear to be most
favourable are made. The trouble is that any analysis of A and B includes only
a small proportion of the actual consequences of doing A and achieving B.
There are also consequences C, D, E, F, and so on. For example, in many places
a town has channelized a river (put it in a straight, deep, concrete-lined bank)
to eliminate floods. This works for the one town but, to everybody's surprise,
it has often caused worse floods downstream. It is often better to allow some
flooding rather than to control it. The construction of the Aswan Dam on the
Nile has destroyed many fisheries, eliminated the annual flooding which
created the rich soils of the valley, and enabled bilharzia, an enfeebling
snail-carried disease, to spread upstream to millions of potential victims. The
Peace River Dam in British Columbia almost destroyed the delta in Lake
Athabaska which supported a large portion of Canada's wildfowl, a thriving
trapping industry for an Indian community, and the forage for the plains
buffalo in Wood Buffalo National Park. These consequences were neither
anticipated nor intended. Diefenbaker Dam on the South Saskatchewan
River was justifiable only on assumptions of extensive use for irrigation and
recreation. The use for irrigation is still very small, and that for recreation

below projections. If present actual use were the basis for analysis, the dam should never have been built.

All human activities have unanticipated and unintended consequences. Sometimes these are good, often bad. Humanity is incapable of the kind of analysis that can follow the outcomes of each possible choice to the point where all consequences are known. Each important choice includes elements of risk and uncertainty. The larger and more unique the project, the more likely that important consequences will not have been anticipated. Small projects are more likely to be similar to other projects for which there is already a record of consequences both anticipated and unexpected; small projects tend to be easier to analyze; and small projects are easier to alter and stop. One of the big problems in controlling environmental degradation is that it is easier and more glamorous for governments to plan and organize one big project than many small ones, but the big projects have the biggest risk of unpleasant surprises. The big organizations of which our society is increasingly made up are dangerous because they like to do big things in a big way. If there were no countervailing factors, the prospects for controlling environmental degradation would be dim.

Two of the driving forces for the economic and technological achievements of western civilization are, first the specialization which enables an organization to concentrate its resources in a narrow direction for a restricted range of goals, and second, the large size of organizations which enables them to mobilize massive resources of manpower, knowledge, energy and money towards this narrow range of objectives. Only by disregarding many consequences because they can be treated as unimportant externalities, and by adopting an oversimplified framework of 'market' economic values, has our civilization achieved its successes. Electrical utilities are successful because they care for the value of electricity, not for the value of rivers, Indians and canoeists; pulp mills and mining companies are successful because the first know how to make paper cheaply, the second know how to extract metals, and neither cares whether it destroys the biology of rivers; irrigation farming is successful because the farmers value the crops, not the rivers; and municipalities thrive on the pollution they pass to other people.

This picture is dismal. But there are good grounds for optimism. The first is that uses of resources do compete and conflict, and that governments increasingly are forced to intervene and resolve these conflicts. The greater the variety of uses which the government must recognize, the more likelihood that some rivers will survive. The Conservation Authorities of southern Ontario have followed this road to improvement. Originally the Authorities' function was to control flooding. They did this by building flood control structures. Gradually they expanded. They bought land for reforestation, dammed and re-created the swamps that had been drained, built small structures to prevent gullies and erosion, and in many other ways restored the natural balancing mechanisms of the ecosphere. After many years of these river regime-regulating activities, they became concerned with wildlife and fishing. Even later they became generally concerned with recreation and water quality. At first their recreational interests were fishing, boating and swimming of the traditional flat water type. In the past few years, however, many Conservation Authorities have become interested in the use of their rivers for canoeing, and have cleared portages, prepared guides and arranged campsites. As a result, many rivers of southern Ontario are now better for canoeing and fishing than they have been in the hundred years since their basins were first cleared for agriculture. The Conservation Authorities are a good organizational innovation for dealing with many aspects of environmental degradation in southern Ontario. The rivers are small, as are the Authorities. The Authorities are sensitive to and responsive to the people of an entire river basin, and represent and try to accommodate many different demands.

Most Canadian rivers are not protected by agencies like Conservation Authorities, however. Northern ones especially seem to be available to the first large-scale user who comes along – electrical utility, pulp mill, or mining company. The only thing which has saved most of them is their remoteness, but this is fast disappearing. As the costs of oil and gas increase, and hydro-electricity becomes correspondingly more attractive as a source of energy, the outlook grows increasingly pessimistic. More northern rivers will be dammed, and if the practices of the recent past are continued the new lake beds will be inadequately cleared, the lakes themselves will, because of fluctuating water levels, have unpleasant shorelines, their downstream flow will be harmed, and the other users of the river and river basin – farmers, Indians, and canoeists – will be damned along with them.

The externalities of exploitation of large northern rivers often do not result in the commercial harm which encourages governments to intervene. The main hope for northern rivers lies in the increasing questioning of hitherto accepted assumptions that more is always better, whether the more be economic growth, population growth, industrial growth or growth of consumption. These are problems of values, and it is possible that out of our present economic and political discontents a different system of values will emerge which places a higher priority on retaining parts of our environment little altered by man. Some rivers, like the Nahanni, have been protected by being made into National Parks. Some provinces have begun to create wild river parks. The Wild Rivers Survey of the federal Parks Branch was in part an examination of rivers which might be preserved in their natural state. These actions are all signs of an increasing concern for the values which are important to canoeists.

There is still a long way to go, however. Social sciences, even though they claim to study human behaviour and welfare, are retarded in understanding problems of values, largely because values are not, at their heart, amenable to rational analysis. Values in modern social science analysis are usually unexamined, crude assumptions. The science is in the analysis, which hangs from and hides these assumptions the way a coat of new paint hides a rusting auto body. One of the best things to come out of the energy crisis might be a reduction in the ease with which governments and industries can commit massive resources to projects like dams and airports. Scarcity of resources increases the need to make careful choices, and the process of taking care includes discovering what values and value conflicts are involved.

Perhaps the most important conclusion that emerges from this look at the problems of rivers today is this: if canoeists want to preserve their rivers they have to argue for their values. They must convince governments that they are not a tiny band of freaks but represent important sectors of the public, and that the wants of large-scale organized commercial organizations, even government organizations like hydro utilities, must not always come first when values conflict. Canoeists also have to be reasonable and insist that only some, not all, rivers should be preserved, and decide which rivers are most important to them. They should aim to ameliorate the bad consequences of dam building and other uses of the rivers. But especially they must prove to governments that their concerns for rivers are not trifles. Governments have no values and no morals apart from those imposed on them by their citizens.

The canoeist must also recognize that his activities can conflict with the spaceship ecology. Many U.S. rivers suffer from overuse. In 1972, when more than 16,000 boaters (mostly in commercial trips in rubber rafts) went down it, the Grand Canyon on the Colorado River had more use than in the hundred years from 1869 to 1969. In the eastern United States, kayakers often have to wait in line for an hour on some of the more popular rivers simply to get a chance to play in an interesting roller. The Nantakala Outdoor Center in North Carolina often has as many as a thousand people through it on a long summer weekend, and canoeists use it like a ski resort, lunching there in a restaurant, taking a shuttle bus to the put-in eight miles upstream, and then

The simplicity and small impact on the environment of the Indians' existence was matched by its discomfort, even as romanticized by Krieghoff.

paddling back to the restaurant. It and some other rivers are used by more than 200,000 canoeists in a year. Because of the pressure of use, a permit system has had to be established on many American rivers, strictly limiting the number of canoeists. Algonquin Park is so far the only area in Canada which faces comparable problems, but Canadians as well as Americans are capable of loving the wilderness to death, and this could become a real 'tragedy of the commons.'

Canoeists can also disagree amongst themselves on values and priorities. Many of the popular canoeing rivers are white water challenges in summer only because their flow is regulated by dams. Wilderness canoeists would rather have no dams and poorer white water; white water racers and enthusiasts in such instances want the dams.

Superficially, it seems evident that the canoeist is on the side of ecological good. He wants the river in its natural state. He is returning to nature, rejecting civilization and technology and all their attendant evils. But he is very dependent on the benefits of technology. He could not enjoy the extended seasons and wide choice of location for river canoeing without modern methods of transportation – particularly the automobile. On a weekend canoeists often make a round trip by road of eight hundred or a thousand miles for twenty miles on the river: in fact modern canoeing could not exist without widespread private ownership of cars. In the north, air transport was needed to launch recreational canoeing. Whereas Franklin and Tyrrell took months to reach the end of civilization where their explorations began, a modern canoeist can fly from Ontario to anywhere in the Arctic in twenty-four hours, and can usually return by regularly scheduled flights from the settlement he finds at the river's mouth. Paddling is still hard work, but modern technology has improved out of all recognition the logistics of canoeing. We can get close to nature and can recreate our history by canoeing, but only by taking every advantage from energy and resource intensive modern technology. The Canadian Department of Energy, Mines and Resources summed this up in a study entitled *An Energy Policy for Canada:*

A man who paddles down a quiet woodland stream 'under his own power' tends to forget that he drove to the stream in a 200-horsepower car whose engine used only one-quarter its energy to move a mass of which he was only a one-fifteenth part; that he sits in an aluminum or fibreglass canoe, produced through the expenditure of considerable energy and used, perhaps, only a few hundred hours in its total lifetime, although the materials are nearly indestructible; that he carries precision instruments like a camera and binoculars that are probably unnecessary to his existence but which required a great deal of energy in their manufacture; that every roll of film he exposes is a heavy consumer of energy in manufacture and processing, etc. He may overlook the fact that while in the woods he left his automatic furnace or humidifier on in his house, his refrigerator running and his porch light burning. In fact, his brief return to simple nature has been accomplished and made worthwhile through the expenditure of more industrial energy than most urban or industrial activities he could have chosen.[6]

It is a weak excuse to say that the canoeist would be consuming more energy if he were in a power boat. In that case he probably would not have driven as far. The canoeist in total consumes as much, or more, energy as the power boater.

The difference is that the canoeist has one foot in the environmentalist camp, even though his other rests on modern technology, whereas the power boater rests both feet on the side of technology. The canoeist is squarely faced with the conflict of values. He can do his part by speaking out for the values that are threatened – those of the wilderness. Modern technology, buttressed by huge influential organizations that spend billions of dollars, is able to look out for itself.

There is in our society a three-pointed conflict between the desire to preserve nature (and leave it alone), the desire to enjoy nature (over-use and love it to death), and the desire to exploit nature (and eventually destroy it by consumption and pollution). In this struggle, some people and organizations emphasize one set of priorities, others a different set. Values can also conflict within the individual and he, like society, must choose how much he wants to consume, how much he wants left alone, and how much he wants to participate in and celebrate the complex integrated beauty of nature, water and life. Society, and many canoeists, do not always have their priorities clear on these issues.

Canoeists can contribute to a sorting out of priorities. If the problems posed by technology are at heart questions of value, the canoeist who lives and tries to understand his canoeing must face these conflicts and work to resolve them, both inside himself and in his life as a member of society. He can be part of the solution as well as part of the problem. The expansion of his understanding through hard work, physical challenge and risk-taking, through knowledge of rivers and nature, will mould and improve his system of values. It can change his life. Father Brébeuf related that on his canoe journeys into the Huron country he was 'sometimes so weary that the body could do no more, but at the same time my soul experienced very deep peace, considering that I was suffering for God; no one knows it if he has not experienced it.'[7] A modern canoeist can also experience a deep peace in the midst of fatigue. It comes to him for the same reason that it came to Father Brébeuf. He also is converting the savage, only now we know that the savage who needs converting is the man from civilization, including the canoeist himself.

'So weary that the body could do no more.'

APPENDIXES

APPENDIX A: Information on canoeing rivers
Although guides now exist for nearly a thousand Canadian rivers, this is only a small fraction of the rivers that are potentially good for canoeing. Most river guides are available from governments, as is the other information which is needed to supplement or substitute for guides.

Canada-Wide Guides
Wild Rivers Survey Between 1971 and 1973 crews from the federal Department of Indian and Northern Affairs canoed sixty-five rivers across Canada to examine their recreational potential. The crews made their trips during the summer months in open canoes, and were experienced, skilled paddlers who obviously enjoyed the challenges of white water. Their descriptions are being edited and published as a series of ten booklets containing outline maps of the rivers (insufficient for canoeing purposes), brief descriptions of their climate, geography, flora, fauna and history, and outlines of the chief features of interest to canoeists, including whether, and how, rapids were run or portages made, possible campsites, conspicuous natural and man-made features and guides to navigation. The necessary topographical maps are listed for each route. Although no data are included on water flow, the numerous photographs in the booklets give a good indication of the rivers' character. When the series is complete it will comprise:
Wild Rivers: Alberta
Wild Rivers: Central British Columbia
Wild Rivers: Saskatchewan
Wild Rivers: Northwest Mountains
Wild Rivers: Yukon Territory
Wild Rivers: The Barrenlands
Wild Rivers: The James Bay/Hudson Bay Region
Wild Rivers: Southwestern Québec and Eastern Ontario

Wild Rivers: Québec North Shore
Wild Rivers: Labrador and Newfoundland.
These booklets are published by Parks Canada in both French and English, and are available by mail from the Publishing Centre, Supply and Services Canada, Ottawa K1A 0S9, at a cost of $1.50 each. They can also be ordered through local booksellers. They are good quality guides, helpful for choosing a route, planning a trip, and on the trail.

Eric W. Morse, *Fur Trade Canoe Routes of Canada / Then and Now* (Ottawa: Queen's Printer 1969, 125 pp.) This book is an outstanding introduction to the geography and logistics of the fur trade, and to the present status of its main canoe routes. Eric Morse has himself canoed most of them. The book can be used as an on-the-trail guide, but it is also valuable as a reference book in planning routes, and in understanding the canoeing history of Canada. It is available from the same government sources as the Wild River Surveys booklets.

Nick Nickels, *Nick Nickel's Canoe Canada* (Toronto: Van Nostrand Reinhold 1976, 256 pp.) Mr Nickels has collected information on an astonishing number of canoe routes across Canada, and this is presented in terse form in this book. A list of maps, but few geographical references, and few indications of the routes' difficulty or interest to canoeists are given. This compendium is, however, a good abbreviated survey covering all of Canada, of help in choosing a route. Many useful addresses and other data are included. It is available in bookstores.

Newfoundland and Labrador
The rivers of Newfoundland are in the eastern maritime region, those of Labrador in the Precambrian. The rivers of Labrador involve remote northern travel. As of August 1975 there were no published guides to canoe routes in Newfoundland and Labrador. However, the provincial Department of Tourism is undertaking canoe route studies and hopes to produce information on pond and river canoeing.

Nova Scotia
The rivers of Nova Scotia are relatively short, and each involves, at most, only three to four days of both wilderness and non-wilderness canoeing. There are many side trips through tributaries and lakes which can lengthen this time, however. The Nova Scotia Department of Recreation has published an index map of the province's canoe routes and strip maps of thirteen of its best canoe waterways. The maps are on a large scale (four inches to the mile) and are

basically aerial mosaic photo interpretations of the routes with such canoeing information as rapids, portages and campsites printed on them. Most of the routes are for simple canoeing. The highest difficulty, only for short stretches, is grade IV. The maps are printed on tear-resistant waterproof paper which floats if dropped overboard. They are available from the Provincial Government Bookstore, 1683 Barrington Street, Halifax, Nova Scotia, at $1.00 each. The index map is free.

Canoe Routes: Nova Scotia This mimeographed booklet was prepared by the Nova Scotia Canoeing Association and printed by Sport Nova Scotia. It contains approximately 100 pages of detailed information on most of the province's canoeable waterways. Comprehensive and helpful, it and accompanying strip maps can be obtained from The Trail Shop, 6260 Quinpool Road, Halifax, Nova Scotia.

Prince Edward Island
There are no rivers of interest to white water canoeists in Prince Edward Island, because of the province's small area and flat topography.

New Brunswick
The rivers of New Brunswick, like those of Nova Scotia, are in the eastern maritime region, but they are longer and many run through near-wilderness. The Department of Tourism in New Brunswick has completed an inventory of the province's canoeing waters, and has prepared a *Guide to Canoe Tripping* with a half-page of information in point form on each river, and a briefer general folder, *N.B. Canoeing.* The Department also has individual reports on each river. These are available only in the province itself.

Canoe tripping on many New Brunswick rivers is discouraged because it conflicts with Atlantic Salmon angling. The Department of Natural Resources has a preservationist policy which is unique in Canada. They wrote to me that: 'We do have excellent canoeing in New Brunswick, covering the full range from white water to still lakes. We consider our canoeable rivers an extremely valuable part of our total wildland recreation potential and, as such, we intend to preserve this asset for New Brunswick citizens, present and future. Although canoe routes have been promoted in the past by the Department of Tourism, it is the current policy of the Department of Natural Resources to prohibit any promotion [of] canoeing outside of the Province. As such, canoe route guides are not currently available. I hope you will respect our preservationist attitude.' Nevertheless, if a canoeist goes to New Brunswick, the Department will provide him with information.

Quebec

Quebec includes some eastern maritime region, some St Lawrence Lowlands, and a great deal of Precambrian Shield. Much of its north is beyond treeline, and is underlain by permafrost. The landscape of most of Quebec is extremely rugged and the rivers are as varied and interesting as the physiography. The main source of information on river canoeing in Quebec is the guide prepared by the Fédération québecoise de canot-kayak, *Guide des Rivières du Québec* (Montreal: Edition du Jour 1973, 288 pp), available only in French. This is a fine book. It has good information on more than 250 rivers, covering rapids, portages, camping, water flow, maps, access and other points of interest. It can be ordered through any good bookseller.

Ontario

Most of Ontario lies in the rugged Precambrian Shield, although the fertile south is in the Great Lakes Lowlands, and other lowlands surround James and Hudson Bay. There is good canoeing in all regions. The Parks Branch of the Ministry of Natural Resources in Ontario has prepared a description of 125 rivers of northern Ontario; outlines of these descriptions, including distance, number of portages, starts and finishes, etc., are provided as a series of printed folders which accompany a map of the region and useful general information in an outfit, *Northern Ontario Canoe Routes*, available for 50 cents from the Ministry of Natural Resources, Queen's Park, Toronto, M7A 1W3. This outfit is helpful in making a first choice of route. Canoeists should then write to the Ministry's appropriate District Manager to obtain the detailed description. Some of the route descriptions were prepared by canoeists who obviously used outboard motors on their craft. The same Branch has prepared an excellent detailed canoeing map of Algonquin Park, which is available at Algonquin Park, Box 219, Whitney, Ontario, K0J 2M0. Maps of Killarney and Quetico Parks have also been prepared, though they do not have the same detail as the Algonquin map. In addition, the Ministry booklet, *Ontario, Canada, Camping Book* has information on outfitters and Ministry offices. The Ministry has lists of canoe routes, publications, a question and answer leaflet about Ontario canoeing, and many other useful publications.

Most of the rivers of Southern Ontario are overseen by regional Conservation Authorities. Each year more of these Authorities publish canoeing guides, which are available directly from the Authority concerned. Among the better guides, and rivers, are those of the Mississippi Valley Conservation Authority, the Moira Valley Conservation Authority, and the Saugeen River Conservation Authority. Conservation Authorities make little effort to publicize canoe routes outside their immediate region. The Parks Branch has also prepared some route descriptions of rivers in the southern part of the province.

Keith Denis, *Canoe Trails Through Quetico* (Toronto: The Quetico Foundation 1959, 86 pp) This excellent book describes canoe routes of the historic and beautiful Quetico wilderness. The detailed descriptions include a map and historical information. Available through booksellers.

Ian Scott and Mavis Kerr, *Canoeing in Ontario* (Toronto: de Pencier Publications 1975, 80 pp) This little book contains an introduction to canoeing, extremely brief route descriptions of rivers in southern Ontario, and small scale maps. Some of the rivers are flat water, while others are suitable only for experienced white water paddlers, but the book gives no suggestion of river grade. Useful information on clubs, canoeing schools, and other matters is in the back pages. This book is skimpy, of little use to the white water canoeist because of the inadequate river description, and could mislead beginning canoeists into thinking that difficult rivers are easy. Widely available at stores throughout southern Ontario.

Ontario Voyageurs Kayak Club, *Ontario Voyageurs River Guide* (Toronto: 1970) This mimeographed booklet of about 150 pages contains guides prepared by members of the Ontario Voyageurs Kayak Club to their favourite rivers in southern Ontario. Most are white water rivers. The club principally uses covered canoes and kayaks, and the guide is written from the perspective of paddlers in these craft. The descriptions are good and detailed, as are the maps. Available from the OVKC Secretary, John Shragge, 166 St Germain Avenue, Toronto, Ontario, price $5.00 for non-members.

Manitoba

Manitoba, except for its southwest portion, is underlain by the Precambrian Shield. The province has much to offer canoeists at all levels of competence. The Parks Branch of the Manitoba Department of Tourism, Recreation and Cultural Affairs has prepared canoe maps for a representative sample of Manitoba rivers, varying from easy to those which should be attempted only by experienced crews. Some are outstanding for wildwater wilderness canoeing. Each map contains great detail on routes, rapids and portages, and human and natural history. They are written for paddlers in open canoes. The Branch is in the process of preparing a guide book. Maps are available from the Parks Branch, 200 Vaughan Street, Winnipeg, Manitoba, R3C 0P8.

Saskatchewan

Major waterways in the southern third of the province are the South Saskatchewan River, Last Mountain Lake, and the Qu'Appelle River. In 1976, canoe trips were charted in some of these areas for use by novice and family groups. The north, which is largely in the Precambrian Shield, was a major trapping region and the location of important fur trade canoe routes. The Saskatchewan Department of Tourism and Renewable Resources has prepared a booklet on canoeing in Saskatchewan which outlines fifty canoe trips in the province. These are primarily in the Churchill River basin, although some are in the Saskatchewan River basin to the south, and a few in the north. Some routes are short and easy, a few long and difficult. They are written for paddlers in open canoes. Detailed guides to routes can be obtained from the Department of Tourism and Renewable Resources, po Box 7105, Regina, Saskatchewan, S4P 3N2.

Alberta

Most of Alberta lies in the mountainous west and the interior plain, and the foothills have good canoeing rivers. A reference map prepared by the Alberta Department of Recreation, Parks and Wildlife is available free of charge. Five trip guide booklets contain more detailed information on each river. The excellent descriptions have most information which a canoeist would want to know, including river and rapid grading, portages and campsites, topographical maps and access points. These are the only river guides in Canada which include the descent in feet per mile, details of geography and charts of river regimes. The rivers vary from easy to very difficult, from those in well-populated country to wilderness trips. Most of the descriptions are applicable to open canoes, although information of interest to paddlers in covered craft is also included. The booklets are printed on waterproof paper. Available for $1.00 each from the Queen's Printer, 11510 Kingsway Avenue, Edmonton, Alberta, T5G 0X5.

British Columbia

British Columbia is mountainous and its rivers are as rugged as its scenery. They offer excellent canoeing at all levels of wilderness and white water challenge.

Canoe Sport British Columbia, *British Columbia Canoe Routes* (New Westminster, BC: Nunaga Publishing Company 1974, 112 pp) This excellent booklet contains descriptions of 92 river and lake routes in British Columbia. The detailed descriptions include nearly all the information a canoeist would want. Good photographs. The routes range from placid lakes to tumultuous river torrents suitable only for experienced white water paddlers in covered craft. The book is available from Western Heritage Supply Limited, po Box

399, 27247 Fraser Highway, Aldergrove, BC, V0X 1H0. The Parks Branch of the Department of Recreation and Conservation has prepared folders on other canoe routes in provincial parks.

Northwest Territories

The Division of Tourism of the Government of the Northwest Territories has route descriptions of the major canoe routes of the Territories. Most come from the federal government's Wild Rivers Survey. These, and an *Explorer's Guide* to the Territories, are available from Travel Arctic, Yellowknife, NWT. Canoeists should supplement them by reading the accounts of early travellers and explorers. Most of the routes are difficult wilderness trips, requiring a charter flight of 250 to 300 miles to the starting point and ending in remote places.

Yukon

The rivers of the Yukon Territory run through remote mountainous regions. Many are surprisingly tranquil, including the Yukon, Teslin and Stewart, for which the Government of the Yukon Territory has prepared guides. The reports of the Wild Rivers Survey on sixteen other rivers are also available from the Department of Tourism and Information, Whitehorse, Yukon Territory. Some of these rivers are extremely difficult white water challenges.

Information on Climate, Waterflow, Geology

A general source of information on climate, waterflow, geology, and other matters is the *National Atlas of Canada*, 4th edition (Macmillan of Canada for the federal Department of Energy, Mines and Resources 1974). At the back of the *Atlas* is a list of sources of the data for each map. These sources cover most aspects of information important to canoeists. Many books on geography, natural history and travel have been written about all areas of Canada and can be found in good libraries. The federal Department of the Environment produces useful studies on the climate in specific regions, and tables of streamflow are produced by both the federal and provincial governments. Most libraries have some of these materials, or at least catalogues of the government publications that are available. I have found government departments very helpful in answering serious inquiries about climate, streamflow, and geography.

Maps and Aerial Photographs

Maps of the many National Topographic Series are available from the Canada

Map Office, 615 Booth Street, Ottawa, K1A 0E9. They cost $1.50 each plus 50 cents for handling. The Map Office gives excellent, speedy service. Index maps are available without charge.

Each provincial government also has a mapping branch which will supply provincial, and normally also the national, maps. Some stores in most large cities also supply the national topographical maps of the region.

Aerial photographs are obtainable from the National Air Photo Library, 615 Booth Street, Ottawa, K1A 0E9. The photos are normally contact prints from a nine-inch by nine-inch negative, covering about four miles on each side. To order, the area of interest must be marked on a suitably scaled topographical map, which should then be sent to the Air Photo Library.

APPENDIX B: Books on canoeing

This appendix describes books on canoeing techniques, camping, wilderness medicine, route finding and survival – including some widely distributed ones that are less than satisfactory. Not included are books on the history of canoeing, expeditions by canoes, personal experiences, or nature watching: these are widely available in bookstores and libraries. Some of these I have enjoyed are cited in the Notes. The *National Atlas of Canada* has an excellent list of books on explorations and the fur trade in its section on sources.

Books on Canoeing Techniques

The following is a small selection from the many manuals now in print on canoeing technique. They are listed progressively from the most elementary to the most technical.

Omer Stringer and Dan Gibson, *The Canoeist's Manual* (Toronto: Dan Gibson Productions 1975, 30 pp) This little booklet is a good introduction to paddling techniques as they are taught at Algonquin summer camps. Stringer is an Algonquin Park old-timer. The recommended kneeling position, with knees together, is not suitable for white water, nor is the pry stroke as it is shown. The photographic illustrations are good.

Ronald H. Perry, *Canoeing for Beginners* (Toronto: G. R. Welch Company 1967, 126 pp) Perry was a canoeing instructor at Ontario summer camps. This book, an updating of his *The Canoe and You*, is a good elementary introduction, with some history, safety, tripping advice, etc. Contains admonitions like 'Don't stand up in a canoe,' and 'Don't shoot rapids.' Well illustrated with drawings.

American National Red Cross, *Basic Canoeing* (American National Red Cross 1965, 67 pp) A condensation of the Red Cross's excellent larger textbook, *Canoeing*. Good coverage of elementary techniques and paddle strokes. The stroke motions in the drawings are exaggerated, and would quickly exhaust a paddler. Some suggestions in it are open to question, such as replacing seats with thwarts, and cleating down the free ends of bow and stern lines.

Wolf Ruck, *Canoeing and Kayaking* (Toronto: McGraw-Hill Ryerson 1974, 96 pp) A good basic introduction to elementary canoeing and kayaking, which also discusses white water strokes, including bracing and Eskimo rolling. There is a section on handling white water, and others on flat water racing and touring. The drawings and photographs are well done. It describes canoeing and kayaking as it is now taught at the summer camps which recognize and welcome the challenge of white water.

Robert E. McNair, *Basic River Canoeing*, 3rd ed. (American Camping Association 1972, 103 pp) A version of an early manual on white water canoeing produced in the United States soon after white water began to gain its popularity in the 1960s. A good introduction to strokes and tactics. It is oriented towards short trips on small rivers in covered two-man canoes.

John T. Urban, *A White Water Handbook for Canoe and Kayak* (Boston: Appalachian Mountain Club 1973, 77 pp) A fine introduction to white water techniques for covered canoes and kayaks. Well illustrated.

Joseph L. Hasenfus, *Canoeing* (American National Red Cross 1969, 496 pp) An authoritative manual for advanced paddling in open canoes, well illustrated, with chapters on white water. Although parts are dated (it was first published in 1956) it is an excellent book which has less popularity than it deserves. It tends to be overly dogmatic, and the paddling style emphasizes arms too much, and shoulders and body too little. Bargain-priced.

Jay Evans and Robert R. Anderson, *Kayaking: The New Whitewater Sport for Everybody* (Brattleboro, Vermont: Stephen Greene Press 1975, 192 pp) Jay Evans was a former U.S. Olympic coach. The authors have produced a fine handbook to kayaking. Their main interest is white water skills, especially those used in first-class slalom competition. The book does not discuss open canoes, although there are brief sections on covered C1s and C2s. An excellent manual on advanced white water techniques in covered craft.

Dean Norman, ed., *The All-Purpose Guide to Paddling* (Matteson, Illinois: Great Lakes Living Press 1976, 218 pp) This excellent book gives an introduction to all aspects of advanced white water and wilderness canoeing, including, among other topics, open canoes, kayaks, surfing, poling, and buying or building. Each chapter is written by an American expert in the field. Good value.

Books on Canoe Camping

The books in this section are for people interested in extended canoe trips. They are listed in what, in my opinion, is ascending order of usefulness.

Ray Bearse, *The Canoe Camper's Handbook* (New York: Winchester Press 1974, 366 pp) A long but not very good book; some errors could seriously mislead a reader. For example, the picture on page 197 shows the wrong feathering on the 'guide' stroke. Bearse calls it his favourite stroke, but he must like going in circles because that is what he would do if he used it. Bearse says that after a dump 'A healthy slug of 151-proof rum and hot water is comforting.' This is bad advice because alcohol can aggravate hypothermia. He also says it is 'advisable' to use spray covers in grade IV rapids! His advice on gear is more useful to campers than canoers.

John Malo, *Malo's Complete Guide to Canoeing and Canoe Camping* (New York: Collier 1969, 278 pp) This paperback is a primitive introduction to canoeing and camping techniques. The illustration on page 75 also has the feathering wrong for the 'guide' stroke. Malo rates canvas as the 'ideal tent material.'

John W. Malo, *Wilderness Canoeing* (New York: Collier 1971, 176 pp) Primarily about planning and conducting trips into the wilderness. The information in it is straightforward and elementary.

Mike Michaelson and Keith Ray, *Canoeing* (Chicago: Regnery 1975, 154 pp) Includes a discussion of basic canoeing techniques and elementary camping. Reasonably comprehensive. Not much wrong, although some things are not quite right. The illustration of tracking on page 109 shows a canoe that is about to swamp because of bad control by two lines, and the packsack in the canoe does not look as though it is tied in.

Bradford Angier and Zack Taylor, *Introduction to Canoeing* (Harrisburg, Pa.: Stackpole Books 1973, 191 pp) Much the same as the previous book.

Carl Monk and Jerome Knap, *A Complete Guide to Canoeing* (Toronto: Pagurian Press 1976, 192 pp) This book adequately covers the elements of basic canoeing and canoe camping.

Robert Douglas Mead, *The Canoer's Bible* (New York: Doubleday, 1976, 164 pp) Another adequate introduction to elementary canoeing and canoe camping.

G. Heberton Evans III, *Canoeing Wilderness Waters* (New York: Barnes 1976, 211 pp) A good guide by an experienced leader of summer campers on wilderness river routes.

James West Davidson and John Rugge, *The Complete Wilderness Paddler* (New York: Knopf 1976, 259 pp) A modern handbook by two recreational white water canoeists. The sections on river tactics and route planning and finding are especially useful. A worthwhile book.

Bill Riviere, *Pole, Paddle and Portage* (New York: Van Nostrand Reinhold 1969, 259 pp) Riviere is an old-time woodsman whose personality and experience suffuse his writing. He convinces the reader that he has tested and tried what he suggests. A good, comprehensive introduction to canoeing and canoe camping techniques.

Calvin Rutstrum, *North American Canoe Country* (New York: Macmillan 1964, 216 pp) Rutstrum, like Riviere, is an old-time woodsman. This book discusses his general approach to the wilderness in terms of both technique and philosophy. Good, vivid descriptions of canoeing experiences in the wilderness, primarily drawn from Rutstrum's experience in northern Ontario and Manitoba.

Books on Camping of Interest to Canoeists

Townsend Whelen and Bradford Angier, *On Your Own in the Wilderness* (New York: Galahad Books 1958, 330 pp) An old-style woodcraft book which includes many no longer environmentally acceptable practices like cutting bough beds and living off the land by hunting. The advice on footwear, clothing and camping gear is also dated. Useful advice on finding your way.

Bill Riviere, *Backcountry Camping* (New York: Doubleday 1972, 320 pp) Also an old-time woodsman's manual, although more oriented towards the interests of modern recreational campers. Little advice suitable for go-light camping.

Richard W. Langer, *The Joy of Camping* (Baltimore: Penguin Books 1973, 320 pp) A lively, reasonably comprehensive introduction to camping techniques, with chapters on canoeing.

Calvin Rutstrum, *The New Way of the Wilderness* (New York: Macmillan 1958, 276 pp) Rutstrum's chapters on wilderness cooking are especially good. The book is a comprehensive introduction with an attractive thoughtful quality, but the sections on equipment need updating.

Colin Fletcher, *The New Complete Walker*, 2d ed. (New York: Knopf 1974, 470 pp) Fletcher is a modern backpacker who experiments with and uses the lightest and best modern equipment and food. Canoeists do not need to take the same extreme care over weight as backpackers, but Fletcher's analyses of alternatives in equipment, materials and techniques are of great help to any camper and canoeist in examining and selecting gear and food. A first-class book, and entertaining in its own right.

Route Finding and Survival

James A. Wilkerson, ed., *Medicine for Mountaineers* (Seattle: The Mountaineers 1967, 309 pp) Covers most of the accidents and ailments that can occur in the wilderness. A layman can understand it.

Bjorn Kjellstrom, *Be Expert with Map and Compass* (Laporte, Indiana: American Orienteering Service 1967, 136 pp) A guide to the use of maps and compasses for orienteering – the sport of car-rallying without a car, on foot, cross-country. It also has a great deal of information on techniques and equipment useful to any wilderness traveller.

Calvin Rutstrum, *The Wilderness Route Finder* (New York: Macmillan 1967, 214 pp) This straightforward introductory textbook on finding your way in the wilderness includes chapters on such topics as maps, compasses, and the use of natural features, as well as some elementary techniques of astronomical navigation. Good, clear and concise.

Canada, Department of Indian and Northern Affairs, *Northern Survival*, (1972, 93 pp) A good introduction to all aspects of wilderness survival in northern Canada, which includes short sections on topics like first aid, hypothermia, other aspects of medicine, travel, shelter, route finding, edible plants and animals, cooking, and equipment.

APPENDIX C: Equipment list

Every canoeist develops his own personal preferences in equipment, gear and clothing. This is the check list I use in preparing for a week-long wilderness trip, assuming the likelihood of cool weather.

Canoeing Equipment (for two)

1 canoe
3 paddles
2 life jackets
1 100 ft. nylon line, 1/4-inch
1 20 ft. nylon line, 1/4-inch
1 roll duct tape
1 fibreglass repair kit (if the canoe is fibreglass) or canoe repair kit
2 canvas canoe packs
1 tent with fly
1 plastic tarp (optional)
1 axe – full size
1 small saw
1 file, for sharpening axe (optional, but necessary on longer trips)

1 whetstone (optional, but necessary on longer trips)
100 ft. 1/8-inch nylon cord for use around camp, etc.
1 roll toilet paper
1 sewing kit
10 green plastic garbage bags
20 small plastic bags
1 box matches in waterproof container
1 emergency kit – includes snare wire and fishing tackle
1 waterproof map case
1 set maps
1 river guide
1 first aid kit
1 candle lantern or flashlight

Cooking Equipment (for two)

1 grill for wood fire
1 small gas stove
1 quart container white gas (naphtha)
2 forks
2 spoons
2 mugs
2 bowls or plates
1 set nesting tins for cooking

1 frying pan
1 spatula (optional)
1 cooking spoon (optional)
1 can opener (or ensure that a pocket knife has a good opener)
cleaning pads
detergent

Clothing (for one)
1 wool underwear, long johns
2 undershorts
2 wool undershirts
2 viyella or light wool shirts
1 heavy wool shirt
1 shell parka
1 cagoule
1 down vest or sweater
2 pairs twill or woollen trousers (one pair of shorts and one pair of trousers in warm weather)
1 belt
1 pair rain chaps
3 pairs wool socks
2 bandannas
1 pair running shoes
1 pair boots
1 pair down booties
1 pair pyjamas
1 pair gloves
1 bathing suit (optional)
1 hat

Personal Gear (for one)
1 sleeping bag
1 foam pad, closed cell (or air mattress)
Insect repellent
1 insect head net (in the spring, or in the north)
1 towel
1 toilet kit
Soap
Knife
Compass
Waterproof match safe filled with matches
Camera equipment (optional)
Binoculars (optional)
1 note book
1 pencil
Fishing tackle (optional)
Emergency rations
Reading material, nature guides, etc. (optional)
Stuff bags for clothing and sleeping bag
Waterproof bag for camera equipment (optional)

NOTES

In many instances reprint editions are cited as being more readily available than the original edition.

Chapter 1 The Canoe

1 Samuel de Champlain, *Works*, edited by H. P. Biggar (Toronto: The Champlain Society 1922), vol. I, pp. 104-5

2 The best description of native Canadian craft is: Edwin Tappan Adney and Howard I. Chapelle, *The Bark Canoes and Skin Boats of North America* (Washington: Smithsonian Institute 1964). Adney, born in Ohio in 1868, spent his life studying native Indian craft and lived for much of his adult life in Woodstock, New Brunswick. He was more a collector of information than a writer, and after his death in 1950 Howard Chappelle of the Museum of History and Technology, Washington, DC, organized his papers for publication. George Frederick Clarke, a long-time friend of Adney, observed: 'In all he made more than a hundred models ... spruce bark canoes, moosehide canoes; the umiak and kayak of the Eskimo – all built to one-fifth scale of actual size. Most of these models he later sold to the Newport News Marine Museum. Why this museum? you may ask. I answer: because none of the several wealthy men he approached in Canada possessed enough sense of their historical value – that in these models rested the whole early story of inland water transportation in North America – to pay the very modest sum his industry was entitled to! Thus, one by one, Canada continues to lose her historical treasures.' *Someone Before Us: Our Maritime Indians* (Fredericton: Brunswick Press 1968) p. 185

3 Samuel Hearne, *A Journey to the Northern Ocean*, edited by Richard Glover (Toronto: Macmillan 1958) p. 62

4 Diamond Jenness, *Indians of Canada*, 7th ed. (Ottawa: National Museum of Canada 1967) pp. 104-5

5 Samuel Strickland, *Twenty-Seven Years in Canada West; or the Experiences of an Early Settler* (Reprinted Edmonton: Hurtig 1970) vol. II, pp. 48-9

6 Alexander Henry, *Travels and Adventures in Canada and the Indian Territories Between the Years 1760 and 1776* (Reprinted Edmonton: Hurtig, 1969) p. 172

7 See H. A. Innis, *The Fur Trade in Canada* (Toronto: University of Toronto Press 1962) pp. 222-3 fn. Innis is mistaken in stating that the canoe factory was at St Joseph's Island. It was actually located at Grand Portage.

8 Adney and Chapelle, *The Bark Canoes and Skin Boats of North America*, p. 153

9 J. W. Anderson, *Fur Trader's Story* (Toronto: Ryerson Press 1961) p. 112

10 J. W. Tyrrell, *Across the Sub-Arctics of Canada: A Journey of 3,200 Miles by Canoe and Snowshoe Through the Barren Lands* (London: Unwin 1898) p. 9

11 *Ibid.* p. 116

12 John Murray Gibbon, in his *The Romance of the Canadian Canoe* (Toronto: Ryerson 1951) p. 133, suggests that the Chestnut canoe was so named because it was made of chestnut wood. This is not correct. The Chestnuts were a prominent Fredericton family of hunting and fishing enthusiasts who began and carried on canoe-making and designing.

13 Edwin Hodder, *John MacGregor ('Rob Roy')* (London: Hodder 1894) p. 250

14 Edwin C. Guillet, *Pioneer Travel in Upper Canada* (Reprinted Toronto: University of Toronto Press, 1963) pp. 30-1

15 A good book on the different modern materials and the making of fibreglass craft is: Charles Walbridge, *Boatbuilder's Manual* (Penllyn, Pa.: Wildwater Designs 1975).

Chapter 2 The Canoe on the Water

1 Anna Brownell Jameson, *Winter Studies and Summer Rambles in Canada, Selections* (Reprinted Toronto: McClelland and Stewart 1965) p. 134

2 Strickland, *Twenty-Seven Years in Canada West*, p. 50

3 Carle W. Handel, *Canoeing* (New York: Ronald Press 1956) p. 58

4 William Francis Butler, *The Great Lone Land: A Narrative of Travel and Adventure in the North-West of America* (Rutland, Vt.: Tuttle 1968) p. 184

5 W. Kaye Lamb, ed., *The Journals and Letters of Sir Alexander Mackenzie* (Toronto: Macmillan 1970) p. 101

6 George M. Grant, *Ocean to Ocean: Sandford Fleming's Expedition Through Canada in 1872* (Reprinted Edmonton: Hurtig 1967) pp. 55-6

7 Léo-Paul Desrosiers, *Les Engagés du Grand Portage* (Montréal: Bibliothèque Canadienne-Française 1969) p. 43. My translation

8 Butler, *The Great Lone Land*, pp. 184-5

9 S. C. Ells, 'White Water,' *Canadian Geographical Journal*, 40, 4 (April 1950) p. 183

10 J. B. Tyrrell, introduction to *David Thompson's Narrative of his Explorations in Western America* (Toronto: Champlain Society 1916) p. lxiii

11 R. M. Patterson, *Far Pastures* (Sidney, BC: Gray's 1963) pp. 181-2

12 Ronald M. Perry, *The Canoe and You* (Toronto: Dent 1948) pp. 14-16

13 Mary G. Hamilton, *The Call of Algonquin: A Biography of a Summer Camp (Toronto: Ryerson 1958)* p. 11

14 Calvin Rutstrum, *Way of the Wilderness* (Minneapolis: Burgess 1946) p. 21

15 See, for example, *On Leaped the Canoe Like A Runaway Horse,* in Cortlandt Schoonover, ed., *The Edge of the Wilderness: A Portrait of the Canadian North* (Toronto: Methuen 1974) pp. 148-9

16 Ottelyn Addison, *Early Days in Algonquin Park* (Toronto: McGraw-Hill Ryerson 1974) p. 95

17 Sigurd Olson, *The Lonely Land* (New York: Knopf 1966) p. 19

18 Eric Morse, *Fur Trade Canoe Routes of Canada / Then and Now* (Ottawa: Queen's Printer, 1969)

19 Ontario, Department of Planning and Development, *Moira Valley Conservation Report,* 1950, 'Recreation,' p. 4

Chapter 3 Turbulence and River Tactics
1 Paul Kane, *Wanderings of an Artist: Among the Indians of North America* (Reprinted Edmonton: Hurtig, 1968) pp. 226-7

2 George Back, *Narrative of the Arctic Land Expedition: to the Mouth of the Great Fish River, and Along the Shores of the Arctic Ocean, in the Years 1833, 1834, and 1835* (Reprinted Edmonton: Hurtig 1970) p. 165

3 J. W. Tyrrell, *Across the Sub-Arctics of Canada,* pp. 39-40

4 R. M. Patterson, *The Dangerous River* (Sidney, BC: Gray's 1969) p. 18

Chapter 4 Canoeing Judgment
1 David Thompson, *Travels in Western North America, 1784-1812,* edited by Victor G. Hopwood (Toronto: Macmillan 1971) p. 139

2 John T. Urban, *A White Water Handbook for Canoe and Kayak* (Boston: Appalachian Mountain Club, 1973) p. 2

3 Vilhjalmur Stefansson, *My Life with the Eskimo* (New York: Collier 1971) p. 167

4 John Fraser, 'Blair Fraser: 1909-1968,' in John and Graham Fraser, eds., *Blair Fraser Reports: Selections 1944-1968* (Toronto: Macmillan 1969) p. xxiv

5 Walt Blackadar, 'Caught up in a Hell of White Water,' *Sports Illustrated* 14 August 1972, p. 43

Chapter 5 Canoe Trips
1 Lamb, ed., *Journals and Letters of Sir Alexander Mackenzie,* p. 97

2 Edna Kenton, ed., *The Jesuit Relations and Allied Documents* (New York: Vanguard 1954) p. 121

3 Grace Lee Nute, *The Voyageur* (St. Paul: Minnesota Historical Society 1955) p. 16

4 W. Kaye Lamb, ed., *Sixteen Years in the Indian Country: The Journal of Daniel Williams Harmon, 1800-1816* (Toronto: Macmillan 1957) p. 197

5 Bil Gilbert, 'Haunting the Arctic,' *Sports Illustrated* 8 July 1974, p. 60

6 Lamb, ed., *Sixteen Years in the Indian Country,* p. 208

7 Archibald McDonald, *Peace River: A Canoe Voyage from Hudson's Bay to the Pacific by Sir George Simpson in 1828,* edited by Malcolm McLeod (Edmonton: Hurtig, 1971) p. 29. Other sources support these figures.

8 Whitefish is calculated at 45 calories per ounce, salmon at 64 calories per ounce, in accordance with figures in: Ontario, Department of Health, *Nutrient Value of Some Common Foods* (Toronto: n.d.). All figures for calorie values of foods in this section are taken from this publication.

9 This approach is adopted from Colin Fletcher's *The New Complete Walker,* 2d. ed. (New York: Knopf 1974) p. 102

10 Kane, *Wanderings of an Artist,* p. 114

11 Frederick Merk, ed., *Fur Trade and Empire; George Simpson's Journal Entitled: Remarks Connected with the Fur Trade in the Course of a Voyage from York Factory to Fort George and Back to York Factory, 1824-25, with Related Documents,* revised edition (Cambridge, Mass.: Harvard University Press 1968) p. 14

12 H. M. Robinson, *The Great Fur Land: Or Sketches of Life in the Hudson's Bay Territory* (New York: Putnam 1879) p. 117

13 Quoted by Alice M. Johnson in 'Edward and Frances Hopkins of Montreal,' *The Beaver,* Autumn 1971, p. 6

14 Merk, ed., *Fur Trade and Empire,* p. 23

15 Vilhjalmur Stefansson, *Unsolved Mysteries of the Arctic* (New York: Colliers 1962) p. 50

16 John D. Robins, *The Incomplete Anglers* (New York: Duell 1944) pp. 10-11

17 Arthur Koestler, 'Drifting on a River,' in *Drinkers of Infinity: Essays, 1955-1967* (London: Hutchinson 1968) p. 125

18 James Dickson, *Camping in the Muskoka Region: A Story of Algonquin Park,* (Reprinted Toronto: Ryerson 1960) p. 43

Chapter 6 The River

1 Hannah Arendt, *Between Past and Future* (London: Faber 1961), p. 78

2 Lao Tzu, *Tao Te Ching* translated by D. C. Lau (London: Penguin 1963) XI, p. 67

Chapter 7 The Canoeist and the River

1 Much of the legal material for this section is derived from G. V. La Forest and Associates, *Water Law in Canada: The Atlantic Provinces* (Ottawa: Information Canada 1973).

2 The references to Professor Ryan's work are to an unpublished commentary on a draft of this chapter. His main point is that the interpretation of what is a navigable river in La Forest is too restrictive.

3 (1853), 3 U.C.C.P. 305

4 (1906), 37 S.C.R. 577

5 (1906), 13 O.L.R. 237

6 Canada, Energy, Mines and Resources, *An Energy Policy for Canada – Phase 1*, vol. I (Ottawa: Information Canada 1973) p. 28

7 Kenton, ed., *Jesuit Relations*, p. 103

CREDITS

Alan Broadbent, pages 98, 103 (top)
Archives of Ontario, page 26
Canadian Pacific: title page, page 108
Canadian Pacific Corporate Archives Collection, pages
    52, 61, 96
Chestnut Canoe Company, page 25 (bottom)
C. E. S. Franks, pages 32, 35, 38 (top and bottom), 69,
    71, 77 (top and bottom), 81, 101, 109 (bottom), 110,
    115, 118, 122, 126, 130, 131, 140, 151, 155, 158, 164, 165,
    179, 199, 206
Glenbow Alberta Foundation, pages 8, 25 (top), 57, 90,
    167
Hudson's Bay Company, pages 21 (top), 64, 85
McCord Museum, page 203
National Museum of Man, pages 11, 14 (bottom), 29
Public Archives of Canada: pages 10, c-16427; 12,
    PA-22095; 13, PA-38008; 14 top, PA-74670; 16,
    PAC-30193; 18, PA-42078; 19, PAC-40073; 21 bottom,
    C-2774; 22, C-16442; 23, PA-45326; 42, C-18506; 45,
    C-11854; 47, C-4574; 49, C-16425; 51, PA-40033; 55,
    PA-19540; 58, C-53425; 79, C-13457; 80, PA-45207; 103
    bottom, PA-44511; 106, PA-49821; 109 top, C-33694;
    120, PA-19500; 135, C-2773; 136, C-38414; 145,
    PA-45374; 153, PA-10580; 157, C-11256; 159, C-25551;
    162, PA-32232; 163, PA-59510; 169, PA-39907; 171,
    PA-19566; 197, PA-12170
Royal Ontario Museum, pages 43, 137, 152
C. N. Stephen, page 170

INDEX

Butler, W. F. 44, 51-2, 222

calorie consumption and measurement 142-51
campfires 149-51
camping: books on 216-17
camps: summer 123; Algonquin 60-3, 214; Kandalore 20; northern Ontario tripping 60; Temagami 62
Canada Map Office 176, 213-14
Canadian House of Commons 51
Canadian Pacific Railway 59, 60, 168
canoes: aluminum 31-3; birch bark 8-15; C1, 36, 38, 39; C2 (open) 36-7; C2 36, 37, 38; canvas and cedar strip 21-2, 24-6, 52; Chestnut 24, 222; prospector 25, 26, 32, 34, 109; cottage 36-7; design 35-6; dugouts 15-17; elm bark 17; fibreglass 33-40, 118-19; flotation 118; fur trade 18-22; *canot du nord* 18-21, 27, 44, 47, 134; *canot de maître* 18-21, 44, 45, 48, 51, 55; Grumman 31-2, 37; Indian 7-18, 121, *see also* Indian canoes; light 134; modern 31-40; Peterborough 23-4; repairs 14, 119, 120; *Rob Roy* 27-31, 59; Rushton 31; *Sairy Gamp* 31; thermoplastic foam sandwich 34-5; wilderness 37, 39, 91
canoeing: and the automobile 204; bush thrash 141; companionship 133-4, 175; diary 176-7; distance and motivation 134-41; *le canotage gastronomique* 150; legal rights 186-93; leisure activity 57-68; purpose 68, 127-8, 141, 178, 205; racing 66, 87, 114, 124, 132, 181, 203; regions 166-72; safety 60-5, 84, 115-28; seasons 129-33; socio-economic history 53-68; techniques: books on 214-15
Canoeing (American National Red Cross) 65, 215
Champlain Provincial Park 20
Champlain, Samuel de 7-8, 17, 221
Champlain Society 56
Chapelle, Howard I. 221, 222
Chats Rapids 45
Chestnut Canoe Company 24, 222
Chesterfield Inlet 23
Clarke, George Frederick 221
clothing 119, 151-9; footwear 119,154
Complete Walker, The (Colin Fletcher) 148, 217
CORTS (Canadian Outdoors Rum Toddy Society) 133, 139, 148-50, 153, 158, 178

Davis, W. M. 160-1
décharge 102
Davidson, James West 216

Hudson's Bay Company 20, 21, 24, 27, 32, 53, 55, 56, 80, 134, 143, 171
Hudson Bay Lowlands 164, 183
Hydro Quebec 196
hypothermia 110-11, 117, 124-5, 153, 216

Indian and Northern Affairs, federal Department of: Parks Branch 184, 207
Indian canoes 7-18, 121; Algonkian 11; Chipewyan 18, 27; crooked 13; Dog Rib 28-9; dugout 15-17; elm bark 17; hybrid 18, 27, 28-9; Kootenay 10-11, 37; Micmac 10, 12, 14; Nahanni 18, 19; Ojibway 11
Indians 53, 102, 116, 120, 129, 134, 136, 143, 144, 183, 199, 200; food and lifestyle 141-2, 147; Iroquois 15, 24, 136; James Bay Cree 13, 90, 196; paddles 41; paddling techniques 41-4; reserves: Caughnawaga 24, 136; Golden Lake 20; West Coast 16-17; *see also* Indian canoes
Information: on rivers 172-5, 178-85, 207-14; over-using 177-8; using 175-7
Innis, H. A. 222
insect pests 129, 130-1
International Joint Commission 194, 196
International River Grading System 105-14

James Bay 20, 26, 27, 68, 90, 196, 207
Jameson, Anna Brownell 41, 222
Jenness, Diamond 15, 221
Johnson, Alice M. 224
Johnson, Samuel 44

Kane, Paul 90, 137, 143, 223, 224
Karras, A. L. 60
kayaks: Eskimo 7, 17-18, 28, 66; modern 36, 38, 39, 66; *Rob Roy* 27-31
Keewatin Power Co. v *Kenora* 188
Kenton, Edna 223, 225
Kerckhoff, Herman and Christa 67, 181; *see also* Madawaska Kanu Camp
Kerr, Mavis 211
Killarney Park: canoeing information 210
Kjellstrom, Bjorn 218
Koestler, Arthur 150, 224
Krieghoff, Cornelius 79, 203

La Forest, G. V. 187-93, 225
Laberge, Charlie 20

Banff National 125; Killarney: canoeing
information 210; national parks 202; Quetico:
canoeing information 210, 211; Samuel de
Champlain 20; Wild River 181, 182; Wood Buffalo 199
Parks Branch: federal Department of Indian and
Northern Affairs 184, 202, 208
Patterson, R. M. 59-60, 104, 223
pemmican 142-4, 147, 148
Perry, Ronald H. 214, 223
Peterborough Canoe Company 24
pièce 51, 135
pipe (voyageurs' measure of distance) 134, 149
politics and canoeing 192-205
pollution: *see* ecology
Port Meadow 197
Portage des roches 91
pose (voyageurs' measure of distance) 135
Precambrian Shield 7, 54, 56, 91, 111, 161-2, 170, 171,
178, 179, 180, 183; canoeing region 166, 168-9, 208, 210,
211, 212
Prince Edward Island: information on rivers 209
Public Lands Act 191
Publishing Centre: Supply and Services Canada 208

Quebec: information on rivers 207, 208, 210
Quetico Park: canoeing information 210, 211

Ray, Keith 216
reading water 82-3
Reg. v *Meyers* 188
repair kits 119
rights, 186-93; camping 187, 191, 192; Crown lands 188,
189, 192; fishing 187, 189, 190, 191, 192; flotability 187,
189; navigation 186, 187-9, 191, 192; portaging 191,
192; riparian 186, 189-90; and ownership 189-92
risk-taking 126-8
rivers: climate 164-5, 174, 213; geomorphology 160-72,
213; grading 105-14, 174-5, 176; guidebooks 107-14,
207-13; navigable 186-93; regimes and
streamflow 164-72, 174, 213; regions 166-72; uses,
competing 186-205; water levels 107, 118, 129-32, 164
Rivers, by name: Abitibi 8, 90, 163; Albany 68, 139, 164;
Athabaska 23, 100; Back 95, 176; Black (Ontario) 68;
Black (Sask.) 120; Bow 59, 150; Churchill 65, 143,
183-4, 212; Colorado 196, 202; Columbia 90, 166;
Coppermine 139, 146, 170, 176; Credit 129, 130, 150;
Crow 139; Dordogne 150; Dubawnt 23, 176; Firth 184;

JEHOVAH-TALK

JEHOVAH-TALK

THE MIND-CONTROL LANGUAGE OF JEHOVAH'S WITNESSES

DAVID A. REED

Baker Books

A Division of Baker Book House Co
Grand Rapids, Michigan 49516

Published by Baker Books
a division of Baker Book House Company
P.O. Box 6287, Grand Rapids, MI 49516-6287

Printed in the United States of America

Library of Congress Cataloging-in-Publication Data

Reed, David A.
    Jehovah talk : the mind-control language of Jehovah's Witnessess / David A. Reed.
      p. cm.
    Includes bibliographical references.
    ISBN 0-8010-5749-3 (pbk.)
    1. Jehovah's Witnessess—Controversial literature. 2. Jehovah's Witnesses—Terminology. 3. Jehovah's Witnessess—Membership. I. Title.
BX8526.5.R43 1997
289.9′2—dc21   97-25140

For information about academic books, resources for Christian leaders, and all new releases available from Baker Book House, visit our web site:
http://www.bakerbooks.com

CONTENTS

A man with Jehovah's Witness relatives wrote to me recently and described his loved ones as being on the other side of an invisible obstacle like a glass wall. He said he could yell, scream, and pound on the glass without getting any response from them—as if they couldn't even hear what he was saying.

This man's experience is not unique. Many who attempt to reason with JW visitors or acquaintances feel that they run up against an invisible obstacle. If you have already read other books on Jehovah's Witnesses and have tried unsuccessfully to share liberating information with them, you may feel discouraged from making further attempts. You may be thinking, "Why should I bother reading more about JWs? I can never get through to them with what I already know. When I talk to them, it's as if I'm not even speaking their language."

If so, you may have correctly identified the invisible obstacle as a language barrier. Yet it is much more than that. The "theocratic language" that Watchtower leaders admit teaching their followers is actually an instrument of mind-control. It is designed to prevent you from getting through to them and to prevent them from accepting the information you are trying to share with them.

7

Having their own unique language is something that Jehovah's Witnesses share in common with other mind-control cults. Yet it is an aspect of the sect that is often missed by Christians, who focus on religious differences or doctrinal errors. And, partly because they fail to take the effects of mind-control into account, these Christians typically find it difficult if not impossible to correct those doctrinal errors in the JW's mind. A direct presentation of clear and simple information fails to penetrate the Witness's thinking because the thinking process itself has become twisted and distorted.

The use of language in mind-control is not necessarily a religious issue. Atheistic communist regimes perfected the technique apart from any religious aspirations and used it as one of the psychological weapons they turned against Americans captured during the Korean War. When a captive audience is coerced into listening, the process is termed "brainwashing." When the same techniques are used minus the coercive element, the more correct terms are thought reform or mind-control. In either case, language plays a key role.

Consider, for example, the effect of a single, well-chosen name. A regime that calls itself "The Democratic People's Republic of Korea" trains people to refer to it by that name in order to influence their thinking. Though it forms only a small part of a large mind-control/propaganda effort, the name itself serves as an obstacle to thinking of the regime as undemocratic. An undemocratic democratic republic is a linguistic contradiction, and the human mind automatically tries to avoid contradictions. Like loaded dice weighted to roll a predetermined number, the "loaded language" of mind-control exerts subtle pressure to induce a predetermined line of thought. To outsiders, exposed to a single euphemistic name or a few vocabulary samples, such words are hardly persuasive at all, but to the actual targets of a mind-control program—people immersed in propaganda twenty-four hours a day and cut off from outside influences—the effect can be overwhelming.

Because the Bible is familiar ground, Christians prefer to study Scripture for answers to Jehovah's Witnesses rather than to study JW mind-control. (That preference apparently accounts for the popularity of my book, *Jehovah's Witnesses Answered Verse by Verse*, with over one hundred thousand copies circulating in English and nearly an equal number in translated editions.) Yet it is that very mind-control that prevents JWs from grasping what Christians show them in the Bible. Later in this book, I discuss the case of a Witness woman who was asked to open her own *New World Translation* of the Bible to Revelation 19:1 to determine whether that verse placed the "great crowd" on earth or in heaven. She read "great crowd in heaven" and concluded it said they are on earth. Mind-control forced her to see the opposite of what actually appeared on the page. This is what Christians are up against when they go to Jehovah's Witnesses with the Bible but without an understanding of the mind-control language that distorts the Witnesses' thinking.

Would you train missionaries in the Scriptures and then send them to China—without also teaching them the Chinese language? Of course not! By the same token you should not expect success if you try to take the gospel to Jehovah's Witnesses without first studying the "J.W.ese" language. This volume will give you the basic information you need.

Acknowledgments

This book is constructed almost entirely from my own vocabulary—the words I was accustomed to speaking and the expressions I regularly listened to during the thirteen years I was an active Jehovah's Witness. Added to these are a few additional terms I have encountered in researching the sect since my departure in 1982: new expressions to accompany "new truths" introduced since then, and some obsolete expressions that had fallen out of use before my 1969 baptism into the Witnesses. The words themselves originate, for the most part, with the Watchtower organization that coined or redefined them. Other terms have sprung up spontaneously from the worldwide body of rank-and-file Witnesses in the form of slang expressions, nicknames, or abbreviations for more complex organizational verbiage.

About a year after I self-published the initial forty-four-page booklet version of this *Dictionary,* and at the time the present book-length manuscript was near completion, I was surprised to discover on the World Wide Web an Internet website dealing with Jehovah's Witness vocabulary. The document, entitled *Glossary of American English Hacker Theocratese,* bears the 1995 copyright of a Mr. Lynn D. Newton, a Jehovah's Witness elder from Arizona who enthusiastically supports the organization and apparently fails to see the sinister aspect of its unique vocabulary. He states under "Purpose and History of the Glossary" that his "initial intent" was to provide "a reference list for some Witnesses whose native tongue is not English." Now, though, he explains that his *Glossary* "has become a labor of love, and a gift to all persons who want to have it." Hence he includes in it this blanket permission: "The 'Glossary' may be redistributed or quoted in whole or in part without asking the permission of the author." Finding it so late in my own work, however, I was able to use the *Glossary* more to verify the completeness of my manuscript than to assist in creating it.

So, my greatest indebtedness for this collection of words and definitions is to those Jehovah's Witnesses who introduced me to "the truth," trained me in "field service," and taught me at "the meetings"—many of whom have since grown old and died, and the remainder of whom disown any connection with me today. And, though, toward the end of my time in the sect, I began to develop an awareness of how language was being used to manipulate me, it was exit counselor Steven Hassan who helped me put this into broader perspective by writing in his book *Combatting Cult Mind Control,* "a destructive cult typically has its own 'loaded language' of words and expressions."

When two Jehovah's Witness ladies deliver their prepared speech at your front door, they take great pains to use plain English in such a way that you will understand everything they say. After all, they hope that you will end up agreeing with them, and, in order to agree intelligently with their message, you must first understand it. They try to speak your language at the door.

However, if you visit a local coffeeshop an hour later when those same two ladies stop for their mid-morning or mid-afternoon break, and you slip into an adjoining booth unobserved, the conversation you overhear may prove completely foreign and unintelligible. (Please note that you would have to sit down unobserved. Witnesses in public places will often start reciting excerpts from their prepared speeches if they notice non-JWs listening.) Their private dialogue might go something like this:

"Did we finish the territory, Sister Daniels?"

"Yes, Julie. Those N.H.'s completed our coverage."

"Good! I'd like to take you to meet my study. She's making good progress. Her husband recently began sitting in, and he just got a theocratic haircut. They're writing their letter to get out of Babylon."

"Isn't he the one who was once an approved associate?"

"Oh, no, sister! I couldn't even count my time on that call."

"Good! I'm auxiliary pioneering and I need to get my time in, but speaking of goats, Julie, I should alert you to a former Bethelite who's new in town."

"That old man who's a member of the evil slave class?"

"You've already heard! Yes, I met him years ago when I was at Brooklyn. He worked in the factory, and he was a b.a. back then, but later he rejected new light and got disfellow-shipped."

"That is so sad! How could anyone leave the truth?"

"It just shows our need to avoid independent thinking, and instead to exert ourselves vigorously to move ahead with the organization."

These two Witness ladies are speaking English, but with so many peculiar terms thrown in that they might as well be speaking another language. Actually, they are speaking what could be called "J.W.ese" (pronounced JAY´DUB•BEL•YOO•EEZ´)—the unique language of Jehovah's Witnesses.

JWs are so accustomed to speaking "J.W.ese" that they have to receive special training to speak plain English at the doors of strangers. Each Witness, whether nine or ninety, remains continually enrolled in the local congregation's Theocratic Ministry School, where he or she practices speaking before an audience on a regular basis. After presenting a talk, the individual's Speech Counsel Slip (report card) is graded on such points as volume, pausing, gestures, fluency, conversational quality, sense stress, modulation, warmth and feeling, personal appearance, and so on. The instructor marks each point either W for "Work on this," I for "Improved," or G for "Good." The student speaker works on two or three points each time up and goes on to other points only after achieving G grades on the current ones. One of the first points of counsel each one works on is listed as "Clear, understandable" on the Speech Counsel Slip. The *Theocratic*

Ministry School Guidebook gives this advice to Witnesses working on this aspect:

> Our study of the Scriptures and the Watch Tower Society's publications has given us a vocabulary of terms quite strange to those unacquainted with our work. If we were to explain the truths of the Bible to some audiences, using terms such as these, either much of what we say would be lost or our speech would be entirely unintelligible. (page 112)

So, Witnesses realize that most or all of what they say might prove "unintelligible" to outsiders without special care on their part to avoid using their normal, everyday "J.W.ese" vocabulary. The speech training book goes on to give specific examples:

> Consider your audience. What is the level of their understanding? How much do they know of our work? How many of these expressions will be as readily understood by them as by the speaker? Terms like "theocracy," "remnant," "other sheep," even "Armageddon" and "Kingdom," can convey either a different thought to the hearer's mind or none at all. Even such terms as "soul," "hell" and "immortality" need to be clarified if the hearer is unfamiliar with our work. (page 112)

Is it simply a matter, then, of listeners being "unfamiliar with [the] work" Jehovah's Witnesses do, just as a lay person might be baffled when overhearing electronics technicians speak to each other about diodes, resistors, ohmmeters, and so on? There is an element of that, as will be discussed later, but much more is involved.

Is it, then, a matter of doctrinal differences, with JWs attaching somewhat different significance to a few abstruse theological terms? Yes, that too is involved—and to an extent most outsiders would find unimaginable, with Christ redefined as the first angel created and the Holy Spirit reduced to an impersonal active force. More will definitely be said about this throughout this book, but there is still much more involved in the unique language JWs speak among themselves.

Yes, it is, in a sense, virtually a language of its own, not just a vocabulary of work-related tools like book bags, car groups, and territory maps (see definitions) or theological terms like archangel, remnant, and little flock. In fact, *The Watchtower* magazine, the principal publication of Jehovah's Witnesses, acknowledges that the Witnesses speak a language of their own. It refers to it as the "pure language," which it says, "has its own vocabulary." The magazine declares further: "The most important term in this theocratic language is the name Jehovah.... Other outstanding terms and expressions in this pure language are theocracy, kingdom, vindication, the Word, dedication, faithfulness, witnessing, Bible study, etc." (*The Watchtower,* April 15, 1953, page 231).

The same article, entitled "The Language Barrier and the 'Pure Language,'" adds that "as the light increases this pure language keeps expanding.... And as the columns of *The Watchtower* throw ever more light on God's Word, Jehovah's witnesses [*sic*] find their vocabulary being enriched, the pure language growing" (page 231). Aware that outsiders are separated from JWs by such a language barrier, *The Watchtower* notes on the same page that "one United States judge once observed that Jehovah's witnesses [*sic*] had their own vernacular."

The full significance and impact of this "J.W.ese" language can be grasped only when it is placed in a wider context and examined from other than simply a religious perspective.

With the use of brainwashing techniques and reeducation camps by totalitarian communist regimes against dissidents among their own people and then during the early 1950s against prisoners of war in Korea, psychiatrists, psychologists, and sociologists began looking more closely at the processes of mental manipulation. Language proved to be a key factor that surfaced in study after study. Experts studying the phenomenon found that brainwashers or thought reformers taught their victims to speak a "loaded language," with words and expressions carefully crafted like loaded dice to push the speaker's thoughts in a predetermined direction. Exit counselor Steven Hassan sums up their findings this way: "A destructive cult typically has its own 'loaded language' of words and expressions . . . controlling certain words helps to control thoughts" (*Combatting Cult Mind Control* by Steven Hassan [Rochester, Vt.: Park Street Press, 1988], pages 61–6).

Actually, though, some time before the terms "brainwashing" and "thought reform" came into popular usage in the Western world, it was the insightful British writer George Orwell who brought the concept fully before the reading public in his 1949 classic novel entitled *Nineteen Eighty-Four.* The all-enslaving "INGSOC" (English socialism) portrayed in this novel with its pervasive reminder that "Big Brother Is Watching You" never materialized in the real world to rule the British Isles—perhaps due in part to Orwell's graphic warning of how terrible it would be—but similar regimes have ruled and still rule parts of the world, and cultic organizations have exercised similar authoritarian rule over their members. Moreover, Orwell's description of the role of the fictional language "Newspeak" in manipulating the minds of his characters has been reflected over and over again in real life.

In February 1982, while a dissident member of the Watchtower organization, I wrote an article drawing parallels between the world of Orwell's *Nineteen Eighty-Four* and the world I lived in as a Jehovah's Witness. The Newspeak word "facecrime" perfectly summed up instructions we had just received to the effect that JW women "must not express disagreement with judicial decisions of the elders *even by their facial expressions*" (see "The Author's Testimony" at the end of this book). Two years later, a dissident Canadian Witness and his wife produced a book that expanded on the parallels I had drawn and demonstrated dozens of other similarities. In their volume entitled *The Orwellian World of Jeho-*

vah's Witnesses (Toronto: University of Toronto Press, 1984), Heather and Gary Botting provide a twelve-page vocabulary and devote six pages to parallels between the JW use of language and the Newspeak of Orwell's novel.

Besides facecrime there is also thoughtcrime in Big Brother's world. The chief purpose of Newspeak is to eliminate the possibility of committing thoughtcrime by eliminating the words necessary to verbalize any sort of challenge to or deviation from Party orthodoxy. If you learn to think only Newspeak words, you cannot commit thoughtcrime, even accidentally. In their book the Bottings draw attention to parallels and cite actual cases of JWs interrogated for thoughtcrimes. Interestingly, *The Watchtower* itself has directly commanded followers to "avoid independent thinking . . . questioning the counsel that is provided by God's visible organization" (January 15, 1983, page 22).

Doublethink is another Newspeak word exemplified among Jehovah's Witnesses. It refers to the mental gymnastics enabling one to know the facts and yet to believe that white is black or that yes means no if the ruling authority says so. The practice of doublethink allows JWs to attach contradictory meanings to certain "J.W.ese" words such as prophet and prophecy so that the organization's predictions for specific dates are God's prophecies while the dates are yet future but were never really promoted as prophetic utterances after they fail to come true—and so that the Governing Body speaks as God's prophet while at the same time the Governing Body has never claimed to be a prophet of God (for examples, see box titled "a prophet yet not a prophet" on page 111).

Like the inhabitants of Orwell's fictional world who see no problem with calling a forced labor camp a joycamp, Jehovah's Witnesses gladly speak of cleaning their church building's toilets as a Kingdom privilege. Only upbeat positive-sounding words can be applied to the organization, while its opponents are automatically—with no consideration as to merit—assigned negative names such as evil slaves or filthy apostates.

In his novel's Appendix, entitled "The Principles of Newspeak," Orwell breaks down that fictional language into various component parts, outlining the mind-control function of each. The same can be done here for the "J.W.ese" language.

"J.W.ESE"—A LANGUAGE WITH A BUILT-IN AGENDA

People unfamiliar with the unique language spoken by Jehovah's Witnesses can understand it more easily if it is broken down into its distinct elements. Some of these categories overlap to one extent or another, but the JW vocabulary can be separated into these general divisions or word groupings:

(1) **Biblical retranslations:** expressions taken from the Watchtower Society's *New World Translation* of the Bible. JWs speak of Christ being nailed to the torture stake rather than the cross.

(2) **JW distinctives:** activities or things that are peculiar to JWs. For example, just as Hindus look up to their swami and worry about their karma, so JWs have their circuit overseer and are concerned about going out in service enough.

(3) **Wedge words:** new names assigned to things JWs share in common with other people. To drive a wedge between Jehovah's Witnesses and their non-Witness relatives and neighbors, Watchtower leaders assign new names to things held in common, thus eliminating potential common ground for friendly communication. So, while others go to church, JWs go to Kingdom Hall.

21

(4) **Redefined words:** common words that take on totally different meanings in Witness usage. Examples include spirit, defined as an inanimate force like electricity, and goat, a person who rejects the sect's message.

(5) **Cloaking expressions:** obscure words used to conceal information from outsiders unfamiliar with the sect. Witnesses resort to such devices when organizational instructions require them to violate tax laws, refuse military conscription, evade child welfare laws, and so on. Falsifications on these matters are not considered lies, but theocratic war strategy.

(6) **Manipulative expressions:** euphemisms, pejoratives, and other slanted expressions—the key linguistic element of mind-control. These expressions shape members' thoughts by controlling the words they use to express them. For example, the expression "evil slave class" automatically passes judgment on certain members who quit the sect.

Since each of these elements of the language functions somewhat differently and serves a somewhat different purpose, it will be helpful to discuss each element separately in some detail.

Biblical Retranslations

One of the first goals a Jehovah's Witness works toward with a prospective convert is to replace the individual's Bible with the Watchtower Society's *New World Translation of the Holy Scriptures.* The practice is often justified by pointing out that the new student will understand this modern translation more readily than the archaic seventeenth-century language found in the *King James* or *Douay* versions. However, JWs are actually just as eager to replace the *New King James,* the *New International Version,* and other contemporary translations. Why? Because hundreds of verses have been changed in the *New World Translation* to agree with Watchtower teachings.

These retranslated verses remove a number of common words from the everyday vocabulary of Jehovah's Witnesses and add a number of new "J.W.ese" words to replace them. Thus JWs speak of Christ's torture stake or stake instead of his cross. They refer to him as being impaled rather than crucified. The crucifixion becomes the impalement. The Holy Spirit is transformed into a holy spirit or active force. Just as there is no hell in Watchtower theology, the word has also been removed from their Bible and from the active vocabulary of Jehovah's Witnesses. In its place they use transliterations of Hebrew and Greek terms—sheol, gehenna, and hades—with special sectarian definitions attached. Even Christ becomes a god instead of God, and the name "Jehovah" is inserted into the New Testament in hundreds of places where Greek manuscripts of the Bible actually have the word for Lord *(kurios)*.

JW Distinctives

Perhaps the least sinister aspect of "J.W.ese" is the use of unique words for things and activities peculiar to Jehovah's Witnesses. Members of mainline Christian churches don't speak of territory maps because they don't cut their community's street map into small pieces to guide small groups in canvassing door to door, and they don't speak of counting their time because they don't have to tally and report hours spent in religious activity. Jehovah's Witnesses do both these things, and so it is only natural that they have come up with nouns and verbs to describe their unique paraphernalia and routines.

A jargon or specialized vocabulary of some sort is employed by many professions, sects, or groups of people united by a common interest or activity. Pipe fitters and insulation installers toss around terms such as short- and long-radius elbows, sweeps, bends, and victaulic couplings—terms foreign to other people's ears. Stamp collectors have words to distinguish the varieties of printing, perforating, and preservation methods associated with postage stamps. Astronomers classify as white dwarfs, red giants, binaries, and so on the tiny twinkling points of light the rest of us are content to refer to simply as stars.

So, it should neither surprise nor offend us that Jehovah's Witnesses have their own words associated with various aspects of selling religious literature from house to house. Outsiders would normally not need to know such words or their meanings, but they are found as entries in our Dictionary section to aid those who do desire that knowledge. The real cause for concern—and the reason for putting this volume together—is the sect's manipulation of other words as an instrument of thought reform, mind-control, or brainwashing. Such abuse (or misuse) of words becomes more apparent as the remaining elements of the "J.W.ese" language are examined.

Wedge Words

To drive a wedge between Jehovah's Witnesses and outsiders, Watchtower leaders assign new names to things held in common. The resulting vocabulary distances JWs from their non-Witness relatives and neighbors. If there are four men living on a small street, for example, the Baptist, the Lutheran, and the Methodist may feel some kinship because they all go to church, they all serve as deacons in their respective churches, and they all take Communion. The fourth man, a Jehovah's Witness, feels set apart from his neighbors because he "does not go to church, does not serve as a deacon, and does not take Communion." In reality, though, he does every one of those things but simply calls them by other names: he goes to Kingdom Hall, he serves as a ministerial servant, and he partakes at Memorial.

The use of different terminology to describe things JWs share in common with believers of other religions serves the purpose of dividing Witnesses from their neighbors and hence keeps them more securely under the Watchtower Society's influence. Like members of other churches, Jehovah's Witnesses attend services but they insist on calling them meetings, they sing hymns but they insist on calling them songs. In such areas that would otherwise be common ground, the artificially created differences of vocabulary serve as a barrier, keeping JWs apart from non-Witness relatives and neighbors.

The use of special words also serves another function for Jehovah's Witnesses: these words act as passwords or verbal I.D. badges, immediately identifying genuine Witnesses and alerting them to outsiders in their midst. A stranger walking into Kingdom Hall who speaks the language is readily accepted as a visiting brother or sister. A stranger, on the other hand, who misuses words immediately reveals himself or herself to be an outsider.

Suppose, for example, that a local Witness greets a stranger standing in front of the corkboard at the back of the auditorium before the Sunday morning meeting. If the visitor says, "Hi! I was just looking at the bulletin board to find the topic of this morning's sermon," the Witness knows right away that this is either a newly interested person or a hostile infiltrator. A JW would have phrased the same thought this way: "Hi! I was just looking at the information board to find the topic of this morning's talk." The term "bulletin board" was stricken from JW vocabulary decades ago due to its supposedly unsavory etymology. (They trace its derivation to the papal bull, and certainly no loyal Witness would want to refer to the Kingdom Hall corkboard as a place for displaying documents issued by the Catholic pope.) Sermon, on the other hand, refers to a prepared message presented on the doorstep during house-to-house work, whereas the

25

forty-five-minute public address given on Sunday morning at Kingdom Hall is a talk in JW terminology.

This invisible linguistic barrier fulfills much the same function as physical isolation. It confines members mentally in the same way that the dense jungles of Guyana physically confined the inhabitants of Jonestown. If the latter had been able to discuss with Catholic and Lutheran neighbors the well-rehearsed and orchestrated mass suicide Rev. Jim Jones was preparing them for, they would no doubt have heard enough cautionary admonitions to escape following that madman to their death. The liberating effect of outside communication was well understood by Soviet dictators, who used sophisticated radio-jamming devices to silence Western broadcasts—and by the free world countries that invested in Radio Free Europe to penetrate that informational blockade. It is also well understood by Watchtower leaders, who encircle their followers with mental barbed wire to cut them off from their neighbors of other faiths.

Redefined Words

This is where the language Jehovah's Witnesses speak becomes confusing. Outsiders assume that familiar words have the meanings normally attached to them. Instead, they find many surprises when listening to JWs speak:

A publisher is not a company that produces books, but an individual—perhaps even a child—approved to go out knocking on doors. A territory is a tiny map section that may be carried in one's pocket. A pioneer is not someone exploring a new frontier, but a JW out knocking on doors fulltime. A young man may talk about being in the service and doing k.p. for his c.o.—without any of the standard military meanings (see definitions). New light appears, not at dawn, but when a book is opened. A man in charge is called a servant, and a little girl may introduce herself as a minister.

26

Add to this the fact that words such as Christ and worship have new meanings assigned to them, and it becomes clear that a special dictionary is needed to interpret JW language. Even with such help, it may not always be immediately clear when a JW is using a given word with its standard English definition or with its unique Watchtower meaning. Both the context and the audience must be considered. If speaking to another JW (and not for the benefit of eavesdropping outsiders) the "J.W.ese" definition is most likely meant. If talking to an outsider involved with the Witness in a Bible study on the subject in question, the JW will likely be speaking "J.W.ese," but if speaking at the door to a new contact, the standard English usage would be employed.

Cloaking Expressions

The use of obscure expressions to conceal information is not unique to religious cults. Two groups well known for using professional jargon to hide what they are talking about are doctors and lawyers. Attorneys who go on to become legislators then see to it that laws are set forth in language beyond the comprehension of ordinary citizens, thus requiring common folk to hire the services of attorneys whenever these laws must be consulted. Lawyers often employ Latin expressions such as *habeas corpus* and *amicus curiae* to make themselves indispensable interpreters. Physicians likewise use Latin terminology to conceal the tricks of their trade. When a patient tells a doctor he has a skin inflammation, and the doctor diagnoses it as dermatitis, he has simply translated "skin inflammation" into another language—for a fee of $50.00 or more. Money is the obvious motive when physicians and attorneys use cloaking expressions to conceal their trade secrets, but with Jehovah's Witnesses there are other factors involved.

JWs use the word "neutrality" as a code word for their teaching that young men must refuse the draft in violation

27

of military conscription laws—and must even refuse "alternative service" work in civilian hospitals. [CORRECTION: As this book was going to press, the May 1, 1996 *Watchtower* dropped the sect's ban on civilian alternative service, while still ruling out participation in the military. Rather than rewrite the paragraph based on this "new truth," I chose to insert this correction to highlight the changeable nature of JW beliefs and practices.] To avoid possible legal problems as a consequence of advising young men to violate the law, Watchtower publications use obscure language meaningful only to Witnesses themselves. Similarly, if a young man complies with the law for conscientious objectors by accepting the draft board's assignment to work in a hospital, and the local JW elders punish him with expulsion from the sect, they announce that he has disassociated himself—to hide the fact that he has actually been put on trial and expelled.

There is even a "J.W.ese" expression for the use of such lying or deception to advance the organization's interests. It is euphemistically called theocratic war strategy.

When a Witness knocks at a door, gives a brief sales pitch, and sells a small book for a dollar, local laws may require him or her to collect sales tax. (A credit report on the Watchtower Bible and Tract Society of New York, Inc., revealed $1.25 billion corporate sales figures for 1991, up from just over $1 billion in 1990.) To evade this obligation the organization instructs JWs to say they did not sell the book; rather, they *placed* it. They did not receive the dollar in payment; rather, the money was received coincidentally as an unrelated donation.

Another illegal activity covered by cloaking expressions relates to violating child welfare laws and ignoring court orders regarding medical treatment. When taking such drastic steps to prevent blood transfusions for sick or injured children JWs commonly refer to their actions as keeping integrity or putting God first.

Manipulative Expressions

Euphemisms or slanted expressions serve the purpose of shaping members' thoughts by controlling the words they use to express them. This technique did not originate with Jehovah's Witnesses, of course. The world of commerce uses it widely in advertising hype and even in naming products: Wonder Bread creates great expectations, and Super Glue is naturally assumed to be better than ordinary glue. Corporate management can make a floorsweeper's job opening more attractive without paying out more in wages—simply by changing the job title to "sanitation engineer."

A similar propagandistic end is accomplished when an aggressive nation bent on foreign conquest names its military arm the "Department of Defense." Loyal citizens who employ this terminology in their conversations tend to view their military actions as defensive, whether they actually are or not, since the name "Defense" is officially attached to these actions. Similarly, when a totalitarian dictatorship takes on the name "People's Democratic Republic of . . .," the name helps shape the thinking of susceptible individuals and pushes them toward viewing the government as democratic. Free citizens, of course, are in a position to subject such political propaganda to open discussion and criticism. Consumers, likewise, learn to take advertising hype with a grain of salt. Manipulative language becomes much more controlling, however, in a totalitarian society or a religious cult where free discussion and criticism are not allowed ("Do you refuse to listen to bitter criticism of Jehovah's organization? You should refuse"—*The Watchtower* May 15, 1984, page 17).

The Watchtower Society makes effective use of manipulative expressions from the very beginning of its training program for new converts. JW recruiters offer a Bible study to people encountered at the doors, but those who accept the offer find themselves actually studying a Watchtower textbook while opening the Bible only occasionally. Yet, because

29

it is called a Bible study, impressionable people are led to think that they are studying the Bible.

Instead of saying, "I've been a member of the organization for ten years," a Witness is taught to say, "I've been in the truth for ten years." Thus, the truth becomes synonymous with the organization in the JW's mind. This helps prevent members from questioning whether the sect's teachings are true or not. After all, how could *the truth* be false? Anyone who questions or disagrees with the truth automatically identifies himself or herself with lies. Other religions opposed to *the truth* are automatically false.

JWs are constantly encouraged to move ahead with Jehovah's organization by accepting doctrinal changes as soon as these are introduced. This attaches to doctrinal changes the positive connotation of progress, even when indecisive leadership actually flip-flops back and forth, as it has on a number of issues. Ephesians 4:14 speaks of people misled so as to be "tossed to and fro, and carried about with every wind of doctrine," but when Watchtower doctrine wavers to and fro, JWs must immediately endorse each change, since failure to move ahead gives the appearance of foolishly resisting progress. Such doctrinal changes are also introduced as new light, implying that failure to accept the new teachings leaves one in darkness.

Cumulative Effects

Combined with other aspects of the Watchtower mind-control program not detailed in this book—indoctrination, social isolation, repetitive meeting programs, rewards and punishments, judicial committee enforcement, and so on—communicating constantly in the "J.W.ese" language helps mold the thinking of Jehovah's Witnesses. Longtime members are ready to accept any new doctrine, to reject any old pattern of thinking, to refuse a needed blood transfusion, and even to cut off dear friends and loved ones, on command from headquarters.

30

A LANGUAGE
THAT CHANGES ON COMMAND

Since Watchtower leaders employ language as an instrument of mind-control, it should not surprise us that this tool can be redirected with a simple turn of the hand. All that it takes for a word or expression to take on totally new meaning is a sentence or two in a *Watchtower* or *Awake!* magazine or a small paragraph in the active Jehovah's Witnesses' internal monthly, *Our Kingdom Ministry.*

Of course, generally speaking, all language bears more resemblance to a meandering river than to a stationary pond. Not only does it flow out of the mouths of speakers, but it also flows down through time, changing form and direction as it goes. Those who have attempted to read the eighth-century epic *Beowulf* know that the English tongue has changed drastically over the course of a millennium. Even the charming verse of the 1611 *King James Version* Bible poses occasional problems for modern readers. Without a dictionary, who would comprehend that Jacob was cooking stew when he "sod pottage" or that a "shambles" was a meat market? (Genesis 25:29, 1 Corinthians 10:25). Our parents' generation thought of a weaver's tool when they heard the word "shuttle," but we think of a spaceship. And our own generation has witnessed the transformation of the primary meaning of "gay" from happy to homosexual.

Yet these transformations have generally occurred haphazardly, without conscious direction. Purposeful manipulation of language by a centralized authority has been rare in human history. The French, fearful of foreign encroachment on their culture, put in place a bureaucracy to prevent undesirable change by excluding alien words from creeping into public dialogue. The Watchtower organization, on the other hand, as noted earlier, follows the pattern of communist "democratic people's republics" and the imaginary state in Orwell's novel *Nineteen Eighty-Four.* Functioning like a totalitarian dictatorship's Ministry of Propaganda, the Writing Department at Watchtower headquarters in Brooklyn manipulates the language Jehovah's Witnesses use, as a tool to control their thinking. And an inescapable aspect of that manipulation is the element of change.

For example, in 1970, the official word went out to begin calling the bulletin board at Kingdom Hall an information board in order to avoid using a word supposedly derived from the papal bull. From that point on, anyone who slipped back into the old habit and said "bulletin board" received either a verbal rebuke or a stern gaze of disapproval from more alert associates.

Jehovah's Witnesses have repeatedly experienced prophetic failure when the world failed to come to an end in 1914, 1918, 1925, and 1975, to name a few of the most prominent dates predicted by Watchtower leaders. (For details and photostatic documentation, see my 1989 book, *How to Rescue Your Loved One from the Watchtower.*) In recent decades the sect had been proclaiming that the generation of people who saw the events of the year 1914 would not pass away before the world's end ("the Creator's promise of a peaceful and secure new world before the generation that saw the events of 1914 passes away"—*Awake!* masthead on page 4 of each issue from March 1988 through October 1995). However, as years passed the 1914 generation grew older and the prophecy grew less credible. The organization responded by repeatedly redefining what it meant by the word "generation." First it referred to those who were "15 years of age" in 1914 (*Awake!* October 8, 1968, page 13); then to ten-year-olds (*The Watchtower,* October 15, 1980, page 31). Although *The Watchtower* had said clearly that "the 'generation' logically would not apply to babies," it later reversed itself and began speaking of "the babies of that generation." (Compare statements in the issues of October 1, 1978, page 31, and May 15, 1984, page 5.) Eventually, however, the babies of 1914 advanced into their eighties and surviving fifteen-year-olds reached the age of ninety-five. Alas, the sect was confronted with that generation's passing and the prophecy's failure, so *The Watchtower* of November 1, 1995 again redefined the meaning of the word "generation"—it refers simply to the peoples of earth who see the sign of Christ's presence but fail to mend their ways, with no time period whatsoever attached.

Whenever the leadership decrees such redefinitions of words, loyal Witnesses are expected to immediately adopt the new usage without complaining or even questioning. In order to do this, they must "avoid independent thinking . . . questioning the counsel that is provided by God's visible organization" (*The Watchtower,* January 15, 1983, page 22). The command goes forth, the thirteen million who attend JW Kingdom Halls worldwide obediently conform—readjusting their speech and even their thoughts—and the "J.W.ese" language changes once again.

DEFINITIONS OF
JW WORDS AND EXPRESSIONS

A

Abaddon *noun* 1. Jesus Christ, the angel of the bottomless pit in Revelation 9:11. 2. *obsolete* Satan the Devil, the angel of the bottomless pit in Revelation 9:11.

Note: This dramatic reversal is found in JW Bible commentaries published just thirteen years apart, demonstrating the change-ableness of the "J.W.ese" language. *See* AJWSBS and JWL.

Abba, Father! *theological* (from Romans 8:15) An expression reflecting the closeness members of the anointed class feel toward Jehovah God. The vast majority of JWs see themselves as part of the "great crowd" of "other sheep" automatically excluded from this experience.

abomination of desolation *obsolete* (from Matthew 24:15 KJV) The League of Nations/United Nations organization, according to Watchtower interpretation, as in "These worldly people are idolaters because they worship the abomination of desolation." JWs today prefer the *New World Translation* rendering, DISGUSTING THING THAT CAUSES DESOLATION.

abomination that maketh desolate *obsolete* (from Daniel 12:11 KJV) The League of Nations/United Nations organization, according to Watchtower interpretation, as in "These worldly people are idolaters because they worship the abomination that maketh desolate." JWs today prefer the *New World Translation* rendering, DISGUSTING THING THAT IS CAUSING DESOLATION.

Abraham *noun* 1. The patriarch, father of Isaac, grandfather of Jacob. 2. Jehovah God, in passages such as Luke 16:23–30. (To negate the concept of punishment after death, the sect makes each of the characters in this passage purely symbolic, with the rich man and Lazarus each representing a class of people, and Abraham representing God.)

Abrahamic covenant *theological* God's arrangement to bless all humankind through a world government administered from heaven by Christ and 144,000 chosen followers.

Abraham's seed *theological* Jesus Christ plus 144,000 chosen followers.

accounts, the *organizational* A local congregation's bookkeeping records, kept on forms and in a format prescribed by the Watchtower Society.

Accounting *organizational* At a circuit or district convention, the volunteer department responsible for handling monies received from contribution boxes (and, formerly, from the sale of food at a cafeteria and snack bars).

accounts servant *organizational* The ministerial servant assigned to handle a local congregation's bookkeeping.

accurate knowledge The beliefs of Jehovah's Witnesses, as in "I was religious most of my life, but I was without accurate knowledge until the brothers came to my door."

action Short for JUDICIAL ACTION, as in, "If Sister Thompson confirms what you've told me about Jerry Smith, the brothers will have to take action."

action, a committee The official disciplining of a JW member by a judicial committee through disfellowshipping or a lesser punishment.

action, judicial An official move to set up a judicial committee and summon before it an individual accused or suspected of wrongdoing.

active *adjective* **1.** *technical* Having reported time at least once during the preceding six months. **2.** *informal* Participating in field service and/or reporting time.

active force *theological* The "holy spirit" (usually not capitalized by JWs), viewed as neither deity nor person, but rather as the invisible force Jehovah God uses to accomplish his will. During creation "God's active force was moving to and fro over the surface of the waters," according to Genesis 1:2 in the *New World Translation.*

active publisher *technical* A Witness who has reported time during at least one of the preceding six months.

activity *noun* **1.** Work performed and reportable as field service, as in "Have you reported your activity this month?" **2.** Scheduled field service, as in "Will you be participating in this afternoon's activity?"

A.D. *obsolete* Anno Domini (In the year of our Lord), an expression avoided by Jehovah's Witnesses today. Following the pattern of *The Watchtower,* they prefer to label dates with the expression COMMON ERA, abbreviated C.E.

Adam *noun* **1.** The first man. **2.** The first human, originally created with both male and female characteristics, later transformed into a man when God took the female characteristics from him to make Eve—a teaching found in the September 1, 1956 *Watchtower,* pages 530–533, and still referenced as current information.

adjust *verb,* **adjustment** *noun* A euphemism JWs use in reference to doctrinal changes or new teachings developed to replace failed prophecies. For example, "In 1980, our thinking on the acceptability of organ transplants underwent an adjustment."

administration *noun* The *New World Translation*'s substitute for "dispensation" at Ephesians 1:10, interpreted by the Watchtower Society as God's heavenly government in the hands of Christ and the 144,000.

advancement *noun* **1.** Spiritual progress as measured by climbing the ladder of success in the Watchtower Society's hierarchy through obtaining a higher position. **2.** Spiritual progress as measured by taking on greater privileges of service, such as by rising from the level of an auxiliary pioneer to that of a regular pioneer.

Note: Only #2 is available to women, since they are excluded from the hierarchy.

after Armageddon   An expression commonly used by JWs today, referring to the anticipated earthly paradise populated exclusively by Witnesses after God wipes out the entire global population of non-Witnesses. Example: "Look at the size of that mansion! A millionaire must live there. That will be my house after Armageddon."

Aid **book, the**   *nickname* The Watchtower Society's 1971 book *Aid to Bible Understanding,* now viewed as obsolete and superseded by *Insight on the Scriptures* (1988).

Note: Our listing of JW expressions includes nicknames of certain books of current interest. For a more complete catalogue of such materials, or for more details about a particular book, see *Jehovah's Witness Literature: A Critical Guide to Watchtower Publications* by David A. Reed (Baker Book House, 1993).

alcoholic beverages   Drinks containing alcohol. Moderate comsumption is approved by Jehovah's Witnesses, but excesses are common—even at high levels of the organization.

alcoholism   *noun* A sinful practice that is definitely not a disease—but that has been widely tolerated in the Watchtower organization, especially at Brooklyn headquarters, where Bethelites have had a reputation for heavy drinking.

Almighty   *adjective* All-powerful—a term JWs formerly applied to Jesus Christ but now restrict to the Father. In JW terminology the Father is the Almighty God, while the Son is only a mighty god. *See* AJWSBS and JWAVBV.

ancient worthies   *chiefly plural; obsolete* Faithful men of pre-Christian times, *especially* those named in Hebrews, chapter 11, whom Witnesses during the 1920s–1950s expected to be resurrected at any moment and to appear among them. *See* JWAVBV, JWL.

angel   *noun* The order of creation to which Jehovah's Witnesses assign Jesus Christ, Satan the Devil, the demons, and obedient spirit creatures. *See* AJWSBS, JWAVBV, INDEX.

Anglo-American world power A fictitious government or nation composed of England and the United States, believed by JWs to be a de facto reality—invented to make biblical prophecies fit Watchtower interpretation.

anniversary *noun* An annual commemoration or celebration sometimes acceptable to JWs. They celebrate wedding anniversaries and the anniversary of Christ's death, but the organization puts on trial and punishes JWs who celebrate the anniversary of Christ's birth (Christmas) or anyone else's birthday. *See* AJWSBS.

announce a disfellowshipping To inform the local congregation, from the speaker's platform, that an individual has been disfellowshipped by a judicial committee—usually seven days after reaching the disfellowshipping decision, if no appeal has been made. After the announcement has been made, other Witnesses must shun the offender.

announcements A service meeting part—usually at the beginning or end of the meeting—devoted largely to communicating schedules of upcoming activities and other mundane matters concerning the local Kingdom Hall, literature supplies, and similar information.

annual meeting, the The official corporate annual meeting of the members (shareholders, or stockholders) of the Watch Tower Bible and Tract Society of Pennsylvania, generally held in Pennsylvania or nearby New Jersey. Besides the limited number of corporate members, admission to the closed meeting is by ticket only.

anointed *adjective* 1. Of or pertaining to a member of the anointed class. *noun* 1. The anointed class, especially with *the,* as in "She is one of the anointed." 2. With *the,* the Messiah or Christ.

anointed class 144,000 faithful Christian believers from the day of Pentecost until the present—believed by JWs to be the only people going to heaven and the only true members of the body of Christ.

anointed remnant 1. The remaining members of the anointed class still alive on earth today or at any particular

39

time during the last days, officially tallied at the annual Memorial and currently reported as numbering between eight thousand and nine thousand. **2.** The tiny minority of JWs who profess the heavenly hope.

anthem, national   A musical piece dreaded by JWs, who view it as representing satanic rulership. Forbidden to stand up when it is played, and often encountering abuse for taking that position, JWs cringe at the sound. *See* AJWSBS.

antichrist, the   *noun* **1.** An unnamed biblical character prefiguring collectively the clergy of Christendom. **2.** The clergy of Christendom, collectively.

Note: Witnesses also refer to clergy of other churches as "the man of lawlessness" and consider them as the worst villains, second only to "apostate" ex-Witnesses.

antitype   *noun* A person, nation, or thing prophetically foreshadowed or prefigured by a biblical character, nation, or thing. Examples: The Watchtower organization is the antitype of Noah's ark, and Christendom is the antitype of unfaithful Jerusalem, according to Watchtower interpretation.

antitypical   *adjective* Foreshadowed or prefigured by. Example: "Antitypical unfaithful Jerusalem is Christendom."

antitypical Babylon   Collectively, all false (i.e., non-JW) religions today, as prefigured by the ancient Babylonian Empire and/or Neo-Babylonian Empire viewed as a prophetic pattern or TYPE.

antitypical Israel   The anointed class of believers supposedly at the core of the JW organization, as prefigured by the ancient nation of Israel.

antitypical Jerusalem   The JW organization, viewed as having been prefigured by the ancient Jewish capital.

Apollyon   *noun* **1.** Jesus Christ, the angel of the bottomless pit in Revelation 9:11. **2.** *obsolete* Satan the Devil, the angel of the bottomless pit in Revelation 9:11.

Note: This dramatic reversal is found in JW Bible commentaries published just thirteen years apart, demonstrating the changeableness of the "J.W.ese" language. *See* AJWSBS and JWL.

apostasy   *noun* Any rejection of, or deviation from, Watchtower teaching, even in relatively minor matters—viewed as the most serious form of sin, equivalent to outright rebellion against God himself. Example: "Sister Johnson, please! Don't question what the Society has said about the year 1914. That could get you disfellowshipped for apostasy."

apostate   *noun* A former Witness who now denies Watchtower doctrine. *adjective* Of, or pertaining to, a former JW who now denies Watchtower doctrine.

Note: Apostate is the most derogatory term in Witness vocabulary. A JW sees apostates as ranking below prostitutes, murderers, and child abusers.

apostolic succession   The Roman Catholic teaching that the position and/or authority of the twelve apostles has been passed on to other men in our day.

Note: Jehovah's Witnesses reject the concept as a false doctrine when promoted by Catholics, but embrace the same concept in viewing their own Governing Body as the modern-day equivalent of the twelve apostles.

appeal   *verb* To request a rehearing of an unfavorable judicial committee decision. For example, the chairman of such a committee may say to the accused at the end of the proceedings, "The committee has concluded that you must be disfellowshipped. However, no announcement will be made for seven days, to allow you opportunity to appeal, if you wish."

appeal committee   *organizational* Three or more elders assigned to form a temporary body to rehear a case previously tried by a judicial committee. The appeal committee's decision is usually final, with no further appeal available.

appointed   *verb, past tense* Placed in position by God. Example: "The appointed servants in a congregation serve as Jehovah's representatives."

appointed times of the nations   A divinely fixed interval of 2520 years set aside for uninterrupted rule by Gentile nations opposed to God, commencing with the alleged desolation of Jerusalem in 607 B.C. and ending A.D. 1914 with the heavenly enthronement and invisible return of Christ. Formerly, the GENTILE TIMES.

> ## "appointed times of the nations"
>
> Acceptance of the "J.W.ese" definition for a word or expression is not optional for Jehovah's Witnesses. Nor is it a mere academic question. I have personally known elderly JWs who were put on trial for doubting the official definition of the "appointed times of the nations." Convicted of such a thoughtcrime, they were sentenced to forced shunning, cutting them off from all contact with children, grandchildren, and lifelong friends.

appointment *noun* Assignment from God, through his organization, to serve in some special capacity. Example: "Appointment to serve as an elder is made by Jehovah God through his organization."

appreciate spiritual things To demonstrate a positive attitude toward the teachings and instructions of the Watchtower Society, as in "We won't let our daughter play with the Johnson girl, because the Johnsons don't appreciate spiritual things."

appreciation Appreciation of spiritual things, as in "She quit pioneering because she's lacking in appreciation."

appreciation of spiritual things A positive viewpoint toward the Watchtower Society's teachings and organizational arrangements.

approved associate *obsolete* An unbaptized person who is studying with Jehovah's Witnesses, who is attending meetings, and who has conformed his or her lifestyle and beliefs to Watchtower standards—and who is hence declared eligible to share in field service and to turn in a report that will be accepted by the organization.

archangel *noun* Michael, alias Jesus Christ, who JWs believe is the first angel created by God. *See* JWAVBV.

ark, the The ark of salvation, God's organization. For example, an elder may tell an inactive Witness, "Get into the ark! Your life depends on it."

ark of salvation   The Jehovah's Witness organization, allegedly prefigured by Noah's ark as the only safe place to be when destruction from God rains down on the modern world.

Armageddon   *noun* God's final war, ending the present wicked world, with the destruction of all human governments and the permanent annihilation and eternal death of all non-JWs. *See* AJWSBS.

artificial blood   An experimental product, Fluosol-DA, which JWs looked to hopefully between 1980 and 1985 when it was proved ineffective.

arrangement, the   In any specific situation or circumstance, the procedural instructions provided by the Watchtower Society through its publications, letters, and appointed representatives. For example, an elder may reject suggestions for an innovative approach to meetings or door-to-door work by replying, "No. Let's just follow the arrangement." This puts the weight of the Watchtower Society and God's invisible heavenly organization behind his words.

assembly   *noun* **1.** A large JW district convention held annually in a rented stadium or convention center for three days or longer with approximately ten thousand to sixty thousand in attendance at each convention site in numerous cities around the globe. **2.** A smaller annual or semiannual JW circuit convention lasting two or three days with approximately five hundred to two thousand drawn from several local congregations in attendance at a JW Assembly Hall or a rented high school auditorium. **3.** Any special gathering of JWs from more than one congregation.

assembly hall   *noun* Essentially an oversized Kingdom Hall, a building with seating capacity to accommodate several congregations at the same time and used for small assemblies.

Note: The Assembly Hall may be owned by one of the Watchtower corporations or by a local legal entity formed for that purpose.

assembly overseer   **1.** A JW elder in each circuit responsible for organizing and directing the various departments handling physical arrangements at a circuit assembly. **2.** The elder caring for similar responsibilities at a district convention or international assembly.

assembly release(s) *noun* New Watchtower books, booklets, tapes, or CDs announced and made available, usually at a district assembly. Example: "We just got home from the convention. Here, let me show you the new assembly releases."

assistant congregation servant *obsolete* A discontinued second-in-command post in the local JW hierarchy. Today's congregation overseer shares some of his power with the congregation secretary and the field service overseer.

association, freedom of A democratic concept advocated by Jehovah's Witnesses insofar as it applies to their organization's legal right to hold meetings, but denied by the organization to individual members who seek outside association. For example, a JW may face trial and punishment for attending a political rally, participating in a town meeting, or sharing in the worship service of another church.

astrologers *noun* The derogatory term JWs use for the "wise men" who brought gifts to baby Jesus. In the Watchtower view it was Satan the Devil who sent the Star of Bethlehem as part of the plot to have Jesus killed in infancy.

attend *verb* To belong to (a specific congregation). Since the concept of membership is offensive to JWs, they usually avoid saying they *belong to* a certain congregation and say instead that they *attend* that congregation.

attendant *noun; technical* An usher (nearly always male) assigned to seat people, to keep order, and to direct traffic at a JW meeting or assembly.

audience contact Eye-contact with listeners; one of the speech counsel points on which JWs are graded when giving student talks in the Theocratic Ministry School.

Auditing Department The division of a circuit or district convention organization responsible for collecting, counting, and dispensing the convention's funds.

aux. pio. *abbreviation* auxiliary pioneer

auxiliary pioneer   *noun* A JW whose application has been accepted for the privilege of full-time service during a single month or a number of consecutive months, currently with a monthly goal of sixty hours. *verb* To hold this assignment, as in "I plan to auxiliary pioneer in April if I can schedule my vacation then."

Awake!   The less doctrinal companion magazine to The Watchtower, designed to capture the attention of people who are not religiously minded. Formerly entitled The Golden Age and Consolation. As of this writing approximately thirteen million copies are produced semimonthly in seventy-five languages.

B

b.a.   *slang* A Bethelite who privately manifests a bad attitude (abbreviated b.a.) through untheocratic thoughts or facial expressions, or by secretly flaunting disregard for organizational authority or authority figures. Use of this term is confined largely to the Bethel family and is seldom heard among JWs in general.

baby   *noun* One of the few acceptable reasons for a woman to stop pioneering or to avoid entering pioneer service. The statement, "She had a baby," carries this immediate implication when a woman's spirituality is being discussed by other Witnesses.

baby shower   A social gathering for the purpose of bestowing gifts on a pregnant woman for her future infant—one of the few acceptable occasions for JWs to hold a party.

Babylon   *noun* 1. Non-Witness religious organizations collectively. Example: "Alice has gone back to Babylon," means, "Alice has resumed her involvement with her non-Witness church." 2. The ancient Neo-Babylonian Empire and/or its capital city. 3. The land of the post-deluge Tower of Babel.

***Babylon book,* the**   *nickname* The Watchtower Society's 1963 publication entitled *"Babylon the Great Has Fallen!" God's Kingdom Rules! See* JWL.

45

Babylon the Great   The "world empire of false religion" comprised of all non-JW religious organizations and their members. *See* AJWSBS.

Babylonish   *adjective* 1. False-religious. Used primarily to describe doctrines and practices of other sects. 2. Characteristic of ancient pagan Babylon.

Babylonish captivity   1. The seventy-year period from 607 to 537 B.C.E. when the leaders and people of Judah were held captive as exiles in the Neo-Babylonian Empire, according to Watchtower interpretation. 2. A similar period from 1914 to 1918, allegedly foretold in Scripture, when Watchtower followers in a weakened spiritual condition compromised with worldly influences, culminating in the 1918–1919 imprisonment of President J. F. Rutherford and other leaders of the sect.

Babylon's fall   1. The Medo-Persian conquest of the Neo-Babylonian Empire in 539 B.C.E. 2. The prophesied defeat of modern Babylon the Great—the non-JW religions—in 1919, when Watchtower leaders imprisoned on sedition charges were released from the Atlanta federal penitentiary.

back call   *obsolete* 1. A return visit to a householder who showed interest when JWs knocked on his or her door on a prior occasion. 2. Such a householder, as in "The woman on the third floor is my back call" (= "The woman on the third floor is someone I visited earlier with the intention of returning.")

back call book   *obsolete* A small pocket notebook used for recording the address and other pertinent information regarding potential and actual back calls.

bad association   1. Any non-Witness, or a JW who is obviously headed for trouble. Example: "It wouldn't be right to go to a restaurant with our worldly neighbors; they're bad association." 2. The act of spending time with a worldly person. 3. *obsolete* A designation equivalent to DISFELLOWSHIPPED PERSON but applied to an unbaptized individual who had begun to engage in congregation activities. (The practice was discontinued, apparently after encountering defamation lawsuits from such individuals.)

bad attitude   *slang* A Bethelite who privately manifests un-theocratic thoughts or facial expressions, or secretly flaunts disregard for organizational authority or authority figures. Use of this term is confined largely to the Bethel family and is seldom heard among JWs in general. (Usually abbreviated b.a.)

bag   *slang* A briefcase or book bag used in field service.

ban   *noun* A governmental prohibition on the door-to-door preaching activity of Jehovah's Witnesses, or, in more extreme cases, a total outlawing of the sect. Example: "Our brothers in Greece were preaching under ban at that time."

Note: Although outsiders refer to the sect's ban on blood transfusions and its past bans on organ transplants and vaccinations, JWs themselves avoid this usage of the term.

baptism   *noun* **1.** A service JWs normally hold two or three times a year, usually as part of a convention, during which new members are baptized. **2.** The act of baptizing such new members.

baptize   *verb* To immerse a new member in water at a baptismal service.

Baptism's significance to Jehovah's Witnesses

JWs view baptism as a public act demonstrating that an individual has privately made a prayer of dedication to serve Jehovah God under the direction of the Watchtower organization.

Battle of Armageddon   The second part of the Great Tribulation; the destruction of all human governments and the rest of Satan's world, following the Battle of Babylon. Jehovah's Witnesses believe that they will be the only survivors and that God will send everyone else—men, women, and children—to eternal destruction.

Battle of Babylon   The first part of the Great Tribulation; the destruction of all non-JW religious organizations, including all the churches of Christendom.

B.C.   *obsolete* Before Christ—an expression avoided by Jehovah's Witnesses. Following the pattern of *The Watchtower,* they prefer to label dates with the expression "Before the Common Era," abbreviated B.C.E.

B.C.E. *abbreviation* Before the Common Era—the expression Jehovah's Witnesses use in place of B.C. or Before Christ. (Although others sometimes use B.C.E. to stand for Before the Christian Era, JWs nearly always read it as Before the Common Era.)

beard *noun* The hair on a man's chin and cheeks. Although Watchtower founder Charles Taze Russell was bearded, beards have generally been unacceptable among Jehovah's Witnesses throughout most of this century. A beard usually marks a man as a non-Witness. In fact, illustrations in Watchtower publications even depicted Jesus as beardless between 1942 and 1968. *See* JWL.

beast(s) *noun* Human governments under the control of Satan the Devil.

beast out of the abyss The League of Nations, and then later the United Nations organization, according to Watchtower interpretations of Revelation 17:8.

beast out of the sea *noun* The worldwide political system of human governments under the control of Satan the Devil, according to Watchtower interpretations of Revelation 13.

beast, two-horned *noun* The Anglo-American world power, an alleged de facto combine of Britain and the United States.

beer *noun* An alcoholic fermented beverage approved by Jehovah's Witnesses for moderate use, but traditionally consumed in large quantities at Brooklyn headquarters.

Before Christ *See* B.C.

Before the Christian Era *See* B.C.E.

Before the Common Era *See* B.C.E.

belong *verb* A term Jehovah's Witnesses avoid using in regard to their local congregation. Rather than say, "I belong to the Downtown Congregation," a Witness would say, "I attend the Downtown Congregation."

Bethel *noun* 1. The Watchtower organization's world headquarters complex, composed of some thirty buildings, in

Brooklyn, New York. **2.** A Watchtower Branch Office complex in another country, particularly when referred to by JWs native to that country. For example, Canadian JWs refer to Toronto Bethel. **3.** Loosely, any of the Watchtower Society's live-in complexes, including outlying farms operated by full-time volunteers. **4.** *obsolete* The four-story brownstone at 124 Columbia Heights, Brooklyn, formerly the residence of Congregational pastor Henry Ward Beecher, purchased by the Society to house its headquarters staff when moving to New York City in 1909. The March 1, 1909 *Watchtower* declared, "The new home we shall call 'Bethel,'" derived from the Hebrew expression for House of God. **5.** *obsolete.* Plymouth Bethel.

Bethel

According to Genesis, Jacob assigned this name (meaning house of God) to the place where God revealed himself to him. Located at the southern end of the ten-tribe kingdom of Israel, Bethel later became one of two cities Jeroboam selected as centers of worship to keep his subjects from making the pilgrimage to Jerusalem's temple in the kingdom of Judah. Hence, Bethel became known as a center of false worship.

Bethel family   **1.** A collective term for the thousands of full-time Brooklyn headquarters, farm, and Branch Office live-in volunteer workers. **2.** The workers at a given location, as in "the Brooklyn Bethel family" or "the Toronto Bethel family."

Bethel Home   **1.** The residence portion of the Brooklyn headquarters complex. **2.** The residence portion of a Watchtower Branch Office complex.

Bethelite   *noun* A full-time live-in worker at Watchtower headquarters or at any of the Society's Branch Offices or farms. Bethelites are unpaid, but receive room and board plus a small monthly allowance for personal items.

Bethel service   A live-in full-time volunteer position at Watchtower headquarters or one of the Society's Branch Offices or farms, ranked above pioneering but below circuit work.

Beth-Sarim   *noun* A San Diego mansion that served as second Watchtower president J. F. Rutherford's winter residence, but that was supposedly held in trust for soon-to-be resurrected Old Testament patriarchs and prophets who would rule the earth from that residence. *See* AJWSBS.

Bible   *noun* **1.** The Watchtower Society's *New World Translation of the Holy Scriptures.* **2.** Any Bible. *See* AJWSBS, JWAVBV, JWL.

Bible-based   Derived from a correct understanding of Scripture—a term usually applied to Watchtower teachings and literature to endow them with biblical authority.

Bible dictionary   **1.** The 1988 Watchtower publication *Insight on the Scriptures* in two volumes. **2.** The obsolete 1971 Watchtower publication *Aid to Bible Understanding.* See JWL. **3.** Any standard Bible dictionary from non-Witness sources. JWs view these as unreliable, but will quote from one if material can be found to support a particular Watchtower teaching.

Bible drama   A stage play put on at a JW convention with amateur actors depicting Bible characters and modern Witnesses—with a definite lesson to be learned. The spoken parts are normally recorded ahead of time by trained Bethel speakers; then local Witnesses pantomime the parts onstage. Though stiff and dry by entertainment industry standards, these brief dramas are the highlights of Watchtower conventions for most JWs, especially the children.

Bible House   *obsolete.* The Watch Tower headquarters building in Allegheny, Pennsylvania.

Bible knowledge   Understanding and acceptance of Watchtower teachings, as in "The church members who agreed to study with us began to gain Bible knowledge."

Bible principles   General rules of conduct set forth in Watchtower publications, citing the Scriptures as authority.

Bible Students   **1.** The name early Watchtower followers used to refer to themselves, abandoned in 1931 in favor of the name "Jehovah's Witnesses." **2.** Members of groups that remained loyal to C. T. Russell's teachings and refused to accept J. F. Rutherford's changes. Prominent among these groups today are the Chicago Bible Students and the Dawn Bible Students. *See* AJWSBS, JWL.

Bible study *noun* **1.** A one-on-one indoctrination session usually held weekly in the home of a prospective convert with paragraph-by-paragraph consideration of a Watchtower textbook. **2.** A prospective convert who takes part in such a study, as in "She's my Bible study," meaning, "She's a prospective convert with whom I conduct a study in one of the Watchtower Society's books."

Bible Study Overseer *obsolete* An elder assigned to oversee disciple-making, return visits, and home Bible studies in a local JW congregation. This was, for a time, the third-ranking position in a local congregation, and the elder holding it was a member of the Congregation Committee.

Bible Study Report *See* Study Report.

binder A permanent storage shell that can be purchased at the literature counter to hold a year's accumulated *Watchtower* or *Awake!* magazines. Binders are used by JWs who cannot afford to purchase bound volumes or who wish to save the personal study notes they made in their original magazines.

birth control Artificial means of preventing pregnancy. Some forms are acceptable to JWs and others are objectionable, as spelled out in *Watchtower* articles on specific methods.

birthday *noun* The anniversary of one's birth—a subject on which the Watchtower Society has flip-flopped over the years, with positions ranging from encouraging celebration to forbidding it as a disfellowshipping offense. Birthday parties and birthday cards are currently forbidden. *See* AJWSBS.

blood card *slang* A "no blood" card. Example: "You won't be able to get the new book at the assembly unless you can show the brothers your blood card."

blood fraction Any of the various components of whole blood, some of which JWs may accept and some of which they must refuse. The Governing Body has ruled that Witnesses may accept albumin, immune globulins, Factor VIII, Factor IX, and their own blood circulated outside the body in a heart/lung or kidney machine, but they must refuse plasma, red cells, white cells, platelets, and their own blood stored outside the body in a bottle or bag.

bloodguilt   *noun* Accountability for violating God's law on the sanctity of blood, incurred by contributing to an untimely death or by accepting a blood transfusion. An elder might counsel a Witness in this manner, for example: "If you hold back from sharing in the preaching work, you will bring bloodguilt on yourself for the people who die without hearing our lifesaving message."

bloodguilty   *adjective* Having incurred bloodguilt.

blood issue   The organizational decree that JWs must refuse blood transfusions, and the controversy that often results.

blood substitute   Usually a plasma volume expander that keeps veins from collapsing due to blood loss, but that fails to perform all the functions of real blood.

body   *slang* The local body of elders. For example, the Presiding Overseer might say to the Circuit Overseer, "Sure, it's okay with me for you to park your trailer at Kingdom Hall, but I'll have to check with the body."

body of elders   Collectively, the elders of a local congregation meeting together in formal session.

book bag   The small briefcase (men) or large purse (women) JWs use to carry their magazines, books, and other merchandise to householders' doors. It also typically contains tracts, handbills, a territory map, a return visit book, and other field service paraphernalia.

book offer, the   The book specified in *Our Kingdom Service* as the one JWs should be presenting at the doors during a given month.

book room   The cubicle or small room used at Kingdom Hall for storing and dispensing Watchtower books, booklets, bound volumes, and other literature with the exception of periodicals—usually equipped with a window or dutch door to provide counter service. Also called a literature room.

book study   The one-hour Congregation Book Study Meeting held weekly in each JW congregation, usually on Tuesday evening, for the purpose of studying a textbook assigned by Brooklyn headquarters. Each congregation usually splits up into book study groups, with several book studies meeting simultaneously in private homes and in various rooms at Kingdom Hall.

book study group   The individuals (usually between ten and thirty) assigned to attend a particular Congregation Book Study Meeting.

bound volume   A hardcover collection of a particular year's *Watchtower* or *Awake!* magazines—the preferred form in which these periodicals are kept for reference.

Branch Office   One of approximately one hundred regional subsidiaries of the Watchtower Society worldwide supervising the sect's operations in a particular country and, in some cases, neighboring countries as well. The Branch Office complex usually includes business offices, living quarters for Branch personnel, warehouse and shipping facilities, and sometimes a literature-production factory.

break   *noun* A mid-morning or mid-afternoon stop for coffee and donuts during field service activity. (The duration of the break is often a bone of contention between reluctant Witnesses, for whom it is the highlight of the morning, and time-conscious auxiliary pioneers eager to get their time started again. Circuit overseers and regular pioneers commonly keep their time running during the break and relax there as long as they want.)

break integrity   To violate God's law (as interpreted by the Watchtower Society), especially in the area of political or medical prohibitions.

bride, the   The bride class.

bride class   1. The 144,000 believed bound for heaven, especially in their role as the bride of Christ. 2. The anointed remnant.

brochure   Any of several thirty-two-page JW booklets with the same dimensions as a *Watchtower* magazine.

Brooklyn   *slang, noun* **1.** The headquarters organization, as in "The elders submitted my question to Brooklyn, and now they are waiting for an answer." **2.** The Watchtower headquarters complex in Brooklyn, New York, as in "We're going to take a tour of Brooklyn next week."

Brooklyn Tabernacle   *obsolete* The Watchtower organization's name for the former Plymouth Bethel, purchased in 1908 to house the Society's new offices in New York City. *See* Plymouth Bethel.

brother, a   *slang* A male baptized Witness.

brothers, one of the   *slang* 1. An appointed elder. 2. A male baptized Witness.

brother, the   *slang* The elder in charge in a given context.

brothers, the   *slang* The congregation elders.

bulletin board   *obsolete* The term "bulletin board" was stricken from JW vocabulary decades ago due to its supposedly unsavory etymology. Witnesses trace its derivation to the papal bull, and certainly no loyal Witness would want to refer to the Kingdom Hall corkboard as a place for displaying documents issued by the Roman Catholic pope. Notices are hung on the INFORMATION BOARD. (It is technically permissible for JWs to use the term "bulletin board" when referring to such an object at their place of employment or at the supermarket, but the habit of substituting the expression "information board" often carries over to this usage as well.)

business territory   Nonresidential streets or blocks occupied by storefronts, offices, factories, or other commercial/industrial buildings, sometimes set aside to be worked by pioneers or others who express a preference for it.

Byington   *The Bible in Living English* by Steven T. Byington (Watchtower Society, 1972). A JW might say, "I took along my Byington to use at that call," meaning "my copy of Byington's translation." (For more information, see pages 130–132 of *Jehovah's Witness Literature: A Critical Guide to Watchtower Publications* by David A. Reed [Baker Book House, 1993].

C

C.E.   *abbreviation* Common Era, the expression Jehovah's Witnesses use in place of A.D. or Anno Domini (in the year of our Lord).

c.o.   *slang* 1. Circuit overseer. 2. *obsolete* Congregation overseer.

   Note: In each case, the resemblance to the secular "c.o.," meaning "commanding officer," is intentional and appropriate.

caesar   *noun* The secular government.

caesar's law   Secular civil or criminal law, viewed as inferior or subordinate to God's law (as interpreted by the Watchtower Society). Example: A JW working as a secretary or clerk in a government office would say to herself or to another Witness, "Caesar's law requires me to keep these records confidential, but I will obey God's law and tell the elders that Medicare paid for a blood transfusion for Sister Johnson."

calendar, the   A colorful calendar printed by the Watchtower Society. JWs superstitiously avoid displaying or using commercial calendars whenever possible, because these commonly feature holidays denoted by religious or patriotic artwork, which they consider to be of satanic origin. (Yet JW calendars feature the standard names for months and days, ignoring the fact that Thursday is named after the Norse god Thor, March after the Roman god Mars, and so on.)

call   1. A return visit. 2. *slang* A person whom a Witness has been visiting to cultivate interest, as in "Skip the second floor when you do that building, because the woman who lives there is my call."

campaign   *noun* A special focus of door-to-door work during certain months, as outlined in *Our Kingdom Ministry.* For example, January and February may be set aside for a subscription campaign, and December for a campaign with the *New World Translation.*

captain, car   *See* car captain.

captivity to Babylon   1. The seventy-year period from 607 to 537 B.C.E. when the leaders and people of Judah were held captive as exiles in the Neo-Babylonian Empire, according to Watchtower interpretation. **2.** A similar period from 1914 to 1918, allegedly foretold in Scripture, when Watchtower followers in a weakened spiritual condition compromised with worldly influences, culminating in the 1918–1919 imprisonment of President J. F. Rutherford and other leaders of the sect.

car captain   The individual, usually an adult male, assigned to direct the occupants of a particular automobile or group of automobiles traveling together to work territory from house to house or to make return visits. (The car captain may assign publishers to work together or send them out alone, and may tell them to start with a certain house and proceed in a given direction.)

car group   The Witnesses riding together to work a section of territory or to make return visits to interested persons.

card   *organizational* A Publisher's Record Card. (For example, an elder in one congregation may say to an elder in another, "Even though her illicit sex took place in our territory, Sister Jackson's card is in your congregation's file, so you will have to set up the judicial committee.") *See* Publisher's Record Card.

cemetery witnessing   Organized witnessing activity in graveyards on Memorial Day or similar occasions. The JWs approach people who have come to visit loved ones' graves, give them a tract, and sometimes attempt to speak briefly with them.

cemetery work   Cemetery witnessing.

Channel   *short for* Channel of Communication

Channel of Communication   The Watchtower Society, viewed as God's mouthpiece or the channel through which God speaks to humankind.

chairman   **1.** The elder presiding over a congregation's body of elders. **2.** The elder presiding over a judicial committee or other committee of elders. **3.** The Governing Body member chairing that body's meetings during the current year on a rotating basis.

Chairman's Committee   The chief subcommittee of the Governing Body, composed of this year's chairman, last year's, and next year's.

chariot   *See* Jehovah's chariot.

choir   A group of singers performing in one of Christendom's false churches. JW Kingdom Halls do not feature choirs, since they are viewed as an invention of Satan the Devil.

Christ   *noun* Michael, the first angel God created, in his role as Messiah following his baptism by John. *See* AJWSBS, JWAVBV.

Christ class   *obsolete* The composite Christ made up of Jesus and his 144,000 heaven-bound disciples, a teaching no longer promoted by the Watchtower Society.

Christendom   The non-JW churches, collectively—viewed as an apostate organization under the leadership of Satan the Devil. *See* AJWSBS.

Christian   *noun* 1. A Jehovah's Witness. 2. A nominal Christian, a non-Witness professing Christianity. *adjective* 1. Of or about Jehovah's Witnesses. 2. Of or about nominal Christians.

Note: Since Jehovah's Witnesses believe themselves to be the only genuine Christians, others who lay claim to the name must be impostors, pseudo-Christians, in their eyes.

Christian Congregation, the   1. Technically, the 144,000-member body of Christ, represented on earth today by a remnant of fewer than nine thousand elderly JWs baptized prior to 1935. 2. Loosely, the worldwide body of Jehovah's Witnesses.

Christian congregation, a   A local church body of Jehovah's Witnesses; JWs almost never use the word "church" to apply to themselves, but prefer the word "congregation."

Christian Greek Scriptures, the   The preferred term among JWs for the New Testament. Use of the expression "New Testament" marks the speaker as a non-Witness in most cases.

Christian Scriptures   Short for the CHRISTIAN GREEK SCRIPTURES.

57

Christian Witnesses of Jehovah   An alternate version of the name "Witnesses of Jehovah," employed in formal talks, when the speaker wishes to emphasize the group's profession of Christianity.

Christianity   1. The religion or beliefs of Jehovah's Witnesses. 2. The religion or beliefs of nominal Christians.

church, a   1. A pseudo-Christian religious organization or congregation. 2. The steepled building such a false congregation meets in. 3. *obsolete* A Kingdom Hall. The first Kingdom Hall was named "New Light Church," but JWs no longer use the word "church" in connection with any of their buildings.

Church, the   1. Technically, the 144,000-member body of Christ, represented on earth today by a remnant of fewer than nine thousand elderly JWs baptized prior to 1935. 2. Loosely, the worldwide body of Jehovah's Witnesses.

churches, the   *slang* The false non-Witness organizations professing Christianity.

circuit   *noun* A collection of between twelve and twenty JW congregations under the oversight of a circuit overseer.

circuit assembly   *technical* An annual or semiannual JW convention for the members of a particular circuit, usually lasting two or three days with approximately five hundred to two thousand in attendance at a JW Assembly Hall or rented school auditorium.

circuit convention   A circuit assembly.

circuit overseer   *technical* An elder in full-time service assigned to oversee a number of congregations (perhaps twelve to twenty). Accompanied by his wife, he usually visits each congregation twice a year for a week at a time, staying with a family in their home and taking meals at the homes of other families that volunteer. The circuit overseer ranks immediately above congregation elders and exercises limited authority over them.

circuit servant   *obsolete* Circuit overseer.

circuit work   The position of a circuit overseer, as in "My son is now in the circuit work."

city overseer A local elder appointed to handle citywide matters in cities with more than one congregation.

class *noun* 1. A composite body of people viewed as fulfilling a particular role foretold in Scripture. For examples, see the CHRIST CLASS, the EZEKIEL CLASS, the JEREMIAH CLASS, and so on. 2. The Watchtower missionaries trained together at Gilead School during a particular year. "Martha was a member of the Gilead Class of 1968."

class worker *obsolete* In the 1930s, a congregation publisher.

clergy, clergyman A distasteful term used to designate prominent paid employees of Satan the Devil's religious organizations. JWs vigorously reject the application of the term to any of their elders or traveling overseers and deny that their organization has any paid clergy—although traveling overseers receive a monthly allowance.

closed-minded *adjective* Characterized by unwillingness to listen to the Watchtower message.

collection plate An item not found at JW Kingdom Halls but employed only at false churches, in the Witness view.

colporteur *obsolete* A full-time, door-to-door *Watch Tower* distributor in the early years of the organization. Today's equivalent is a PIONEER or SPECIAL PIONEER.

come into the truth, to To become a Jehovah's Witness. "I came into the truth in 1991. When did you come into the truth?"

comment *noun* A remark from a member of the audience called on to answer a question during a congregation meeting. *verb* To participate from one's seat in the audience during a meeting.

committee, the 1. The Congregation Service Committee. 2. A judicial committee. 3. A special committee.

committee action, a The official disciplining of a JW member by a judicial committee through disfellowshipping or a lesser punishment.

committee business 1. Information of a confidential nature that must remain within the confines of a judicial committee or the congregation committee. For example, an elder serving on such a committee might say to his wife, "I can't discuss with you the relationship between Fred Thompson and the Jackson girl because it has become committee business." **2.** An issue to be decided or a task to be handled by the congregation committee.

committee matter   An offense requiring action by a judicial committee. For example, an elder might explain to the parents of a teenage couple, "If you caught the kids kissing, you parents can discipline them, but if they were engaged in heavy petting or other loose conduct, then it becomes a committee matter and the brothers will have to look into it."

Common Era   The expression Jehovah's Witnesses use in place of A.D. or Anno Domini (in the year of our Lord). Usually abbreviated C.E.

Communion   *obsolete* JWs celebrate the Lord's Evening Meal annually at their Memorial service, but they avoid calling it Communion.

complete donation arrangement   *technical* Procedures and terminology designed to disguise monies received for Watchtower publications as free gifts totally unrelated to the materials distributed—a policy instituted in the United States following a 1990 Supreme Court ruling against Jimmy Swaggart Ministries in a California sales tax case. (The Watchtower Society had entered the Swaggart case as a "friend of the court" by joining the International Society for Krishna Consciousness of California, the National Council of Churches of Christ, the Evangelical Council for Financial Accountability, and other religious organizations in filing *amicus curiae* briefs with the high court. The justices' January 17 ruling against Swaggart was followed by a February 9 letter from Watchtower headquarters instructing Witnesses to stop naming specific sales prices for literature offered from house to house.) *See also* contribution.

conditional donation   Money donated to the organization on the condition that it may be returned to the donor in extreme circumstances.

congregation   A local body of JW believers usually composed of between 50 and 150 publishers and their families.

congregation, the Christian   1. Technically, the 144,000-member body of Christ, represented on earth today by a remnant of fewer than nine thousand elderly JWs baptized prior to 1935. **2.** Loosely, the worldwide body of Jehovah's Witnesses.

congregation accounts   Financial records of a local congregation's income and expenses maintained by the Accounts Servant on forms provided by the Watchtower Society.

congregation committee   Congregation Service Committee

congregation overseer   1. *obsolete* The top elder in charge of a congregation prior to the rotation arrangement introduced during the early 1970s. **2.** *slang* Presiding overseer.

Congregation of Jehovah's Witnesses, the (specific locality)   The name of a local JW church body always takes this form as in, for example, the East Boston Congregation of Jehovah's Witnesses or the Freeport Heights Congregation of Jehovah's Witnesses.

congregation publisher   A rank-and-file Jehovah's Witness who reports time in field service but does not pioneer or serve in any other special capacity.

congregation servant   *obsolete* Congregation overseer.

Congregation Service Committee   *technical* The top three elders in each local JW congregation—the presiding overseer, secretary, and service overseer—who sign routine forms and occasionally perform other tasks as a body.

conscience matter   An area of personal conduct in which organizational rulings allow for some freedom of choice without falling into disfavor. Compare PERSONAL DECISION.

continuous auxiliary pioneer   One who serves as an auxiliary pioneer month after month, indefinitely.

contribute   *verb* 1. To make a free-will donation to the Watchtower Society or the local congregation. **2.** To give money to purchase literature or other items—treated as a donation to evade taxes.

contribution   *noun* 1. A free-will donation to the Watchtower Society or the local congregation. **2.** Money for the purchase of literature or other items, handled as a donation to evade taxes.

contribution box A receptacle for receiving money at a JW Kingdom Hall or assembly site. There may be a general contribution box as well as boxes to receive money for specific purposes—to pay for literature, meals at assemblies, and so on. JWs view passing the collection plate at other churches as a false religious practice; they see no resemblance between their contribution boxes and church collection plates.

convention *noun* 1. A large JW district assembly held annually in a rented stadium or convention center for three days or longer with approximately ten thousand to sixty thousand in attendance at each convention site in numerous cities around the globe. 2. A smaller annual or semiannual JW circuit assembly lasting two or three days with approximately five hundred to two thousand drawn from several local congregations in attendance at a JW Assembly Hall or a rented high school auditorium. 3. Any special gathering of JWs from more than one congregation.

convention department A division of the temporary organization set up to run a district or circuit convention—usually manned by volunteer appointees supervised by a local elder or, in the case of larger conventions, a circuit overseer. Examples: Rooming Department, Food Service Department, Auditing Department.

convention overseer The elder in charge of the temporary organization running a circuit assembly or district convention.

convention report *obsolete* A booklet or paperback book published between 1904 and 1969 in connection with a large district or international convention, featuring photographs taken at the gathering and promoting new publications released there. Also called "souvenir convention report."

convention release(s) 1. *noun* New Watchtower books, booklets, tapes, or CDs announced and made available, usually at a district convention. Example: "We just got home from the assembly. Here, let me show you the new convention releases." Also called simply "release(s)."

conversational quality   A point of speech counsel in the Theocratic Ministry School emphasizing the use of natural-sounding speech that is not "preachy"—both from the speaker's platform and in door-to-door ministry.

counsel   Corrective or instructive advice based on the Bible and/or Watchtower publications and offered by one JW to another, regardless of whether solicited or not.

counsel point   A quality of speech among those enumerated in the Theocratic Ministry School for students to work on.

Counsel Slip   *See* Speech Counsel Slip.

count time, count (one's) time   1. To classify an interval of time as field service that can be reported in the "hours" column of a field service report. Example: "You can't count your time on that visit to Martha because, although irregular, she was still an active publisher." 2. To be in a situation where the clock is running on reportable time. "These letters I'm writing are to worldly people, so I'm counting time right now."

Note: Jehovah's Witnesses speak of themselves as counting time in much the same way that a factory worker who has punched-in his or her timecard is now on the clock. It is also similar to the situation of a taxi driver when the meter is running. The Witness receives no financial remuneration, of course, but views the accumulating time as valuable in itself.

cover (a congregation's territory)   To finish visiting all the homes in door-to-door ministry, as in "How often does your congregation cover its territory?"

coverage   The frequency with which all the homes in a congregation's territory are visited in door-to-door work. For example, a Witness might ask another from the other side of town, "What's your congregation's coverage?" and the other might answer, "Three times a year. What's yours?"

cross   *noun* A pagan phallic sex symbol falsely adopted by the apostate churches to idolatrously represent Christ, who died on an upright stake rather than a cross according to Watchtower teaching. The *New World Translation* eliminates the word "cross" and substitutes "stake" or "torture stake." *See* AJWSBS, JWAVBV, JWL, INDEX.

crowd, great   *See* great crowd.

crucify   *verb* To go along with removing the word "cross" the *New World Translation* eliminates "crucify" and substitutes "impale."

crucifix   *noun* Like the cross, JWs view a crucifix as a pagan idol that should be smashed or destroyed. *See* cross.

crucifixion   *noun* To go along with removing the word "cross," the *New World Translation* eliminates "crucifixion" and substitutes "impalement." *See* cross.

current magazine(s), the   The *Watchtower* and/or *Awake!* issues closest to the date in question.

Note: Watchtower magazines are dated the first and fifteenth of each month, and *Awake!* magazines the eighth and twenty-second. Those dated the first and eighth are usually offered together as a set, as are those of the fifteenth and twenty-second.

current offer, the   The book, magazines, subscription, or other item designated by the internal monthly *Our Kingdom Ministry* as the one to be featured on the day in question. A particular book is commonly featured for a month at a time.

cut off   1. Kill, as in "Evildoers will be cut off at Armageddon." 2. Shun, as in "You must cut off disfellowshipped family members."

D

date   *noun* A specific time set by the Watchtower Society for the world to come to an end, as in "It is not advisable for us to set our sights on a certain date," after predictions regarding 1975 proved false (*The Watchtower,* July 15, 1976, page 441).

Dawn, the   The Dawn Bible Students, or members collectively.

Dawn Bible Students, the   A breakaway group loyal to the teachings of Watchtower founder Charles Taze Russell, but regarded by Jehovah's Witnesses as part of the evil slave class. The group took its name from Russell's *Millennial Dawn* book series.

Dawnites   Individual members of the Dawn Bible Students.

deacon   *obsolete* An office and term not used by Jehovah's Witnesses. Instead, they employ the expression "ministerial servant," found in the *New World Translation,* where other Bibles say "deacon."

Death Warrant   *slang used by JW b.a.'s and non-Witness relatives* The Power of Attorney each Witness signs granting an elder or other mature Witness life-and-death authority to refuse blood transfusions and blood products for the signer.

dedication   *noun* The decision and commitment through prayer to serve Jehovah in association with his organization, preceding baptism. This approximately parallels a Christian's decision for Christ and saying the sinner's prayer. JWs speak of making one's dedication, as in "Has he made his dedication yet?"

deity   *noun* The quality of being superhuman. Thus, a JW who says, "I acknowledge the deity of Christ," may mislead a Christian who understands this to mean Jesus is God.

delegate   *noun* A JW attending an assembly or convention.

demo   *slang; noun* A demonstration.

demonized   Possessed by or inhabited by evil spirit persons, as in "The scarf she bought at a yard sale was demonized, and that's why Sister Miller has been so sick these past few months," or, "Don't go to that house. The people who live there all speak in tongues, so they're probably all demonized."

demons, the   Evil spirits, collectively, as in "Our worldly relatives think Jack's problem is psychological, but we know it's the demons."

demonstration   A role-playing enactment of a Witness speaking to a worldly person, using a presentation or technique outlined in *Our Kingdom Ministry* or an assembly part outline. For example, a JW woman might say, "I'm a householder in a demonstration in Brother Beck's part on the Service Meeting."

Devil   Witnesses believe Satan the Devil to be a cherubic angel who was appointed overseer of the newly inhabited earth, but who then rebelled against God by misleading Eve into tempting Adam to sin.

65

Devil's organization, the   Non-Witness religions, all of earth's governments, commercial and educational institutions form part of Satan the Devil's organization, which JWs believe embraces the rest of humankind in its membership. "Everyone belongs either to Jehovah's organization, or to the Devil's," is typical Witness thinking.

Diaglott, the   *The Emphatic Diaglott* by Benjamin Wilson, a Greek-English interlinear translation of the New Testament used by Pastor Russell and still published by the Watchtower Society.

different   Unlike the surrounding worldly people, usually in regard to dress and grooming, but sometimes also in regard to conduct or speech. For example, a JW father might say to his teenage son, "Robbie, you have to get a shorter haircut because Jehovah's people must look different from the world. Right now you look just like the worldly kids in this neighborhood." JWs in authority often apply a double standard, as in the example here where the father's grooming may be identical to that of the worldly businessmen he works with, while the son must look "different from the world."

disappointed, disappointment   *euphemism* Failure of the Watchtower Society's prophetic dates for the end of the world in 1914, 1925, 1975, and so on. Rather than say, "The Society's dates proved false," a JW confronted with the information would say, "Some of God's people were disappointed in that year," or "experienced disappointment at that time."

disassociate   *verb* 1. To separate oneself voluntarily from the Watchtower organization. 2. To be declared by a judicial committee to be voluntarily separated from the Watchtower—even when this is involuntary on the individual's part. When a young JW joins the military (regardless of whether this is through recruitment or conscription), the elders announce that he "has disassociated himself" from the JW organization. This wording is used apparently to avoid having the congregation disfellowship or expel one who joins the military, as such disciplinary action might be seen as a violation of the law. *See* AJWSBS.

disassociated person One who has voluntarily separated from the Watchtower organization or who has been expelled by the elders under the guise of disassociation.

disassociation *noun* The act of voluntarily separating oneself from the Watchtower organization.

disassociation letter A signed document from an individual declaring his or her intention to separate from the Watchtower organization. Elders on a judicial committee often request such a letter from someone they wish to remove from the congregation, especially in situations where expelling the person might prove embarrassing or illegal—as in the case of JWs who embrace Christianity or join a military organization.

disfellowship *verb* To declare an individual expelled from the Watchtower organization and henceforth subject to compulsory shunning by Jehovah's Witnesses. A judicial committee takes this action in private, following a closed-door hearing or trial, and then the disfellowshipping announcement is read to the congregation at a Kingdom Hall meeting, usually the Service Meeting on Thursday evening.

disfellowshipped person A JW who has been formally expelled from the Watchtower organization.

disfellowshipping offense, a A violation of Watchtower rules that can result in an unrepentant offender being expelled from the sect.

Mind your P's and Q's

The official *Watchtower Publications Index 1976–1980*, a separate volume indexing topics covered in Jehovah's Witness publications during that period, lists references to "disfellowshiping" and "disfellowshiped" persons, but the *Watch-*

---

tower Publications Index 1981 issued the following year refers to "disfellowshipping" and "disfellowshipped" persons. Notice the difference? The words are now spelled with two p's instead of one. Alert English-speaking JWs worldwide immediately picked up on the change and conformed their own spelling to the Watchtower Society's new usage. Any who missed the point or forgetfully fell into old spelling habits were chided by others as failing to keep up with the Society—or literally failing to mind their P's and Q's! (Interestingly, the September 15, 1981 *Watchtower* article referenced in the new Index actually uses the old spelling.)

disgusting thing that causes desolation (from Matthew 24:15 NWT) The League of Nations/United Nations organization, according to Watchtower interpretation, as in "These worldly people are idolaters because they worship the disgusting thing that causes desolation."

disgusting thing that is causing desolation (from Daniel 12:11 NWT) The League of Nations/United Nations organization, according to Watchtower interpretation, as in "These worldly people are idolaters because they worship the disgusting thing that is causing desolation."

disloyalty The serious sin of failing to uphold the Watchtower organization in some thought, word, or deed—seen as equivalent to turning against God.

district *noun* A territory formed by a dozen or more circuits, under the supervision of a district overseer.

district assembly A large JW convention held annually in a rented stadium or convention center for three days or longer with approximately ten thousand to sixty thousand in attendance at each convention site in numerous cities around the globe.

district convention A large JW convention held annually in a rented stadium or convention center for three days or longer with approximately ten thousand to sixty thousand in attendance at each convention site in numerous cities around the globe.

district overseer   *technical* An elder in full-time service assigned to oversee a number of circuits (perhaps twelve to twenty). Accompanied by his wife, he usually visits each circuit once or twice annually, staying with a family in their home and taking meals at the homes of other families that volunteer—or staying in an apartment constructed for that purpose at a JW Assembly Hall. The district overseer ranks immediately above the circuit overseers in his district and exercises limited authority over them. He, in turn, reports to the Service Department at Brooklyn headquarters or to the Branch Office having oversight over the country where he serves.

district servant   *obsolete* District overseer.

divine   *adjective*, **divinity** *noun* The quality of being superhuman. Thus, a JW who says, "I acknowledge the divinity of Christ," or ". . . that Christ is divine," may mislead a Christian who understands this to mean Jesus is God.

do (a house, street, territory)   To visit all the homes (of the house, street, territory), as in "When are you going to do that street?" or "We did that territory two months ago."

domestics   The members of the anointed remnant, as recipients of the spiritual food that they distribute through the Governing Body.

donation   *noun* **1.** A financial or other valuable gift to the Watchtower organization. **2.** Money received as the sale price for Watchtower publications at a Kingdom Hall literature counter or at a householder's doorstep—termed a donation to deny sales activity in jurisdictions where taxed or otherwise restricted. **3.** *obsolete* Money received as the price of a meal at a JW convention cafeteria or snack vending booth—termed a donation to evade meals tax in certain states and localities, from March 11, 1990, through the end of 1994, when the sale of food at conventions was discontinued altogether.

double life   Many teenagers and younger children in JW families acknowledge among themselves that they live what they call a double life, playing the role of a Witness at home

69

and at Kingdom Hall, but acting as a worldly person at school and among friends in the neighborhood.

doubt   *noun* An inward questioning or feeling of uncertainty about a teaching of the Watchtower Society. Example: "Sarah has been staying home from the meetings because she has doubts." *verb* To question the truthfulness of one or more Watchtower teachings. Example: "Fred has started doubting lately, and that is why he isn't giving talks."

Note: To doubt or entertain doubts is viewed as a symptom of spiritual sickness bordering on sin.

dress   *noun* Styles of dress are a major concern for both male and female JWs. Both are subject to reprimand from the elders if their dress is deemed inappropriate. At various times certain styles—such as men's bellbottom pants and women's pantsuits—have been ruled unacceptable.

E

elder   *noun* One of the men appointed by the Watchtower Society to a position of oversight in a Jehovah's Witness congregation.

elder body   *slang* The body of elders of a local JW congregation.

elders, the   The body of elders of a local JW congregation.

emblems, the   The red wine and the unleavened bread (often, Jewish kosher matzo) used in the JW version of Communion at their annual Memorial meeting.

eternal life   The reward, given only to the faithful, of living forever—in heaven for 144,000 chosen ones and on earth for additional millions. This is not IMMORTALITY, but life continues uninterruped because the causes of death have been removed.

everlasting life   *See* eternal life.

evil slave   1. An individual belonging to the EVIL SLAVE CLASS. 2. *loosely* A former JW who now attacks or criticizes the Watchtower Society.

evil slave class   Members of the anointed remnant of the 144,000 who become unfaithful and turn against the Watchtower Society (from Matthew 24:48). The term is applied principally to elderly persons who left the organization many years ago.

expectations   *See* premature expectations.

Ezekiel class, the   The anointed remnant allegedly at the core of the Watchtower organization—supposedly prefigured by the prophet Ezekiel.

F

factory, the   1. The mammoth printing plant at the Watchtower Society's New York headquarters, as in "My son the Bethelite works in the factory." 2. The printing plant at any of the Society's Branch Offices or farms.

faithful and discreet slave   1. The remnant of the 144,000 anointed ones in their role as God's channel of communication in fulfillment of Matthew 24:45–47. 2. *loosely* The JW Governing Body serving as spokesman for the anointed remnant. *See* AJWSBS, JWAVBV.

fall of Babylon, the   1. The Medo-Persian conquest of the Neo-Babylonian Empire in 539 B.C.E. 2. The prophesied defeat of modern Babylon the Great—the non-JW religions— in 1919, when Watchtower leaders imprisoned on sedition charges were released from the Atlanta federal penitentiary.

fall of Babylon the Great, the   The prophesied defeat of the non-JW religions in 1919, when Watchtower leaders imprisoned on sedition charges were released from the Atlanta federal penitentiary.

false prophet, a   1. A self-proclaimed spokesman for God whose predictions fail to come true. 2. A term wrongly applied to Jehovah's Witnesses by their enemies. Example: "Jehovah's Witnesses, in their eagerness for Jesus' second coming, have suggested dates that turned out to be incorrect.

Because of this, some have called them false prophet."
(*Awake!* March 22, 1993, page 4).

Note: Although Jehovah's Witnesses themselves have predicted the end of the world for several different dates—1914,
1918, 1925, and 1975 being the most prominent—and recently dropped their longstanding proclamation of "the Creator's promise of a peaceful and secure new world before the
generation that saw the events of 1914 passes away" (*Awake!*
masthead on page 4 of each issue from March 1988 through
October 1995)—they are taught to believe that the term "false
prophet" does not apply to them, because they never claimed
to be prophets in the first place. However, see the box titled
"a prophet *yet* not a prophet" on page 109.

false prophet, the   The dual world power composed of
Britain and the United States (the Anglo-American world
power), allied with Satan the Devil and the United Nations
organization, but finally destroyed in the Lake of Fire, according to Watchtower interpretations of the Bible's apoca-
lyptic prophecies.

false religion   All the world's non-JW religions, collectively. Example: "The great tribulation will begin with the Battle of Babylon and the destruction of false religion, followed by the Battle
of Armageddon and the destruction of human governments."

false religionist   A member or adherent of a non-Witness
religion.

farm, the   1. The Watchtower Farms complex at Wallkill, New
York, as in "My son the Bethelite works at the farm."

Note: The farm includes a massive printing factory where
English-language *Watchtower* and *Awake!* magazines are
produced. 2. Any of the Society's farm facilities staffed by full-
time Watchtower personnel who live in dormitories on site.

field, the   The non-JW community viewed as a territory for
witnessing, as in "After you have developed your presentation, the next step is to try it out in the field."

field service   *technical* Door-to-door literature distribution,
return visits, home Bible studies, and other activity reportable to the Society.

field service report   1. A printed form that each Witness fills out weekly or monthly and turns in to the local congregation to report his or her hours spent in field service, number of books distributed, number of magazines distributed, and so on. 2. The figures listed on such a report. Example: "My field service report was low this month because I was down with the flu for two weeks."

first resurrection   The raising to life of dead JWs and first-century saints, alleged to have occurred in 1918, when these individuals were supposedly given spirit-bodies to live in heaven.

flock, little   The 144,000 heaven-bound Jehovah's Witnesses as prefigured by Jesus' words in Luke 12:32. *See* AJWSBS, JWAVBV.

flood, the   The worldwide deluge of Noah's day.

Fluosol-DA.   *See* artificial blood.

Food Service Department   *obsolete* The department responsible for preparing and serving food at a JW convention, staffed by volunteers. Stands selling hamburgers and snacks plus a cafeteria serving meals—usually for meal tickets sold in advance—were standard features of JW assemblies for decades. Starting in the early 1990s food was no longer "sold" but was made available on a "donation" basis. Then, commencing in 1995, the food service arrangement was dispensed with, and the Society instructed JW families to bring their own food to conventions.

force, active   The Holy Spirit. *See* active force.

free home Bible study   A regularly scheduled discussion conducted by a JW with a prospective convert, usually in the prospect's home for an hour each week, featuring a paragraph-by-paragraph examination of a Watchtower publication—not the Bible itself. Although Witnesses usually refer to this among themselves as simply "a study," they generally say "free home Bible study" when offering it to an outsider.

friends, the   *always plural* Jehovah's Witnesses, collectively, as in "I'm having some of the friends over to my house for a get-together," or "Some of the friends were upset by a remark you made from the platform."

full-time service   The status and activity of a Witness formally appointed to serve as PIONEER devoting sixty or more hours each month to public preaching in the territory.

G

Gehenna   *Greek (taken from Hebrew)* Second death, extinction, the Lake of Fire in which the unrighteous dead are instantly annihilated and permanently destroyed. *See* AJWSBS and JWAVBV.

generation   *noun* **1.** *current definition* "Rather than providing a rule for measuring time, the term 'generation' as used by Jesus refers principally to contemporary people of a certain historical period, with their identifying characteristics."—*The Watchtower,* November 1, 1995, page 17. **2.** *obsolete* "The Hebrews . . . reckon seventy-five years as one generation."—*Awake!* April 8, 1988, page 14. **3.** *obsolete* "It does not refer to a period of time, which some have tried to interpret as 30, 40, 70 or even 120 years, but, rather, it refers to people, the people living at the 'beginning of pangs of distress' for this condemned world system."—*The Watchtower,* October 15, 1980, page 31. **4.** *obsolete* "A 'generation' might be reckoned as equivalent to a century (practically the present limit) or one hundred and twenty years."—*Studies in the Scriptures,* volume 4, 1908 edition, page 604. **5.** *obsolete* "Or . . . it would not be inconsistent to reckon the 'generation' from 1878 to 1914—36 1/2 years."—*Studies in the Scriptures,* volume 4, 1908 edition, page 605.

generation, the   *obsolete* Short for "the 1914 generation," or "the generation that saw 1914" as in "We know Armageddon is coming soon, because the generation has nearly passed away."

generation, this   The people Jesus allegedly pointed forward to in our day when he said, "Verily I say unto you, This generation shall not pass away, till all be fulfilled" (Luke 21:32 KJV). *See* box.

generation, the 1914   *obsolete* Short for "the generation that saw 1914" as in "We don't have much longer to wait, brothers, because the 1914 generation is getting well up in years now."

generation that saw 1914, the   *obsolete* Collectively, the people born before 1914 who saw the events of that year—and who were expected to live to see the end of the world and the establishment of a New Order worldwide under Christ's millennial reign. This expression became obsolete when the November 1, 1995 *Watchtower* revised the prophetic interpretation of Jesus' words in Luke 21:32.

---

the 1914 generation

From the 1960s through late 1995, Jehovah's Witnesses had been taught "the Creator's promise of a peaceful and secure new world before the generation that saw the events of 1914 passes away" (*Awake!* magazine's masthead, page 4 of each issue, March 8, 1988 through October 22, 1995) During the late 1960s and early 1970s, Witnesses connected this with other predictions in their publications to the effect that the end would occur in the autumn of 1975, when the generation who were teenagers in 1914 would be in their mid-70s and close to passing away. ("are we to assume from this study that the battle of Armageddon will be all over by the autumn of 1975?"—*The Watchtower,* August 15, 1968, page 499). Afterward, the organization stretched the generation by applying it to the babies of 1914 rather than the teenagers. And, when it could no longer be stretched, the prophecy was finally dropped at the end of 1995.

Gentile times   *obsolete.* The 2,520-year period from 607 B.C. to A.D. 1914, allegedly foretold by Christ in Luke 21:24 as a fixed interval between the desolation of the Davidic kingdom in ancient Jerusalem and the restoration of this kingdom under Christ. On this basis, early Watch Tower leaders prophesied the world's end for October 4/5, 1914; the Society teaches today that Christ took power as king in heaven on that date. Now called ᴛʜᴇ ᴀᴘᴘᴏɪɴᴛᴇᴅ ᴛɪᴍᴇs ᴏꜰ ᴛʜᴇ ɴᴀᴛɪᴏɴs.

get your time in   *slang* To spend sufficient time in field service to reach one's goal of reportable hours—an expression used primarily in reference to ᴘɪᴏɴᴇᴇʀs who have assigned monthly or annual goals.

Gilead or **Gilead School**   *noun* The Watchtower Society's school or training program (of several weeks' duration) for full-time missionaries sent to foreign lands at the organization's expense.

Gilead Class   The missionary-trainees, collectively, who attend Gilead in a particular year, as in "Brother Smith and Brother Jones were both members of the Gilead Class of '68"—comparable to a college's graduating class.

go out   *slang* Engage in field service activity, as in "I go out every Saturday morning."

goal   *noun* The number of hours set by the organization as a monthly or annual target for JW pioneers or publishers. Formerly, ǫᴜᴏᴛᴀ. (When I pioneered from 1969 through 1971, a ʀᴇɢᴜʟᴀʀ ᴘɪᴏɴᴇᴇʀ's assigned goal was 1,200 hours per year.—*author*)

goat   *slang* A worldly person who has firmly rejected the message preached by Jehovah's Witnesses. (Derived from the Watchtower interpretation of Matthew 25:32–46.)

god   *noun* An angelic or superhuman created being. This usage may be difficult to discern in oral speech, as when a JW is shown evidence that Jesus is God and responds by saying, "Yes, I am aware that the Bible refers to Jesus as god."

god, a   *noun* An angelic or superhuman created being. The JW *New World Translation* renders John 1:1 as, "the Word was a god." *See* JWAVBV and *The Jehovah's Witnesses New Testament* by Robert Countess.

God   *noun* The one true Supreme Being. JWs restrict this term to God the Father and believe that he must be addressed by the name "Jehovah."

god and God

"I'm not interested in hearing your message, because you people deny the deity of Jesus Christ," a householder says to the Jehovah's Witnesses who show up on her doorstep. "Whoever told you that was mistaken," one of the Witnesses responds. "We have always believed in the divinity of Christ."

If the householder accepts this and consents to listen to the JW message after all, it is only because each party to the conversation understands the words differently. In actuality, when Witnesses use the terms "deity," "divine," or "god" in reference to Christ, they mean merely that he is "a god" in the sense that all angels are superhuman beings or godlike ones, or in the sense that Satan the Devil is "the god of this world" (2 Corinthians 4:4).

They realize that outsiders take this as an acknowledgment that Christ is the Almighty, the Creator, and the Witnesses sometimes use this confusion to their advantage, postponing confrontation over this issue in order to establish a foothold first on other matters that they can more easily teach a prospective convert.

God's earthly organization   1. The Watch Tower Bible and Tract Society of Pennsylvania and its related corporate entities. 2. The corporation together with its followers.

God's heavenly organization   Christ, those of the 144,000 already in heaven, and the angels, all functioning together as an organized body.

God's organization   1. The Watch Tower Bible and Tract Society of Pennsylvania and its related corporate entities. 2. The corporation together with its followers. 3. God's universal organization embracing all faithful creatures: Christ, those of the 144,000 already in heaven, the holy angels, and JWs alive on earth.

God's universal organization   All faithful creatures— Christ, those of the 144,000 already in heaven, the holy angels, and JWs alive on earth—functioning together as an organized body under divine direction and represented on earth by the Watchtower Society.

God's wifely organization   God's universal organization, as pictured by the symbolic woman of Revelation 12:1–6.

God's woman   God's wifely organization.

good luck   Since Witnesses avoid using this expression, anyone who says, "Good luck!" can usually be assumed not to be a JW.

good news, the   *This* good news, the JW "gospel" message which is different from the gospel or good news preached by Christians down through the centuries. *See* this good news.

good progress   Acceptance of Watchtower teaching and obedience to the Society's dictates, as in "My student is making good progress and will be baptized at the next assembly."

good standing, in   The status of a baptized Witness who has not been disfellowshipped, nor recently reproved, and is not under any accusation of misconduct.

Governing Body or **governing body**   The ruling council for Jehovah's Witnesses worldwide, seen as the successors to the twelve apostles. Until the early 1970s the Governing Body was synonymous with the Board of Directors of the Watch Tower Bible and Tract Society of Pennsylvania. Then it was expanded and placed above the various JW corporate entities. In recent years the Governing Body's membership has varied from ten to eighteen men.

grace   *obsolete* Jehovah's Witnesses never speak of God's grace. They use the expression "undeserved kindness," which replaces "grace" in the *New World Translation.*

grace or undeserved kindness

People who are well acquainted with the Watchtower organization realize that it is not simply the word "grace" that is missing from the vocabulary of Jehovah's Witnesses; the concept of God's free gift is missing too. In fact, JWs are so accustomed to earning God's alleged favor though obedience to the sect's works program that hardly an eyebrow was raised when their internal publication *Our Kingdom Ministry* declared, "We want to give *deserving* ones the opportunity to learn of Jehovah's *undeserved* kindness and the Kingdom hope" (December 1993, page 7, emphasis added).

great crowd   Collectively, the vast majority of JWs whose hope is to live forever on an earth restored to paradise (derived from Revelation 7:9). *See* AJWSBS.

great tribulation, the   God's final two-part execution of judgment against the non-JW world, consisting of the Battle of Babylon in which all other religious groups will be destroyed and then the Battle of Armageddon in which all human governments and all surviving non-Witnesses will be annihilated.

Greek Scriptures   Short for the *Christian Greek Scriptures,* the name Jehovah's Witnesses use for the New Testament.

grooming   *noun* Men's hairstyles, beards, moustaches—all are of great concern to JWs. At various times certain male hair, beard, and moustache styles have been ruled unacceptable for JWs. In most areas Witness men are required to be clean-shaven—or in some cases small moustaches are allowed—in order to receive any "privileges" in the congregation. Hair over the collar or over the ears has generally been prohibited.

group, car   *See* car group.

H

hall, the   Kingdom Hall

hall cleaning   A weekly group cleaning activity usually assigned to various book study groups by rotation.

Hebrew Scriptures   The Old Testament. (Use of the term "Old Testament" immediately identifies one as a non-Witness in most cases.)

headquarters   *noun* The Brooklyn, New York corporate headquarters complex of the Watchtower Bible and Tract Society—also referred to as BETHEL or BROOKLYN BETHEL.

headship   *noun* 1. The biblical principle assigning the family leadership role to the husband, as interpreted by the Watchtower Society. 2. Biblically assigned leadership roles in the local congregation and in the wider organization.

hearing   *noun* A judicial committee hearing.

heaven   1. The place in outer space where God dwells and where the 144,000 go following their resurrection. 2. *obsolete* The Pleiades star cluster, in particular, its brightest star Alcyone, long taught by the Watchtower Society to be the location of God's throne. *See* RESCUE.

Hebrew Scriptures, the   The preferred term among JWs for the Old Testament. Use of the term "Old Testament" marks a person as a non-Witness.

hell   *theological* 1. An imaginary place of torment thought to exist by WORLDLY people but actually nonexistent because humans have no immoterial soul or spirit capable of surviving death. 2. The common grave of dead humankind, a figurative term rather than an actual place. *See* AJWSBS.

higher education   Postsecondary school training—an expression with strong negative connotations, since college education for the children of Jehovah's Witnesses is viewed as a waste of time and, worse yet, a satanic snare.

Holy Ghost   A term intentionally avoided by Jehovah's Witnesses, since they deny the Spirit's deity and personality. *See* holy spirit.

Holy Spirit   *See* holy spirit.

holy spirit   *not capitalized in JW usage* God's active force: the invisible, impersonal, and inanimate force Jehovah uses to accomplish his will.

home Bible study   A regularly scheduled discussion conducted by a JW with a prospective convert, usually in the prospect's home for an hour each week, featuring a paragraph-by-paragraph examination of a Watchtower publication—not the Bible itself.

householder   *noun* 1. A non-Witness visited in door-to-door ministry. 2. A Witness playing the part of a non-Witness in a demonstration on a meeting part at Kingdom Hall.

hymn   *noun* 1. A disgusting song sung in mock worship at Christendom's churches. 2. *obsolete* A song sung at JW worship services during the late 1800s and early 1900s. Today's JWs sing SONGS and are highly offended if these are referred to as hymns.

hymnal   *noun* 1. A book of disgusting songs sung in mock worship at Christendom's churches, 2. *obsolete* A songbook published by the Watchtower Society and used at JW worship services during the late 1800s and early 1900s. *See* JWL. Today's JWs use SONGBOOKS and are highly offended if these are referred to as hymnals.

I

IBSA   *technical* The International Bible Students Association.

immortality   *theological* Deathlessness and indestructability—a quality possessed only by Jehovah God in Witness theology, since wicked men and angels will be annihilated, while the righteous will be rewarded with ETERNAL LIFE.

impale   *verb* To hang upon a stake. In order to agree with its denial of the cross, the *New World Translation* substitutes impale for crucify.

imperfect, imperfection   The condition of fallen human beings, inclined toward error and evil—roughly equivalent to the Christian term "sinner."

in good standing   *See* good standing, in.

in the truth   *slang* Associated with the Watchtower organization. Examples: "I've been in the truth ten years; how long have you been in the truth?" "I was born in the truth."

inactive   *adjective; technical* Having no time reported in field service for the preceding six months.

inactive publisher   *technical* A Witness who has not reported any time for the preceding six months.

Note: Only active publishers are considered for appointments and for certain privileges.

inappropriate facial expression   *technical* A point of counsel addressed when a student in the Theocratic Ministry School is working on "personal appearance" while giving a student talk.

individual choice   The alleged freedom of each JW to decide for himself or herself on such matters as whether or not to receive a blood transfusion, whether or not to vote in an election, and whether or not to obey a draft board's order to report for military service. In actuality JWs making the "wrong" choice are put on trial and punished. *See* personal decision.

information board   The term "bulletin board" was stricken from JW vocabulary decades ago due to its supposedly unsavory etymology. Witnesses trace its derivation to the papal bull, and certainly no loyal Witness would want to refer to the Kingdom Hall corkboard as a place for displaying documents issued by the Roman Catholic pope. Notices are hung on the information board. (It is technically permissible for JWs to use the term "bulletin board" when referring to such an object at their place of employment or at the supermarket, but the habit of substituting the expression "information board" often carries over to this usage as well.)

Insight   The two-volume Watchtower book *Insight on the Scriptures* published in 1988 as a replacement for the *Aid* book. *See* JWL.

inspired   *adjective* Directed or controlled by a superhuman source, especially God.

inspired, yet not inspired

Jehovah's Witnesses believe that the Watchtower organization is God's channel of communication, God's spokesman to humankind. Yet, whenever critics bring up the sect's long record of prophetic failures and doctrinal flip-flops, Witnesses typically respond that the organization has never claimed to be inspired. This is a classic example of Orwellian doublethink—and plain doubletalk.

instruction talk   A talk of fifteen to twenty minutes delivered at the beginning of the Theocratic Ministry School meeting by a capable adult male.

integrity   *noun* Faithfulness to God through full compliance with all Watchtower Society requirements.

integrity keeper   One who maintains faithfulness to God through full compliance with all Watchtower Society requirements.

***Interlinear,* the**   The Watchtower Society's *Kingdom Interlinear Translation of the Greek Scriptures.*

International Bible Students Association   *technical* 1. The organizational name Pastor Russell instructed his followers to use to identify themselves and to advertise their meetings. 2. The British corporation formed by Pastor Russell in 1914, which continues to function as the sect's legal arm in Britain.

invisible presence   *theological* 1. Christ's second coming, unseen by human eyes, in the year 1914. 2. *obsolete* Christ's second coming in the year 1874, unseen by human eyes, as proclaimed by *Zion's Watch Tower and Herald of Christ's Presence.*

irregular   *adjective, technical* Failing to report time during one or more of the previous six months.

irregular publisher   *technical* A JW officially approved to participate in field service but who has failed to report time during one or more of the previous six months.

J

JW   *abbreviation* Jehovah's Witness or Jehovah's Witnesses—an acronym commonly used by outsiders and finding some slang usage by Witnesses themselves but seldom found in Watchtower publications.

Jehovah   *noun* 1. The name of the true God, the God of the Bible, as found in the *King James Version* in Exodus 6:3 and Psalm 83:18. 2. God the Father, in Jehovah's Witness usage, not the Son or the Holy Spirit.

Notes: 1. Watchtower publications have admitted that Jehovah is an incorrect rendering of the Hebrew YHWH, often rendered Yahweh in other modern translations. *See* JWAVBV, AJWSBS.

2. To reinforce their antitrinitarian teaching, JWs restrict the use of the name "Jehovah" and apply it exclusively to God the Father. So, when a Christian tries to establish the deity of Christ and tells a Witness, "Jesus *is* Jehovah," the JW hears this as, "Jesus is *the Father*"—a thought contrary even to traditional orthodox theology and ridiculous to the JW's ears.

3. Because Jehovah's Witnesses are accustomed to referring to the Deity always by the name "Jehovah," when they hear non-Witnesses speak about God they are often left with the feeling that this is someone else, not their Jehovah. The divisive effect of this word-usage pattern contributes to the overall religious and social isolation of sect members from outsiders, one of the goals of any mind-control language.

4. As part of their systematic effort to slant their *New World Translation* to conceal the deity of Christ, Watchtower leaders insert the name "Jehovah" over two hundred times where Greek manuscripts actually say *kyrios* (Lord). Therefore, many verses that Christians would turn to in a theological discussion take on a completely different meaning for JWs. For example, the familiar words of Colossians 3:23–24 read this way in the *New International Version* (NIV): "Whatever you do, work at it with all your heart, as working for the Lord, not for men, since you know that you will receive an inheritance from the Lord as a reward. It is the Lord Christ you are serving." But the *New World Translation* changes the meaning in the eyes of JWs by having those verses say, "Whatever you are doing, work at it whole-souled as to Jehovah, and not to men, for you know that it is from Jehovah you will receive the due reward of the inheritance. Slave for the Master, Christ."

Jehovah Witness [*sic*] *erroneous* A common but incorrect form never used by the JW organization itself but often used in error by outside observers. Occasionally a poorly educated Witness will also use this expression.

Jehovah's chariot   Jehovah's universal organization, as pictured by the chariot in Ezekiel's vision.

Jehovah's Christian Witnesses   Jehovah's Witnesses. An alternative form of the sect's name, employed when there is a need or special desire to emphasize that they profess Christianity.

Jehovah's earthly organization   1. The Watch Tower Bible and Tract Society of Pennsylvania and its related corporate entities. 2. The corporation together with its followers.

Jehovah's heavenly organization   Christ, those of the 144,000 already in heaven, and the holy angels, all functioning together as an organized body.

Jehovah's organization   1. The Watch Tower Bible and Tract Society of Pennsylvania and its related corporate entities. 2. The corporation together with its followers. 3. God's universal organization embracing all faithful creatures: Christ, those of the 144,000 already in heaven, the holy angels, and JWs alive on earth.

Jehovah's universal organization   All faithful creatures— Christ, those of the 144,000 already in heaven, the holy angels, and JWs alive on earth—functioning together as an organized body under divine direction, and represented on earth by the Watchtower Society.

Jehovah's Witness, a   To refer to someone as a Jehovah's Witness usually identifies the speaker as a non-Witness; a JW is taught to say "one of Jehovah's Witnesses," thus affirming that the expression is a descriptive term rather than a denominational name. *See* Jehovah's Witnesses.

Jehovah's Witnesses (also Jehovah's witnesses)   Second Watchtower president Joseph F. Rutherford asked assembled members to approve this new name in 1931 to distinguish the sect from other Russellite "BIBLE STUDENTS." A lowercase "w" was often used by Rutherford and later writers to emphasize the claim that this is not a denominational

name but a description of what the members actually are—
witnesses of God.

Jehovah's Witnesses, not Jehovah's Witnesses

Roughly thirteen million people worldwide attend Jehovah's
Witness Kingdom Halls as their place of worship and, as a re-
sult, are viewed in their communities as Jehovah's Witnesses.
Yet the Witnesses themselves, if asked, will tell you that seven
million of these are not Jehovah's Witnesses. They count as
JWs only the five million who share in their door-to-door work.
"If one does not preach he is not a minister of God and is not
one of Jehovah's witnesses [sic] and is not recognized by the
Society as such."—*Qualified to be Ministers*, 1955 edition,
page 355

Jehovah's wifely organization   Jehovah's universal organization, as pictured by the symbolic woman of Revelation 12:1–6.

Jehovah's Witnesses, one of   JWs use this expression to affirm that they are actually witness-bearers of God rather than
members of a denomination named Jehovah's Witnesses. JWs
are taught to use this expression in place of "a Jehovah's Witness."

Jehovah's woman   Jehovah's wifely organization.

Jeremiah class, the   The anointed remnant allegedly at the
core of the Watchtower organization—supposedly prefigured by the prophet Jeremiah.

Jesus   *noun* The name Michael the Archangel—the first spirit
creature God created—took on when he was miraculously
transferred to the womb of the Virgin Mary to be born as a
human. As an angelic creature, Jesus is a god but not God.
See JWAVBV.

Jesus Christ   = Jesus the Messiah, or Jesus the Anointed One,
a title not correctly applied to Mary's son until he was thirty

years old and anointed with "holy spirit" at the time of his baptism by John. *See* AJWSBS.

Jonadab, a *obsolete* In JW terminology of the 1930s a Jonadab was a member of the great crowd—a Jehovah's Witness with the earthly hope—held to be prefigured by Jehonadab son of Rechab, who mounted Jehu's chariot to ride with him (2 Kings 10:15 NWT).

judicial action An official move to set up a judicial committee and summon before it an individual accused or suspected of wrongdoing. Example: "When the gossip in the congregation started to get out of hand, the brothers had to take judicial action."

judicial committee An officially appointed body of three (occasionally more) elders assigned to investigate and judge a JW suspected or accused of wrongdoing. Essentially a panel of judges in an ecclesiastical court, but with broad powers to investigate and interrogate an individual, call eyewitnesses, compel testimony, pass judgment, and execute punishment. A judicial committee is case-specific, so that in a congregation with elders A, B, C, D, and E, at a given moment in time A, B, and C may constitute a judicial committee investigating John Smith for adultery, B, C, and E may constitute a judicial committee investigating Jane Doe for cooking Thanksgiving dinner, and if Joe Witness is accused of smoking a new committee must be appointed.

judicial committee hearing A formal ecclesiastical court trial in which a JW accused or suspected of wrongdoing faces a panel of judges—elders who act together as investigator, prosecutor, judge, jury, and executioner.

judicial committee meeting A formal session held by the (usually) three elders forming a judicial committee. Besides actual hearings with others present, meetings may also be held by the committee members alone to plan strategy, arrive at a judgment, and so on.

judicial decisions Rulings made by a congregation judicial committee in regard to persons placed on trial as to their disfellowshipping, disciplining, reinstatement, and so on.

judicial matter Misconduct that can result in the individual being summoned before a judicial committee. Examples: An elder might tell his wife, "I can't answer your question about why Peter Rogers walked out in the middle of the meeting last night, because it involves a judicial matter." Or, a father might tell his teenage son, "If you put your hands all over Susan like that, it's more than I can handle through family discipline; it's become a judicial matter."

Judge, the Judge Rutherford

Judge Rutherford Joseph Franklin Rutherford (1869–1942), the Watchtower Society's second president, who exercised one-man rule over the JW organization from Pastor Russell's death in 1916 until his own demise. He authored most of the sect's books and other materials published during his administration.

K

KIT or **K.I.T.** *abbreviation* The Watchtower Society's *Kingdom Interlinear Translation of the Greek Scriptures.*

K.M. *abbreviation* The internal monthly publication, *Our Kingdom Ministry.*

k.p. *slang; abbreviation* Kingdom privilege, often used sarcastically to describe Kingdom Hall cleaning or other undesirable assignments. Resemblance to the military use of "k.p." is both intentional and appropriate.

keep integrity To live in strict obedience to all God's laws (as interpreted by the Watchtower Society) without deviation.

Kingdom Hall The local meetingplace of a JW congregation—sometimes a rented room or building, but usually a structure owned by the sect through some corporate or trusteeship arrangement. The typical Kingdom Hall seats between fifty and three hundred people and, viewed externally, resembles surrounding buildings, regardless of whether these are commercial or residential. Kingdom Halls do not have steeples; if a former church is purchased as a Kingdom Hall, the steeple is removed.

kingdom interests   Field service, meeting attendance, personal study, and other Witness-related activities, as in "Avoid letting hobbies assume too much importance, lest they cause you to push kingdom interests aside!"

Kingdom Interlinear   The Watchtower Society's Kingdom Interlinear Translation of the Greek Scriptures, featuring the Greek text accompanied by an interlinear English rendering in one column and the *New World Translation* in another column. *See* JWL.

kingdom message, the   The "good news" preached to the public by Jehovah's Witnesses.

Kingdom Ministry   *obsolete or shortened form of Our Kingdom Ministry,* an internal monthly publication of four or eight pages featuring instructions for field service and other aspects of life as a JW. This publication's name was changed from *Kingdom Ministry* to *Our Kingdom Service* in 1976, when the Society began teaching that rank-and-file JWs were not ministers. It was renamed *Our Kingdom Ministry* in 1982, when the Society flip-flopped back to the old teaching. Witnesses often omit the word "Our" from the title in casual speech and even from the speaker's platform at Kingdom Hall, as in "I forgot to take my *Kingdom Ministry* with me to the meeting." *See* JWL and AJWSBS.

Kingdom Service, Our   *See Our Kingdom Ministry.*

Kingdom Ministry School   *technical* A training program for elders, with classes held either at a central location or at local Kingdom Halls and with sessions lasting from one day to four weeks.

kingdom privilege   *slang* A sarcastic description of Kingdom Hall cleaning or some other undesirable assignment. Resemblance to the military's "k.p." is both intentional and appropriate.

L

last days   *theological* 1. The predetermined interval of time from 1914 to the Battle of Armageddon. 2. *obsolete* The harvest period from 1874 to 1914.

lead, those taking the   1. The elders in the local congregation. 2. Anyone assigned oversight. Use of this wording from Hebrews 13:17 (NWT) reminds JWs of the verse's command to "be obedient" and "submissive" to such ones.

leader   *noun* Jesus Christ. JWs adamantly refuse to refer to anyone in the organizational hierarchy as a leader, insisting that they have no leader but Christ—in spite of their referring to such office holders as those taking the lead. Thus JWs dispute the fact that, by definition, those taking the lead are leaders.

legal corporation, the   The Watch Tower Bible and Tract Society of Pennsylvania and/or one of its incorporated Branch Offices, as opposed to the wider, unincorporated spiritual entity of Jehovah's Witnesses. Example: "The government could close down the legal corporation, but they could never shut down Jehovah's organization."

library, the   1. The Kingdom Hall library featuring Watchtower Society publications, including annual bound volumes of *The Watchtower* and *Awake!* going back several decades. Since JWs must live by the Society's interpretations and instructions, the library is consulted often. 2. The room at Kingdom Hall used to house the library, but also often used for elders' meetings and judicial committee hearings.

lie   *noun* A falsehood presented to someone entitled to know the truth of a matter. *verb* To present a falsehood to someone entitled to know the truth. Deception used to safeguard Witnesses in danger or to lead a potential convert into the safety of God's organization is not considered lying. *See* INDEX.

life   *noun* Eternal life in the paradise earth after Armageddon, as in "You must stick close to Jehovah's organization if you want to gain life."

light   *noun* Enlightenment or clarification received from God though the Watchtower Society.

light, new   A revised teaching that replaces previously held ideas.

light got brighter, the   God revealed new information to replace previously held viewpoints. Based on the Watchtower interpretation of Proverbs 4:18, this is the excuse most commonly offered by JWs who are shown the organization's doctrinal changes. *See* RESCUE and JWAVBV for effective responses.

listening ear, a   A non-Witness willing to receive instruction from Jehovah's Witnesses, as in "Sister Cramer was invited in at that door and has not yet come out; she must have found a listening ear."

literature   Publications of the Watchtower Society, especially those offered to the general public, as in "I've spent a lot of time in service this month, but I haven't placed much literature."

literature servant   The ministerial servant appointed by local elders to handle the Society's publications other than magazines. He is responsible for requisitioning and stocking this literature, and for dispensing it to Witnesses at Kingdom Hall. The literature servant works under the direction of the Field Service Overseer and places orders for literature through the congregation's Secretary.

literature room   The cubicle or small room used at Kingdom Hall for storing and dispensing Watchtower books, booklets, bound volumes, and other literature, with the exception of periodicals. It is usually equipped with a window or dutch door to provide counter service. Also called a book room.

little flock   *theological* The 144,000 heaven-bound anointed ones.

long hair   A male hairstyle that overlaps the collar or extends over the tops of the ears—a forbidden style that would usually disqualify a male Witness from any privileges in the congregation and that could bring more severe consequences. Actually, it is not length that makes hair long in the JW view: an elder whose greased, slicked-down hair measures twelve inches or longer as he combs it straight back from his forehead over the top of his head to a point where it stops just above the back of his collar may initiate official action to punish a young man who wears his hair one or two inches long but who allows it to hang over his collar or over the tops of his ears.

Lord's Evening Meal, the   The JW equivalent of Communion, served annually after sundown on the Jewish calendar date of Nisan 14 (usually in March or April), with partaking of the cup and loaf limited to the anointed remnant. The sect reported worldwide attendance of 12,288,917 in 1994, with a mere 8,617 partaking. *See* AJWSBS.

lovingkindness   The *New World Translation*'s rendering of a Hebrew term variously translated as love, goodness, or mercy in other Bibles, leading JWs to use this more awkward expression in their everyday speech.

luck, lucky   Fortune, fortunate. Witnesses avoid saying "luck" or "lucky" due to their belief that the expression gives recognition to "the god of Good Luck" (Isaiah 65:11 NWT). Yet they will wish someone "the best" and call someone "fortunate"—expressions that mean the same thing.

M

magazine(s)   *noun* The Society's *Watchtower* and *Awake!* magazines.

magazine day   A day set aside for door-to-door distribution of *The Watchtower* and *Awake!* magazines—usually a certain Saturday or Saturdays.

magazine room   The cubicle or small room used at Kingdom Hall for storing and dispensing *Watchtower* and *Awake!* magazines—usually equipped with a window or dutch door to provide counter service.

magazine route   A JW's collection of addresses where the occupants routinely purchase the latest *Watchtower* and *Awake!* magazines when visited every two weeks.

magazine servant   The ministerial servant appointed by local elders to handle the Society's magazines. He is responsible for requisitioning and stocking them, and for dispensing them to Witnesses at Kingdom Hall. The magazine servant works under the direction of the Field Service Overseer and places orders for magazines through the congregation's Secretary.

magazines, the   *The Watchtower* and *Awake!*

making good progress   Readily accepting Watchtower indoctrination without objections or problems, as in "My study, Mrs. Jones, is making good progress and will soon be attending meetings, I'm sure."

man of lawlessness, the   1. An unnamed character of Bible prophecy prefiguring the clergy of Christendom. 2. The clergy (of non-Witness churches) as a class [from 2 Timothy 2:3 in the *New World Translation*].

Note: Witnesses also refer to clergy of other churches as "the antichrist" and consider them as the worst villains, second only to "apostate" ex-Witnesses.

manuscript talk   A public lecture given by a speaker who is supplied by the Watchtower Society the complete word-for-word text, rather than a mere outline. Witnesses usually pay special attention to manuscript talks, on the assumption that the matter is of such great importance that the Society must be sure of its exact wording.

map   *See* territory map.

mark   *verb* To single out a Witness for exclusion from social activities due to misbehavior that does not merit disfellowshipping. The individual is still greeted as a "brother" or "sister," but is viewed as "undesirable association."

marking talk   A service meeting part in which an elder representing the body identifies an individual's conduct as disapproved, without actually naming the offender. Listeners who recognize the situation then mark that person.

meat   *noun* Deeper teachings normally reserved for students who have already made good progress—such as complex prophetic or chronological calculations, or the requirements to refuse military service, to abstain from voting, and to allow one's child to die rather than receive blood plasma or platelets.

meeting   *noun* Any of the five services held regularly each week at Kingdom Hall: the Public Talk and the *Watchtower* Study, usually held consecutively on Sunday morning; the Ministry School and the Service Meeting, usually held consecutively on Thursday evening; and the Congregation Book Study, usually held on Tuesday evening in a number of smaller groups, one or more at Kingdom Hall and the others at private homes.

meetings, the   The five weekly services of the local congregation, collectively, as in "Marge must be spiritually sick, because she's stopped coming to the meetings."

meeting for service   A brief fifteen-minute to thirty-minute session held at Kingdom Hall or another meeting place for service prior to departing for the territory. This usually consists of discussion of the daily text and/or suggested presentations. Not to be confused with Service Meeting.

meeting place for service   A private home where Witnesses gather for a brief formal session prior to departing for the territory. This is usually the same place where a Congregation Book Study Meeting is held on Tuesday nights. Formerly called a RENDEZVOUS.

member   *noun* A JW will vehemently deny being a "member of the Jehovah's Witnesses." He will insist that he is actually a witness-bearer for Jehovah God, not a mere member of a denomination. In a fine distinction, however, he may admit to being a member of the local congregation.

Memorial   *noun* The JW equivalent of a Communion service, held annually after sundown on the Jewish calendar date of Nisan 14 (usually in March or April), with partaking of the cup and loaf limited to the anointed remnant. The sect reported worldwide attendance of 12,288,917 in 1994, with a mere 8,617 partaking. *See* AJWSBS.

mental regulating   Jehovah's Witness indoctrination, especially of children—an expression drawn from the *New World Translation*'s rendering of "admonition" (KJV) or "instruction" (NIV) in Ephesians 6:4.

Michael   *noun* 1. The first angel God created, who became like a son to him, helped with the rest of creation, and entered Mary's womb to be born as Jesus. Upon his resurrection and return to heaven, Christ resumed the role of Michael the archangel. 2. *especially among young African American JWs during the 1980s* Popular singer Michael Jackson, who was a Jehovah's Witness in good standing until mid-1987, when he "disassociated himself" according to the sect's spokesmen, or was forced out for suggestive dancing and occult practices according to other sources.

mighty God   Jesus Christ, the first angel God created, who became like a son to Him. In JW terminology, the Father is the Almighty God, while the Son is only a mighty god. *See* AJWSBS and JWAVBV.

milk   *noun* Elementary biblical knowledge suitable for new converts, such as the non-Trinitarian nature of God, the limitation of heavenly life to 144,000, and the apostate nature of all non-JW churches.

minister   *noun* 1. A Jehovah's Witness. Prior to 1976, and now since 1982, the Watchtower Society has been teaching that all JWs are ministers. 2. *obsolete* A JW appointed to an official position in a JW congregation, such as an elder or ministerial servant, according to the teaching that prevailed from 1976 to 1982. This doctrinal flip-flop was reflected in name changes of the internal publication now entitled *Our Kingdom Ministry. See* AJWSBS and JWL.

ministerial servant   *organizational* A man appointed to a position in a Jehovah's Witness congregation roughly equivalent to that of a deacon in a church that also has teaching elders. Ministerial servants operate the book room and the magazine room at Kingdom Hall, supervise the sound amplification equipment, handle the congregation accounts, direct the attendants, maintain and assign territory maps, and assist the elders in other ways.

ministry   *noun* 1. The service performed by a Jehovah's Witness. Prior to 1976, and now since 1982, the Watchtower Society has been teaching that all JWs share in ministry. 2. *obsolete* The work of a JW appointed to an official position in a JW congregation, such as an elder or ministerial servant, according to the teaching that prevailed from 1976 to 1982. This flip-flop was reflected in name changes of the internal publication now entitled *Our Kingdom Ministry. See* AJWSBS and JWL.

ministry school   1. The Theocratic Ministry School, usually in session at Kingdom Hall one hour weekly on Thursday or Friday evening and open to most meeting attenders

95

to train them in door-to-door work and public speaking. **2.** The Kingdom Ministry School, a training program for elders, with classes held either at a central location or at local Kingdom Halls and with sessions lasting from one day to four weeks.

miracle   *noun* A supernatural act performed by God as recorded in the Bible. JWs believe God no longer performs miracles, except in rare instances of providing miraculous protection for Witnesses under persecution.

Miss   A title used in addressing or speaking about an unmarried WORLDY woman. *See* Mr., Mrs.

missionary   *noun* A JW trained at Gilead School for full-time ministry in foreign lands at the organization's expense.

model prayer, the   The Lord's Prayer.

modern-day Witnesses of Jehovah   Watchtower followers from the time of C. T. Russell's break with his Adventist mentors until now, as distinguished from faithful Old Testament characters, first century Christians, and true believers down through the ages—all of whom were "Witnesses of Jehovah," or "Jehovah's Witnesses," according to the sect.

mouthpiece, God's   **1.** The Watchtower Society in its role as God's spokesman. **2.** *obsolete* Charles Taze Russell, before his successor J. F. Rutherford revised the teaching to mean the Watchtower Society.

move ahead   Usually as part of the expression *move ahead with Jehovah's organization,* meaning *readily accept 'new truths' as these are revealed through the Watchtower Society.* This is a prime example of the leadership using "loaded language" to put a positive slant on doctrinal changes, with the implication that any who do not instantly conform are left behind for foolishly rejecting progress.

Mr., Mrs.   A title used in addressing or speaking about a WORLDLY person. For example, a JW saying to another Witness, "John, I'd like you to meet *Mr.* Jenkins," is telling John that Jenkins is not a JW; if Jenkins had been a JW, it would have been phrased, "John, I'd like you to meet *Brother* Jenkins." Similarly with *Mrs.* or *Miss* and *Sister.*

Ms. A title Witnesses find offensive and avoid using in addressing women, because they view its use as submission to the influence of the feminist movement. If a JW does refer to someone in the third person as "*Ms.* Parker," the intent is to label her as a feminist.

***Mystery* book, the** Short for the book *Then Is Finished the Mystery of God,* a commentary on portions of Revelation published by the Watchtower Society in 1969, but replaced by another book a dozen years later. (While the *Mystery* book was current, an observer overhearing one Witness say to another, "I spent my time at the beach reading the *Mystery* book," might have incorrectly assumed that meant a genre novel.)

N

name, God's *Jehovah,* the rendition of the Tetragrammaton officially endorsed by the Watchtower Society.

name, the or **Name, the** *Jehovah. See* God's name.

national anthem A musical piece dreaded by JWs, who view it as representing satanic rulership. Forbidden to stand up when it is played, and often encountering abuse for taking that position, JWs cringe at the sound. *See* AJWSBS.

nations, the A disparaging term JWs use for non-Witnesses, reminiscent of the Pharisees' view of Gentiles.

need, the *noun* The lack of a sufficient number of active Witnesses to cover a given territory satisfactorily—as determined officially by the Watchtower Society. Example: "Sister, you are to be commended for uprooting your family and relocating to serve in an area where the need is great."

neutrality *noun* 1. Refusal to take sides in international disputes or other worldly conflicts. 2. Refusal to accept induction into the armed forces (or into civilian alternative service prior to May 1996) under conscription. In situations where such a stand by a religious organization compelling obedience on the part of young male members may be illegal, "neutrality" often serves as a convenient code word to conceal the official position of Jehovah's Witnesses when discussing these matters in the hearing of others.

new light   A revised teaching that replaces previously held ideas.

New Order   The post-Armageddon world in which only Jehovah's Witnesses remain alive and paradise has been restored.

new person   Someone just beginning to attend the meetings of Jehovah's Witnesses, as in "The Watchtower Study Conductor knows better than to call on a new person for the answer to such a difficult question."

new personality   Collectively, the improved behavior, changed mannerisms, revised thought patterns, new vocabulary, and reformed attitudes that result from complete submission to the Watchtower indoctrination and training program.

new system   The post-Armageddon world in which only Jehovah's Witnesses remain alive and paradise has been restored.

New Testament   *obsolete* Jehovah's Witnesses refer to the New Testament as the Christian Greek Scriptures or, simply, the Christian Scriptures. Use of the term "New Testament" marks the speaker as a non-Witness.

new truth   A revised teaching that replaces previously held ideas, or a completely novel thought just introduced by the Watchtower Society.

New World   The post-Armageddon world in which only Jehovah's Witnesses remain alive and paradise has been restored.

New World Bible Translation Committee   The anonymous group in charge of producing the *New World Translation of the Holy Scriptures.*

New World Society   *obsolete* The JW organization and its worldwide membership—a term used frequently during the presidency of Nathan Knorr.

New World Translation   The shortened form JWs usually use instead of *New World Translation of the Holy Scriptures.*

New World Translation of the Holy Scriptures The Bible version produced and published by the Watchtower Society with hundreds of verses changed to conform to JW doctrine.

N.H.'s *abbreviation* Not-at-homes.

newspaper gospelling *obsolete* The dissemination of Pastor Russell's weekly sermons through syndication in as many as two thousand secular newspapers in 1913.

nineteen-fourteen generation *See* the generation of 1914.

"no blood" card A business-card-sized medical document Jehovah's Witnesses carry in their wallet or purse declaring their refusal to accept a blood transfusion or blood products if found unconscious and bleeding. Signed, dated, and witnessed with the signatures of two other JWs, the card is intended to serve as a legal document preventing the administration of blood in an emergency.

not-at-homes *slang* A list of addresses where no one answered the door during house-to-house work. Not-at-homes must be visited repeatedly, and the list reduced in size, before the territory can be considered properly worked.

NWT *abbreviation* The JW *New World Translation* of the Bible.

O

obituaries, do the Witnessing by letter to the families of the deceased listed on the obituary page of the local newspaper, when it is possible to obtain their address. This sort of activity is popular among JW shut-ins, but is also resorted to by PIONEERS who are short on their hours as the clock approaches midnight on the last day of the month. Example: "The weather is terrible today, and I feel like I'm catching a cold, so I think I'll stay in and do the obituaries."

objections Arguments raised by a householder interrupting a Witness's door-to-door sermon or presentation. The

most common examples include, "I'm busy," "I'm not interested," "I have my own religion," and "You people were just
here a short time ago." Other objections heard less frequently
include, "You're Communists!" "I'm going to get my gun,"
and "Get off my property, before I call the police!"

Note: JWs are trained to respond to initial objections with
well-rehearsed replies, but to abort their efforts and depart
if objections continue or are threatening in nature.

offer, the   The book or other item specified in *Our Kingdom
Service* as the one JWs should be presenting at the doors during a given month.

O.K.S.   *obsolete abbreviation* The initials of *Our Kingdom
Ministry,* the official title of *Our Kingdom Ministry* between
1976 and 1982.

old light   A former teaching abandoned in favor of a new
doctrinal viewpoint.

old order, the   The evil and corrupt world of today dominated by Satan's political, commercial, and religious organizations—soon to be replaced by a New Order of righteous-
ness and peace when God destroys the non-Witness
population at the Battle of Armageddon.

old system, this   The evil and corrupt world of today dominated by Satan's political, commercial, and religious organizations—soon to be replaced by a new system of right-
eousness and peace when God destroys the non-Witness
population at the Battle of Armageddon.

Old Testament   *obsolete* Jehovah's Witnesses refer to the Old
Testament as THE HEBREW SCRIPTURES. Use of the term "Old
Testament" marks the speaker as a non-Witness.

old world, the   The evil and corrupt society of today dominated by Satan's political, commercial, and religious organizations—soon to be replaced by a New World of right-
eousness and peace when God destroys the non-Witness
population at the Battle of Armageddon.

one of Jehovah's Witnesses   JWs use this expression to
affirm that they are actually witness-bearers of God rather
than members of a denomination named Jehovah's Wit-

nesses. JWs are taught to use this expression in place of "a Jehovah's Witness."

open-minded   An expression applied in door-to-door work to describe favorably a householder willing to listen to Jehovah's Witnesses and to reexamine his or her own religious beliefs; not applicable to a Witness investigating the possibility of leaving to join another religion.

opposer   *noun* A knowledgeable non-Witness who speaks against the sect.

order   *See* New Order, old order.

organization, God's   *See* God's organization, God's earthly organization, God's heavenly organization, and God's universal organization.

organization, Jehovah's   *See* Jehovah's organization, Jehovah's earthly organization, Jehovah's heavenly organization, and Jehovah's universal organization.

organization, Satan's   The entire world outside Jehovah's universal organization. Specifically, all human governments, all non-Witness religious bodies, and all non-JW-owned commercial entities are seen as branches of Satan's organization, and all individuals not part of Jehovah's organization are seen as members of Satan's organization.

organization, the   The Watchtower Bible and Tract Society and its various corporate entities and associated congregations.

other sheep   *theological* Those who will eventually inhabit the earthly paradise, i.e., all true worshipers not of the little flock (from John 10:16).

Our Kingdom Ministry   The current title of an internal monthly publication of four or eight pages featuring instructions for field service and for other aspects of life as a JW.

Note: This publication's name was changed from *Kingdom Ministry* to *Our Kingdom Service* in 1976, when the Society began teaching that rank-and-file JWs were not ministers. Then it was renamed *Our Kingdom Ministry* in 1982, when the Society flip-flopped back to the old teaching. *See* JWL.

Our Kingdom Service   *obsolete* The name of *Our Kingdom Ministry* between the Watchtower Society's 1976 and 1982 doctrinal flip-flops on the proper definition of MINISTER. *See* JWL.

---

overcoming objections

A conversation between a Witness at the door and a householder raising objections might start out something like this:
Witness: "Good morning! My friend and I are calling to share some good news that . . .
Householder: "I'm afraid I'm busy right now. I can't talk."
Witness: "Yes, we realize that people are busy these days, so we just want to tell you briefly that . . ."
Householder: "If you're Jehovah's Witnesses, I'm not interested. I have my own religion."
Witness: "It's encouraging to hear that you do believe in God. So, even though you're not interested in Jehovah's Witnesses, I'm sure you would be interested in the good news that God will soon be intervening in humankind's affairs to . . ."

---

out in service   Engaged in field service, as in "I go out in service every Saturday morning."

outline talk   A public lecture given by a speaker who is supplied a detailed outline, rather than a word-for-word manuscript, by the Watchtower Society.

overcome objections   To answer or put aside arguments raised by a householder that would otherwise put an end to a door-to-door presentation.

overcomer   A Witness who succeeds in remaining faithful despite obstacles.

overseer   *noun* An elder appointed to a position of responsibility. Within the local congregation these are, in descending order of rank, the Presiding Overseer, the Secretary, the Service Overseer, the *Watchtower* Study Conductor, and the Theocratic Ministry School Overseer.

overseer, the   1. The Presiding Overseer or the Congregation Overseer responsible for a particular congregation. 2. The elder in charge in a given situation.

oversight   *noun* The responsibilities or assignment of an overseer or ministerial servant, as in "Brother Dugan has been given oversight over the book room."

Elders and Overseers

The men appointed to the body of elders in a local Jehovah's Witnesses congregation hold that position for life unless disqualified. From among them, individuals are selected to serve indefinite terms as Presiding Overseer, Secretary, Service Overseer, *Watchtower* Study Conductor, and Theocratic Ministry School Overseer. In a congregation with fewer than five elders, some may hold two or more of these positions, while in a congregation with more than five elders, some may not hold a position of oversight.

P

paradise, the spiritual   The condition in which Jehovah's Witnesses find themselves today, enlightened and cared for by God's earthly organization.

paradise, the   1. The post-Armageddon world with perfect conditions restored, inhabited only by JWs and resurrected persons. 2. The original Garden of Eden.

paradise earth, the   The post-Armageddon world with perfect conditions restored, inhabited only by JWs and resurrected persons.

paradise of God, the   The heavenly realm inherited by the 144,000 anointed ones.

parousia   *theological* (Greek="coming"; Matthew 24:3 KJV) 1. Christ's second coming in 1914, unseen by human eyes. 2. *obsolete* Christ's second coming in 1874, unseen by human eyes, as proclaimed by *Zion's Watch Tower and Herald of Christ's Presence.*

part, a A speaking or acting part on a JW meeting or assembly program—considered a privilege, and hence often handed out as a favor or reward by the overseer in charge.

partake *verb* To drink from the cup and eat some of the unleavened bread at the annual Memorial service—a privilege reserved for the remnant of the 144,000.

partaker, a Someone who professes to be of the anointed remnant and who demonstrates this by drinking from the cup and eating some of the unleavened bread at the annual JW Memorial service—a privilege reserved for the 144,000. The sect reported worldwide attendance of 12,288,917 in 1994, including 8,617 partakers. *See* AJWSBS.

pastor *obsolete* Although still employed with regard to Charles Taze Russell ("Pastor Russell"), the term "pastor" has no other current usage among Jehovah's Witnesses and is intentionally avoided when referring to modern JW clergyman—who claim to be untitled and not clergymen.

Pastor Russell Charles Taze Russell (1852–1916), founder and first president of the Watchtower Bible and Tract Society. After associating with Adventists for ten years and serving as assistant editor of an Adventist paper, in 1879 he led a splinter group that broke from that denomination to publish his new magazine *Zion's Watch Tower.* To these "Russellites" he assigned the name International Bible Students Association. Using interpretations from the Bible and the Great Pyramid of Egypt, Russell predicted future events, including the rapture of the church and the end of the world, for various dates in the early 1900s. He died shortly after all of these proved false. Today his body lies buried next to the Society's huge stone pyramid marker in a Pittsburgh, Pennsylvania cemetery. When successor J. F. Rutherford tried to lead the BIBLE STUDENTS off into a new direction, they split up into several factions: various independent Bible Students groups, and Rutherford's followers, whom he renamed Jehovah's Witnesses.

perfect, perfection   *noun* The state of sinlessness and restored health to be achieved by obedient humans toward the end of Christ's thousand-year reign. Example: "The tendency to overeat will be gone when we reach perfection," or "when we become perfect."

persecution   *noun* Any speech or act perceived as hostile toward Jehovah's Witnesses or directed against an individual Witness on account of his religion. *See* box.

---

persecution

Most outside observers would agree that Jehovah's Witnesses suffered persecution when imprisoned in Nazi concentration camps along with Jews, homosexuals, and groups Hitler targeted. But JWs also cry "Persecution!" when refusal to sell cigarettes results in dismissal from a store clerk's job. They invoke the same expression when a judge issues a court order for a blood transfusion to be administered to a Witness child who would die without it. Also, when householders awakened early on a weekend morning become enraged at Witnesses ringing doorbells. Yet, although they view such "persecution" as hostility provoked by Satan the Devil, JWs welcome it and rejoice whenever persecuted because they have been taught to see this as proof that theirs is the one true religion.

---

personal decision   **1.** A matter left to the individual conscience with no binding directive issued by the organization. *Compare* conscience matter. **2.** Ostensibly, a choice left up to each individual's free will, but actually forced by organizational dictates. Examples: whether or not to accept a blood transfusion, or whether or not to accept employment banned by the sect.

Note: When this expression is used in Watchtower publications, it is usually necessary to examine the context in order to determine which definition is meant. Even then, the wording may be so subtle that only experienced Witnesses, such as elders, can discern clearly the intended meaning. Consider, for example, these instructions regarding compulsory military service found in the May 1, 1996 *Watchtower* on page 19:

What, though, if the Christian lives in a land where exemption is not granted to ministers of religion? Then he will have to make a personal decision following his Bible-trained conscience. (Galatians 6:5) While taking the authority of Caesar into account, he will weigh carefully what he owes to Jehovah. (Psalm 36:9; 116:12–14; Acts 17:28) The Christian will remember that the mark of a true Christian is love for all his fellow believers, even those who live in other lands or those belonging to other tribes. (John 13:34, 35; 1 Peter 2:17) Further, he will not forget the Scriptural principles found in texts such as Isaiah 2:2–4; Matthew 26:52; Romans 12:18; 14:19; 2 Corinthians 10:4; and Hebrews 12:14.

When this appeared in print, even some experienced countercult workers told me they understood it to mean JWs could now choose for themselves whether or not to accept military service. But I explained to them that language and verses cited proved that such was not the case at all. The Watchtower Society meant this the same way it meant similar statements that it is up to each JW to decide whether to take a blood transfusion—that is, it is up to each one to decide whether or not to break the rules and get expelled from the organization and condemned by God.

personal study   Examination of Watchtower books and magazines with a view toward finding in each paragraph the answers to questions printed at the bottom of each page, as well as reading articles that lack such study questions.

pew   *noun* A benchlike seat found in pseudochristian churches but not in Jehovah's Witness Kingdom Halls—or at least not called by that name when a JW meetingplace does feature similar seats, temporarily, before other seating can be arranged. Metal-and-plastic folding chairs or linked-together chairs are most common in American Kingdom Halls.

phonograph record A recording of one of Judge Rutherford's talks played at householders' doors on a windup portable machine prior to the institution of Theocratic Ministry School speech training for rank-and-file Jehovah's Witnesses.

pioneer *noun* A witness assigned the privilege of full-time service either permanently or temporarily. For the various categories of pioneer, *see* auxiliary pioneer, regular pioneer, special pioneer, temporary pioneer, vacation pioneer. *verb* To engage in full-time service.

pioneer partner A pioneer permanently working in service with another; pioneer partners often room together as well.

pioneer rate *obsolete* The deeply discounted price pioneers paid for magazines and books to be resold to the public at list price, with the greater profit margin aiding the pioneer financially to help him or her remain in full-time service. For example, the price list issued by the Watchtower Society to literature servants in each congregation might have indicated that a certain book with a twenty-five-cent list price should be sold to CONGREGATION PUBLISHERS for twenty cents but to PIONEERS for five cents each.

pioneer work Full-time service as an appointed PIONEER, as in "I'm so glad that your son has taken up the pioneer work!"

pioneering Serving as a pioneer.

place *verb* To sell—a euphemism to avoid the sales connotation and any related taxes, licenses, restrictions, and so on. Example: "I managed to place two books this morning, one with a man who contributed five dollars and one with a woman whose donation consisted of a large can of soup."

placement(s) *noun* Watchtower literature sold to non-Witnesses, as in "My placements for the month amounted to eighteen magazines and three books."

plan In current JW thinking only humans make plans or plan for the future, whereas God has a purpose and therefore he purposes things for the future.

Note: Contrast *The Divine Plan of the Ages,* volume one of Watchtower founder Charles Taze Russell's *Studies in the Scriptures,* written well before his successors introduced this semantic distinction.

platform, the   The speaker's platform at Kingdom Hall. JWs say "the platform" in much the same way that churchgoers say "the pulpit," as in "It would be inappropriate to make such a crude remark from the platform."

Plymouth Bethel   *obsolete* The 13-17 Hicks Street mission building of Brooklyn's Plymouth Congregational Church (once pastored by Henry Ward Beecher), purchased in 1908 by the Watchtower organization to house new offices in New York as well as an auditorium. The structure was renamed "Brooklyn Tabernacle," and the "Bethel" name was transferred to the four-story brownstone at 124 Columbia Heights, which had served as Beecher's residence and which was purchased as livingquarters for the Watchtower Society's headquarters staff.

Power of Attorney   A legal document each JW is expected to prepare giving power of attorney for life-and-death medical matters to another Witness, usually one's mate if married, but often an unrelated elder in the local congregation. (Non-Witness family members have been heard to refer to this document as the Witness's *Death Warrant.*)

preach   *verb* To speak to non-Witnesses about religious matters in door-to-door work, at home Bible studies, or informally at other opportunities.

preacher   *noun* Anyone who shares in the work of spreading the JW message from house to house or at other opportunities.

preaching work, the   The house-to-house ministry and home Bible study ministry carried on by Jehovah's Witnesses.

premature expectations   *euphemism* The Watchtower Society's false prophecies concerning the end of the world. For example, instead of saying, "The Society proved wrong in its prediction that the autumn of 1975 was the likely time for Armageddon," Witnesses who are forced to comment on the

---

On Sunday, *preachers* listen from their seats.

In Jehovah's Witness terminology the elder who addresses the congregation for forty-five minutes on Sunday morning is not the preacher preaching a sermon from his pulpit as would be said in other churches; rather, he is the speaker giving or delivering a public talk or public lecture from the platform. Most of the people listening in the audience, however, are preachers because they preach by delivering their sermons on householders' doorsteps in the public preaching work in their territory.

---

situation at all would be more likely to put it this way: "Some of Jehovah's people entertained expectations for that year that proved to be premature."

presence *theological*   1. Christ's second coming in 1914, unseen by human eyes. 2. *obsolete* Christ's second coming in 1874, unseen by human eyes, as proclaimed by *Zion's Watch Tower and Herald of Christ's Presence.*

presentation   *noun* A prepared sales pitch found in *Our Kingdom Ministry* or developed independently and used when offering literature door to door.

presiding overseer   The head elder in a local JW congregation, appointed to preside over meetings of the body of elders and in other ways to provide leadership.

princes, the   1. Men who will rule on earth as visible representatives of the heavenly kingdom of God during Christ's thousand-year reign after Armageddon. 2. *obsolete* Old Testament patriarchs and prophets expected to appear by resurrection during the 1930s and 1940s to rule the earth from the Watchtower Society's Beth-Sarim mansion in San Diego. *Note:* The second definition was dropped in favor of the first after a 1950 JW convention at Yankee Stadium, where Watchtower Vice President Frederick Franz announced that the "princes of the new earth" had finally arrived and were present at the stadium—only to silence the wild applause of his audience with the further announcement that many of these

109

princes would be appointed from among the sect's modern-day members there assembled, rather than exclusively from resurrected Old Testament personalities as previously taught.

private reproof The mildest form of discipline handed down by a judicial committee to a JW found guilty but repentant—essentially a scolding by the elders in private with no announcement made to the congregation. This may be accompanied by loss of privileges in the congregation.

privilege 1. Any sought-after position, assignment, or responsibility in the organization, such as pioneering, serving as an overseer, or carrying microphones to the audience at a Kingdom Hall meeting. 2. *sarcastic* An undesirable assignment such as washing dishes at a convention kitchen or cleaning Kingdom Hall toilets.

probation *obsolete* An old version of reproof in which emphasis was placed on good behavior during a fixed probationary term.

program, the The series of speaking parts, songs, announcements, and so on, composing a JW meeting at Kingdom Hall or at an assembly, as in "Brother Rollins assigned me a five-minute part on this afternoon's program."

progress *noun* Growing acceptance of Watchtower teachings (by a prospective convert).

progressive understanding *euphemism* The Watchtower organization's changing teachings and doctrinal flip-flops.

Prohibition *obsolete* An evil satanic plot. Watchtower President J. F. Rutherford devoted a major radio address to denouncing Prohibition and then published the denunciation in booklet form. Known to insiders as a heavy drinker, Rutherford reportedly used the organization's Canadian branch to smuggle liquor across the border for his own consumption during Prohibition.

prophecy *noun* 1. A prediction of future events made by a genuine divine spokesman or by an impostor. 2. A term that does *not* apply to the Watchtower Society's failed predictions that the world would end in 1914, 1918, 1925, and then 1975 because "Jehovah's Witnesses, in their eagerness for Jesus' second coming" merely "suggested dates that turned out to be incorrect." (*Awake!* March 22, 1993, page 4. Amazingly, on the same page featuring this denial *Awake!*'s masthead proclaims this obvious prophecy: "the Creator's promise of a peaceful and secure new world before the generation that saw the events of 1914 passes away.")

prophet   *noun* **1.** Any of the Old Testament characters, such as Ezekiel and Jeremiah, who acted as God's spokesmen, performed miracles, and foretold future events. **2.** The Jehovah's Witness organization today, in its claimed role as God's spokesman or channel of communication. **3.** A role the JW organization says it has *never* claimed for itself.

Note: Although definitions #2 and #3 contradict each other, both must be accepted and believed. The organization employs definition #2 when asserting its authority over members and definition #3 when trying to escape responsibility for failed predictions.

a prophet *yet* not a prophet

In a classic example of Orwellian doublethink, Jehovah's Witnesses learn to think of their organization as God's prophet and, at the same time, *not* a prophet at all. These contradictory notions, both of which must be believed simultaneously, are reflected in these quotes from *The Watchtower:*

"Whom has God actually used as his prophet? . . . Jehovah's witnesses are deeply grateful today that the plain facts show that God has been pleased to use them."—January 15, 1959, pages 40–41

"Thus this group of anointed followers of Jesus Christ, doing a work in Christendom paralleling Ezekiel's work among the Jews, were manifestly the modern-day Ezekiel, the 'prophet' commissioned by Jehovah . . . these followers of Christ embraced the name 'Jehovah's Witnesses' . . ."—April 1, 1972, pages 198–99

"Jehovah's Witnesses . . . do not claim infallibility or perfection. Neither are they inspired prophets."—May 15, 1976, page 297

(For several similar quotes, see INDEX, pages 112–13.)

Public Lecture   The public talk, the talk given at the Pᴜʙʟɪᴄ Mᴇᴇᴛɪɴɢ.

Public Meeting   A Kingdom Hall session usually held on Sunday morning or afternoon featuring a forty-five-minute address aimed at the general public (although non-JW visitors in the audience are normally very few).

public reproof   A moderate form of discipline more severe than private reproof but milder than ᴅɪsғᴇʟʟᴏᴡsʜɪᴘᴘɪɴɢ, handed down by a judicial committee to a JW found guilty but repentant in a case that the congregation already knows about or that must be brought to the attention of the congregation—essentially a public announcement that an individual has sinned but has also repented and been forgiven. This is usually accompanied by loss of privileges in the congregation.

public speaker   A male Witness, usually an elder from the local area, who delivers the public talk, usually on Sunday morning.

Public Talk   A forty-five-minute address prepared with a non-Witness audience in mind and given at the Sunday Public Meeting at Kingdom Hall.

publications, the   Books and magazines produced by the Watchtower Society, as in "You can't expect to stay spiritually healthy if you don't read the publications."

publications index   A reference work published annually by the Watchtower Society indexing significant contents of the prior calendar year's publications, or one published every few years referencing publications released during a span of five years or longer.

publisher file   A collection of Pᴜʙʟɪsʜᴇʀ's Rᴇᴄᴏʀᴅ Cᴀʀᴅs maintained by each congregation, containing information on active Witnesses and others associated with the congregation.

publisher   A JW or associated individual approved to participate in field service and for whom a Pᴜʙʟɪsʜᴇʀ's Rᴇᴄᴏʀᴅ Cᴀʀᴅ exists in the local congregation's files.

publisher rate   *obsolete* The discounted price congregation publishers paid for books to be resold to the public at list price, with the small profit margin helping toward the cost of driving an automobile to the territory, and so on. For example, the 1968 book, *The Truth That Leads to Eternal Life*, was sold to the public at the list price of twenty-five cents but was sold to congregation publishers for twenty cents.

publisher's card   *See* Publisher's Record Card.

Publisher's Record Card   An index card maintained by the local JW congregation for each individual approved to participate in field service. The card features the person's name, address, telephone number, date of birth, and other vital information, and is used for permanently recording the number of hours he or she reports in field service each month. Also noted on the card are special privileges of service, such as pioneering, and any disciplinary actions taken by the congregation. If an individual transfers to a different congregation or moves to another city, the elders of the new congregation must receive the PUBLISHER'S RECORD CARD before accepting the person into the congregation.

pulpit   The speaker's stand from which a clergyman addresses his flock in church—hence a word with negative connotations for Jehovah's Witnesses. Their elders speak from THE PLATFORM, never from a pulpit, in Witness terminology.

pure language   Biblical truth, as defined by the beliefs, practices, and lifestyle of Jehovah's Witnesses. "Why should you be concerned about speaking the pure language? For one thing, because your life depends upon learning and speaking it" (*The Watchtower,* May 1, 1991, page 13). This term is taken from Zephaniah 3:9, "For then will I turn to the people a pure language, that they may all call upon the name of the LORD, to serve him with one consent" (KJV). *Compare* theocratic language.

purple triangle, *Purple Triangles*   **1.** The patch of purple cloth that identified Jehovah's Witnesses in Nazi concentration camps. **2.** *Purple Triangles* is the title of a Watchtower video about JWs imprisoned in the Nazi camps.

purpose   In current JW thinking only humans make plans or plan for the future, whereas God has a purpose and therefore He purposes things for the future.

Note: See the 1974 Watchtower book *God's "Eternal Purpose" Now Triumphing for Man's Good.*
See JWL.

Q

question, to; questioning   Any admission by a Witness that he or she has doubts or uncertainties about the validity of one or more Watchtower teachings. To question the Watchtower organization or its teachings is seen as an indication of disloyalty attributable to spiritual weakness or unfaithfulness.

Question Box   A column featured frequently in the internal monthly *Our Kingdom Ministry* and used to issue instructions regarding organizational policy and procedure as well as personal conduct. Topics have included such matters as these: whether a Witness may properly associate with a congregation if he or she lives outside its territory boundaries (March 1976); the attitude to display when asked to leave a building (November 1965); eligibility to perform marriage ceremonies (December 1981); and whether Witnesses may properly display the Tetragrammaton on jewelry, automobiles, or other items (September 1974). Answers are held to be authoritative and binding unless or until superseded by a later Question Box or article on the same subject.

questions, the   After going over the questions (more than a hundred doctrinal questions listed in an organizational manual) with one or more elders, a new convert is accepted for baptism.

Questions from Readers   A column featured frequently in *The Watchtower* magazine used to issue new teachings or clarifications of old teachings regarding doctrine or doctrinally related issues of personal conduct. Issues addressed have included these: whether Adam and Eve were predestined to die (March 15, 1985); whether to stand during the playing of the national anthem (January 15, 1974); when dinosaurs were created and when they became extinct (July 15, 1973); whether a Witness may raise or lower a flag (January 15, 1977); why Jesus cursed the fig tree (February 1, 1972); and whether it would be proper to use pet food containing blood (October 15, 1981). Answers are held to be authoritative and binding unless or until superseded by a later Questions from Readers or other articles on the same subject.

quick build, quick built A Kingdom Hall constructed by volunteer labor over a three-day weekend. Example: "The North Ridge Kingdom Hall was a quick build put up last year."

quota *obsolete; noun* The number of hours set by the organization as a monthly or annual target for JW pioneers. Now referred to as a goal.

R

rate, pioneer *See* pioneer rate.

rate, publisher *See* publisher rate.

reaching out *verb* A male JW is reaching out when he is exerting himself to prove worthy of a privilege of service in the congregation.

reference Bible or **reference edition** The *New World Translation of the Holy Scriptures With References,* the current JW Bible with copious footnotes, cross-references, and supplementary articles.

Regional, the The area's Regional Building Committee.

Regional Building Committee Elders who direct the quick-build Kingdom Hall construction projects in a particular area.

regular *adjective* (A publisher) having reported time for each of the preceding six months.

regular auxiliary pioneer One who serves as an auxiliary pioneer month after month, on a continuing basis.

regular pioneer A Witness appointed permanently to the category of full-time service with an annual goal of one thousand hours (formerly twelve hundred hours).

regular publisher A Witness who has reported time for each of the preceding six months.

Note: Only regular publishers are considered for appointments and certain privileges.

regulating   *See* mental regulating.

reinstate, reinstated, reinstatement   Restoration to fellowship after a period of shunning due to being disfellowshipped. One elder might say to another, "The judicial committee decided to reinstate Jerry Johnson; his reinstatement will be announced at tonight's meeting."

release(s)   1. *noun* New Watchtower books, booklets, tapes, or CDs announced and made available, usually at a district convention. Example: "We just got home from the assembly. Here, let me show you the new releases." 2. *verb* To make such new items available. Example: "We're anticipating that the Society will release at least one new book at this convention."

religion   *obsolete* False religion. Prior to 1951, the organization taught that the word "religion" applied only to the false variety. So, JWs practiced true *worship,* whereas all other sects represented *religion*—a satanic counterfeit of true worship.

Note: It was with this definition in mind (and ignoring the ordinary reader's understanding of the word) that second Watchtower president J. F. Rutherford's 1929 book *Life* declares in its Publisher's Preface, "This is not a religious book." JWs did not see this as a lie, due to their private definition of the term. However, they knew the sense in which the word was used by the rest of the population to whom they offered the book.

religionist   *noun* A member or adherent of a false religion (any religion other than Jehovah's Witnesses).

remaining ones   *See* remnant.

remnant   The remaining ones of the anointed class still alive on earth today or at any particular time during the last days, officially tallied at the annual Memorial and currently reported as numbering between eight thousand and nine thousand—the tiny minority of JWs who profess the heavenly hope.

rendezvous   *obsolete; noun* A private home used as a place for JWs to meet prior to going out in field service. Now called a meeting place for service.

report   *noun* 1. A form listing a JW's field service hours and literature placements, usually turned in monthly. 2. *verb* To hand in such a form. Example: "I'm now an irregular publisher, because I failed to report in September."

report time   To hand in a field service report listing activity for the month.

representative   *noun* One sent by or acting as an agent for another. However, JWs visiting people's homes are *not* representatives of their organization. *See* box.

Do JWs represent their organization?

As agents representing the Watchtower Society individual JWs solicit monies from door to door, and the local congregation then sends these monies on to the headquarters organization. Furthermore, according to *The Watchtower* of February 1, 1952, page 79, it is "Through its legal agency, the Watchtower Society," that the JW leadership "provides the spiritual food in printed form, arranges for meetings, organizes service activities, sends out special traveling representatives and missionaries," and so on.

Yet the Witnesses who are sent out knocking on doors with those printed materials are instructed to "avoid representing themselves as agents or representatives of the Watchtower Bible and Tract Society" (their internal monthly *Our Kingdom Ministry,* February 1989, page 3).

Why this contradictory use of language? The very next sentence in *Our Kingdom Ministry* begins, "In case of an accident or an emergency or if problems are encountered while working trailer parks, apartments, or certain other territory . . ." Evidently the Watchtower Society wants to avoid any legal liability for its "representatives" in case of accidents, so they must then deny being its "representatives."

---

reprints   *noun* Bound volumes collecting the 1879–1919 issues of Zion's Watch Tower.

reproof   *noun See* public reproof *or* private reproof.

reprove   To give public reproof or private reproof. Example: "The judicial committee decided not to disfellowship Janice, but rather to reprove her privately."

research   Research *in Watchtower publications* is understood when JWs say simply that they are going to do some research.

resolution   A formal motion proposed by the elders and voted on by a local congregation—usually approving a special expenditure of congregation funds or a change in meeting times.

restriction   A limitation placed by a judicial committee on the privileges or activities of a reproved or reinstated Witness. Example: "The elders have lifted all of Tom's restrictions, except that he still can't represent the congregation in prayer, and he mustn't allow himself to be alone with Maria."

Rev., reverend   A clergyman's title never employed by JW clergy (who claim not to be clergy) and omitted by JWs when referring to clergymen of other faiths.

return visit   *noun* A planned stop at the home of a householder who has previously shown interest. The number of return visits made is to be entered on a monthly report.

ridiculer   *noun* An opposer (from 2 Peter 3:3 NWT).

Rooming Department   The division of a district convention organization responsible for securing accommodations for the tens of thousands who will attend, and assigning families and individuals to rooms. The department negotiates group rates with hotels and motels but also secures less expensive rooms in private homes, sometimes by door-to-door solicitation.

run ahead, to   The disloyal act of speculating or expressing a personal opinion on a matter of biblical prophecy or interpretation not covered by or explained differently by the Watchtower Society's publications.

Russell   Charles Taze Russell founded the Watchtower organization and served as its first president. *See* Pastor Russell.

Russellite, a   A follower of Pastor Russell—a term originally applied by outsiders to persons associated with the Watchtower organization, but now applied by Jehovah's Witnesses to members of the Bible Students groups that rejected J. F. Rutherford's leadership.

Rutherford   Joseph Franklin Rutherford (1869–1942), the Watchtower Society's second president, exercised one-man rule over the JW organization from shortly after Pastor Russell's death in 1916 until his own demise. He authored most of the sect's books and booklets published during his administration.

S

S-3   The Study Report form, occasionally referred to by this form number.

S-4   The Field Service Report form, occasionally referred to by this form number.

salvation, saved   Survival of the Battle of Armageddon to live in the restored earthly paradise to follow. Hence JWs do not regard salvation as presently attainable; their aim is to maintain loyalty to the organization until Armageddon, so that their lives may be saved at that time.

Satan   Witnesses believe Satan the Devil to be a cherubic angel who was appointed overseer of the newly inhabited earth, but who then rebelled against God by misleading Eve into tempting Adam to sin.

Satan's organization   Non-Witness religions, all of earth's governments, as well as commercial and educational institutions form part of Satan the Devil's organization, which JWs believe embraces the rest of humankind in its membership. "Everyone belongs either to Jehovah's organization, or to the devil's," is typical Witness thinking.

SCE:SSE   (example) Code identifying the desk and the individual writer of an anonymous letter from Watchtower headquarters. Both form letters and personal correspondence responding to congregations and to individuals are usually anonymous and are signed with a rubber stamp signature, such as "Watch Tower B&T Society" or "The Governing Body."

school, the   1. Usually, the Theocratic Ministry School. **2.** In some contexts, Gilead School, the Kingdom Ministry School, Pioneer School, or another special educational program run by the Society.

second death, the   Annihilation in the Lake of Fire or Gehenna. *See* JWASBS and JWAVBV.

Secretary   *noun* The title of the elder appointed to care for all correspondence between the local congregation and the Watch Tower Society's Branch Office. Because he can put his own twist on letters to the Society, the Secretary is the second-most-powerful elder, next to the Presiding Overseer.

Seed of Abraham   *theological* Jesus Christ plus 144,000 chosen followers.

sell   *verb* JWs vehemently deny that their literature distribution constitutes selling, even when the item is imprinted with a price and is exchanged for that amount of money.

separating work   1. *current definition* Helping people now to choose which side they will be on when God destroys the rest of humankind and preserves only Jehovah's Witnesses at Armageddon. **2.** *obsolete* Sharing under angelic direction in Christ's work of separating the sheep from the goats since 1914 in fulfillment of Matthew 25:31–33. (JWs who had believed this separating work was in progress ever since 1914 were suddenly told in the November 1, 1995 *Watchtower* that the sheep and goats would not be separated until later.)

sermon   *noun* A prepared message presented on the doorstep during house-to-house work. In JW usage, the forty-five-minute public address given on Sunday morning at Kingdom Hall is not a sermon but a talk.

servant   A male JW appointed to a position of responsibility in the Watchtower organization—nowadays usually in the lower ranks of the hierarchy in local congregations. Examples: ministerial servant, literature servant, circuit servant (obsolete), district servant (obsolete), and so on.

service *noun* 1. Field service—door-to-door literature distribution, return visits, home Bible studies, and other activity reportable to the Society. 2. Any activity performed for the Society, such as at a Watchtower printing factory or farm, or in the district or circuit work.

service bag *See* book bag.

Service Department The division of the headquarters organization that oversees the local congregations and the circuit and district overseers. Handling questions from local elders by letter and by telephone, the Service Department sometimes becomes involved with local judicial committee cases.

Service Meeting A one-hour weekly gathering at Kingdom Hall, usually on Thursday or Friday evening, providing instruction in field service activity and in daily conduct. *Our Kingdom Ministry* provides outlines and some detailed information for each meeting. Of all the congregation meetings, the Service Meeting is the one least aimed at the visiting public and most strongly directed at Witnesses themselves. Not to be confused with the MEETING FOR SERVICE.

service year The period from September 1 through August 31 of the following year—used in place of the calendar year for accumulating and reporting field service activity, in much the same way that a fiscal year is used by businesses or an academic year by schools. (For example, the 1998 service year begins September 1, 1997, and ends August 31, 1998.)

setting The imaginary circumstances in a role-playing segment on the service meeting or in a woman's student talk in the Theocratic Ministry School. Example: "My setting is at the outside door of an apartment building in house-to-house ministry."

sheep, a *slang* A worldly person who appears to be responding favorably to the message preached by Jehovah's Witnesses (derived from the Watchtower interpretation of Matthew 25:32–40).

sheep, other *theological* Those who will eventually inhabit the earthly paradise, all true worshipers not of the little flock (from John 10:16).

sheol   *Hebrew* Humankind's common grave, actually nonexistence rather than a place where the dead are conscious. *See* JWASBS and JWAVBV.

sick   *See* spiritually sick.

simplified literature distribution arrangement   An alternative name for the COMPLETE DONATION ARRANGEMENT. Rather than acknowledge tax evasion as a financial motive for the new approach to literature distribution, the Watchtower Society introduced it to followers as a simplified arrangement that would facilitate accomplishing the work. *See* complete donation arrangement.

sister   *slang* A female baptized Witness.

Note: When a male JW addresses a female Witness as "Sister," this sometimes carries the connotation of putting her down, reminding her that her proper role is that of subjection to male direction—although in most contexts there is no negative connotation attached to this term, as when "brothers and sisters" are spoken of in the third person.

six-month average   The average hours from a Witness's field service reports for the previous six months. Example: "The elders have called me to meet with them because my six-month average has dropped to three hours."

Society, the   **1.** The headquarters organization in Brooklyn. **2.** Collectively, the Watchtower Bible and Tract Society and associated corporate bodies

Society's reprints, the   A 1919 seven-volume hardcover collection of articles reprinted from the 1879–1919 *Watchtower* magazines.

Son of God   **1.** Michael, the first angel God created, who became like a son to him and who later entered Mary's womb to be born as Jesus. **2.** Adam, the first man created to live in the Garden of Eden. **3.** Any of the 144,000 anointed Witnesses.

song   *noun* A hymn used at Kingdom Hall. Today's JWs insist on calling these songs and are highly offended if these are referred to as HYMNS, although they were freely called that at Watchtower meetings during the late 1800s and early 1900s.

songbook *noun* A book of hymns published by the Watchtower Society and used at Kingdom Hall. During the late 1800s and early 1900s these were called HYMNALS, but today's JWs call them songbooks and are highly offended if anyone calls them hymnals. *See* JWL.

sons of God 1. The 144,000 anointed ones. 2. The angels.

soul *noun* 1. A living human or animal. 2. A person's life or an animal's life.

Note: Jehovah's Witnesses are taught to totally reject the concept of an immaterial soul that survives the death of the body. *See* AJWSBS and JWAVBV.

sound servant The ministerial servant or helper responsible for operating the microphones and amplifier at Kingdom Hall or at a JW convention.

souvenir convention report *obsolete* A booklet or paperback book published between 1904 and 1969 in connection with a large district or international convention, featuring photographs taken at the gathering and promoting new publications released there (also called simply "convention report").

speak *verb* 1. To deliver a Sunday public talk to a congregation. 2. To handle any speaking assignment at a congregation meeting or convention.

speaker, the *noun* The male Witness, usually an elder, who delivers a Sunday public talk to a congregation.

special pioneer A JW appointed to the position of full-time service with the highest goal in hours, 140 hours per month. Special pioneers are usually very effective at what they do and are often sent into relatively virgin territory not regularly covered by a JW congregation. This is the highest organizational position open to a large number of women, ranking immediately below missionaries and traveling overseers' wives.

Speech Counsel Slip A Watchtower form issued to each Witness enrolled as a student in the Theocratic Ministry School and used by the school overseer to grade the student's performance in giving talks.

Spirit, the   The Holy Spirit, though usually not capitalized in Jehovah's Witness usage. *See* holy spirit.

spirit   *noun* **1.** The impersonal life-force found in each of the body cells of both humans and animals. (JWs deny that humans have a spirit that survives death. Rather, the human spirit is seen as equivalent to the electricity powering a machine: it leaves the body at death in much the same way that electricity leaves a machine that is shut off, but it does not continue to exist apart from the physical body.) **2.** God's holy spirit or impersonal active force by which he accomplishes things. **3.** A living being with an immaterial body. Examples: Jehovah God is a spirit, angels and demons are spirits, and Christ was raised a spirit, according to Watchtower teaching. **4.** An individual's dominant characteristics, as in "Joanne has a humble spirit and always puts others ahead of herself." *See* AJWSBS and JWAVBV.

spiritual food   The publications and meeting programs provided by the Watchtower Society.

spiritual Israel   The 144,000 spirit-anointed believers from Pentecost, A.D. 33 to present.

spiritual Israelite   A member of the 144,000.

spiritually sick   Having a poor relationship with God and a poor moral character, as evidenced by failure to maintain field service activity and meeting attendance, or by abandoning one or more Watchtower teachings.

spiritually weak   Experiencing difficulties in maintaining a good relationship with God and in danger of slipping morally, as evidenced by low or declining hours reported in field service activity or by failure to study Watchtower publications regularly.

split   *verb* Divide into two congregations. Example: "When we increased to 150 publishers, the Boxtown Congregation split to form the North Boxtown Congregation and the South Boxtown Congregation."

Note: A JW congregation will split when warranted by growth beyond recommended numbers or limited seating capacity in an existing Kingdom Hall. A congregation will not split over dissention, as this would simply result in the expulsion of dissenting individuals.

spokesman, God's   The Watchtower organization in its role as the channel of communication from God.

stake   *noun* The upright pole, without a crossbeam, on which Christ was impaled, according to the Watchtower Society and its *New World Translation*. Also called torture stake.

stand, take (one's)   To declare oneself on Jehovah's side by dedication and baptism, or verbally declaring one's intention to join Jehovah's Witnesses.

star of Bethlehem   In the JW view of the Christmas story, a supernatural manifestation produced by the Devil to lead evil astrologers to the baby Jesus as part of a satanic plot to have the Christ-child killed.

start your time   To make your first call of the day or of a particular witnessing period, since reportable time is measured from your first call to your last call. Example: "Brother Jones, you'll be driving fifteen minutes before we reach the territory. Please pull over right now, so I can start my time by leaving a tract at one of these homes we're passing." Pioneers with a set goal to reach are usually the Witnesses most concerned with starting their time.

steeple   *noun* An obscene phallic symbol drawn from pagan sex worship and used to adorn Christendom's churches as an indication of their satanic orientation. JW Kingdom Halls do not have steeples; if a former church is purchased as a Kingdom Hall, the steeple is removed.

street witnessing   Field service activity accomplished by standing on a busy sidewalk and displaying Watchtower literature (usually magazines) or by walking with the foot traffic, approaching pedestrians and offering them literature. *Note:* Street witnessing is typically carried on by pioneers who try to reach their monthly goal in hours by starting their time early in the morning, perhaps at 7 A.M., outside a subway station. This enables them to witness to commuters at an hour when it would be considered rude to be ringing doorbells.

street work   *slang* See street witnessing.

student   *noun* 1. A prospective convert with whom a weekly Bible study is conducted. **2.** An individual enrolled in the Theocratic Ministry School.

student talk   A five- or six-minute presentation given at the Theocratic Ministry School by a sister or by a young or inexperienced brother, after which the School Overseer offers constructive criticism.

study   *noun* 1. A weekly lesson conducted by a Witness with a non-Witness or unbaptized child. **2.** A non-JW receiving such lessons, as in "Did you meet my study, Janice, who came to last night's meeting?"

study article   An article in *The Watchtower* magazine featuring study questions for each paragraph at the bottom of the page. Two or three study articles usually form the core of each issue of *The Watchtower* and serve as the focus of discussion in the weekly Watchtower Study Meeting.

Study Report   A Watchtower form Witnesses use to report the home Bible studies they conduct with prospective converts. The overseers who collect the reports thus learn the name and address of each new student, as well as details concerning the material studied and progress made.

study questions   The numbered questions corresponding to numbered paragraphs and found at the bottom of pages in most of the Watchtower Society's books and *Watchtower* magazine STUDY ARTICLES.

stumble   1. *verb; transitive* To cause someone to lose faith in or draw away from God's organization, as in "You stumbled my new student by the ethnic jokes you made after the meeting." **2.** *verb; intransitive* To lose faith in or draw away from God's organization, as in the prayer "Jehovah God, please help me not to stumble over these doctrinal changes!"

stumbling block   Something that causes someone to stumble, as in "The blood issue became a stumbling block to Mr. and Mrs. Roberts, and they stopped their study."

subjection   *noun* Submissive obedience, as in "A theocratic sister will always show that she is in subjection to her husband."

subscription(s)   *noun* Enrollments to receive *The Watchtower* and / or *Awake!* magazines regularly, usually through the mail. For example, a Witness returning from a morning of door-to-door work might gleefully exclaim, "I obtained four subscriptions!"

Note: Prior to April 1990, *The Watchtower* and *Awake!* listed "$5.00 (U.S.) per year" as their subscription price. Now a set price is no longer charged.

suggested contribution   The euphemistic expression used instead of "price" during the period when the Society attempted to charge a set amount for literature without "selling" it.

suggested donation   The euphemistic expression used instead of "price" during the period when the Society attempted to charge a set amount for literature without "selling" it.

Sunday school   A feature of Christendom's churches foreign to Jehovah's Witness Kingdom Halls, where separate programs for children are regarded as inappropriate.

Sunday meetings   The public talk and Watchtower Study meetings, usually but not always held on Sunday morning or afternoon.

symbolize ... dedication   To get baptized, as in "You will have opportunity to symbolize your dedication at the assembly."

T

tacking   The Watchtower Society's pattern of back-and-forth changes in doctrine, described in positive terms as comparable to a sailboat's "tacking into the wind," as illustrated in the December 1, 1981 *Watchtower* magazine on page 27.

talk   *noun* **1.** A forty-five-minute public address given at the Sunday public meeting at Kingdom Hall. **2.** Any of the assigned presentations given from the platform at a meeting or assembly.

Note: JWs never refer to such a talk as a sermon. They reserve the term "sermon" to refer to a prepared message presented on the doorstep during house-to-house work.

talk, the   The forty-five-minute public address given at the Sunday Public Meeting at Kingdom Hall.

telephone witnessing   Jehovah's Witness telemarketing, carried on primarily by Witnesses physically unable to go from house to house, and occasionally by pioneers struggling to reach their goal of hours.

telephone work   Telephone witnessing.

temporary pioneer   *obsolete* Auxiliary pioneer.

territory   *noun* 1. A geographical area assigned for field service, such as the towns assigned to a congregation or the city blocks assigned to an individual JW. **2.** A map defining such an area.

territory envelope   A cardboard, paper, or plastic sleeve used to store and protect a territory map.

territory map   1. A small map section of a few streets or blocks cut from a town street map and assigned temporarily to an individual or a book study group for field service. **2.** A city or town street map showing a congregation's assigned area for field service.

territory servant   A ministerial servant responsible for storing and assigning territory maps.

theocracy, the   The kingdom of God, perceived by JWs as a present-day functioning government headed by God himself and represented on earth by the Watchtower Society.

Theocrat, the   Almighty God, Jehovah (God the Father, alone, according to Witness theology).

theocratic   *adjective* 1. Connected with God's rulership. 2. Showing appreciation for God's rulership by obedience to organizational instructions.

theocratic brother   A serious-minded male JW who works hard in field service, a model Witness.

theocratic haircut   Any short, 1950s-style men's hair style, as in "Instead of conforming to this world, you should demonstrate your desire to please God by getting a theocratic haircut."

theocratic language   The unique vocabulary and word usage peculiar to Jehovah's Witnesses, viewed positively from their standpoint as a superior language supplied by God and required of those who truly serve him. (Yes, JWs recognize that they speak J.W.ese, but they call it their theocratic language.) *Compare* pure language.

Theocratic Ministry School   A Kingdom Hall meeting usually in session one hour weekly on Thursday or Friday evening and open to most meeting attenders for the purpose of training them in door-to-door work and public speaking.

theocratic order   Adherence to organizational arrangements ("God"'s way of doing things) in obedience to the Watchtower Society's instructions.

theocratic organization, the   The JW organization—with God as head.

Theocratic School   Theocratic Ministry School—from 1976 when the Society began teaching that rank-and-file JWs were not ministers until 1982 when the Society flip-flopped back to the old teaching. *See* AJWSBS.

theocratic sister   A serious-minded female who works hard in field service and demonstrates subjection to the brothers—a model Witness.

theocratic war strategy   Hiding truth from persons not entitled to it, or deceiving outsiders to advance the organization's interests. Falsehoods presented to "God's enemies" are not considered lies, due to the state of war existing between God's forces (the JWs) and Satan's (the rest of the world).

this good news   The message Jehovah's Witnesses preach, namely, that Christ returned invisibly in 1914 and will soon destroy most of humankind, leaving only Jehovah's Witnesses alive to experience the transformation of this planet into a global paradise.

Note: This expression is taken from Matthew 24:14, where Jesus speaks of "this gospel" or "this good news." In the JW interpretation his use of the word *this* means he was speaking of a gospel or good news other than the one generally spoken of in the New Testament—a special gospel message (*this* good news) to be preached only during the time of the end. (Compare Galatians 1:8–9.)

this system   The present wicked world, before Armageddon, in which Satan rules all of humankind with the exception of Jehovah's Witnesses.

this world   The present wicked system of things, before Armageddon, in which Satan rules all of humankind with the exception of Jehovah's Witnesses.

Thursday night meetings   The Theocratic Ministry School and the Service Meeting, typically held on Thursday nights.

time   Hours in field service, as in "Have you got your time in this month?"

time of the end   *theological* The predetermined interval of time from 1914 to the Battle of Armageddon.

time slip   A form listing a JW's field service hours and literature placements, usually turned in monthly. *See* Field Service Report.

torture stake   *noun* The upright pole, without a crossbeam, on which Christ was impaled, according to the Watchtower Society and its *New World Translation*. Also called simply stake.

'Tower   *short for* Watchtower or *Watchtower*. Example: "I've already studied my *'Tower*."

traveling brother   A circuit or district overseer.

traveling overseer   A circuit or district overseer.

traveling work   The work of a circuit or district overseer or his wife.

tribulation, the   The final destruction visited upon this world by God.

Trinity   In the JW view, a three-headed false god invented by Satan the Devil.

true worship   The Jehovah's Witness religion.

Truth book, the   The 1968 Watchtower book *The Truth That Leads to Eternal Life*.

truth, new   A revised teaching that replaces previously held ideas, or a completely novel thought just introduced by the Watchtower Society.

truth, the   The JW organization, as in "I've been in the truth since 1981."

Tuesday meeting, the   The Congregation Book Study, typically conducted on Tuesday evening.

type   *noun* A biblical character, nation, or thing that serves as a prophetic pattern illustrating or prefiguring a later person, nation, or thing, called its antitype. Example: Unfaithful Jerusalem serves as a prophetic type foreshadowing Christendom, according to Watchtower interpretation.

typical Babylon   The ancient Babylonian Empire and/or Neo-Babylonian Empire viewed as a prophetic pattern or *type* prefiguring all false (i.e., non-JW) religions today, collectively.

typical Israel   Ancient Israel viewed as a prophetic pattern or type prefiguring a religious body today.

U

unassigned territory   A town, county, or other geographical area not assigned to any congregation of JWs for regular door-to-door coverage.

unbaptized associate   A new convert who understands and accepts the basic JW teachings and who has brought his or her life into conformity with JW standards (quit smoking, resigned from unacceptable employment, etc.), but has not yet begun reporting time in field service, nor been baptized.

unbaptized publisher   A new convert who understands and accepts the basic JW teachings and who has brought his or her life into conformity with JW standards (quit smoking, resigned from unacceptable employment, etc.), has therefore been approved to begin sharing in door-to-door work, and who has actually begun reporting time in field service, although not yet baptized.

unbeliever   *noun* A non-Witness, irrespective of any profession of belief in Christ that such an individual may have made or membership in another church.

unbelieving mate   *noun* A non-Witness married to a JW.

underlining   Drawing a pen or pencil line under the words in a paragraph that best answer the study question at the bottom of the page—the most common form of personal study JWs do in preparation for meetings that will discuss the material studied. Example: "I'm all set for Sunday's meeting; I've already done my underlining."

undeserved kindness   The expression that replaces "grace" in the *New World Translation* of the Bible. *See* box at *grace*.

unevenly yoked   Married to a non-Witness.

unity   The uniformity in belief and practice that is the most highly prized characteristic of the Watchtower organization, in the eyes of Jehovah's Witnesses—achieved by unquestioning obedience to the Brooklyn leadership.

universal organization, God's   The vast network of angels in heaven and Jehovah's Witnesses on earth, all working together as an organized body under God's direction.

Universal Sovereign, the   God

V

vacation pioneer   *obsolete* Auxiliary pioneer.

victorious organization   The Watchtower organization viewed as the earthly part of God's universal organization, hence assured of ultimate victory over hostile political, religious, and social elements opposed to Jehovah's Witnesses. "Put Faith in a Victorious Organization!" declared the front cover of the March 1, 1979 *Watchtower* magazine.

vindication   *theological* **1.** Final proof that God is truthful and good, thus disproving the accusations made by Satan the Devil. **2.** *capitalized* A three-volume book by that title written by J. F. Rutherford and published by the Watchtower Society in 1931 and 1932. *See* JWL.

Note: While traditional Christianity has generally focused on human salvation as its main concern, Witnesses are taught that the vindication of Jehovah's name is the most important issue.

W

wait on Jehovah   To put up with perceived injustices, errors, wrong practices, and so on, in the Watchtower organization, in the expectation that God will either intervene to rectify matters or will correct one's viewpoint.

Watchtower, The   The principal doctrinal magazine of Jehovah's Witnesses.

Watchtower Bible and Tract Society   *informal* The organization that governs Jehovah's Witnesses. This general name encompasses a number of similarly named legal corporations, the most prominent of which are listed here.

Watchtower Bible and Tract Society of New York, Inc.   The branch organization in charge of JWs in the United States.

Watchtower Society   *short* for Watchtower Bible and Tract Society.

***Watchtower* Study, the**   The weekly meeting devoted to paragraph-by-paragraph discussion of a Watchtower study article.

Watch Tower, The   *obsolete* Former name of *The Watchtower* magazine. *See* JWL.

Watch Tower Bible and Tract Society   The Pennsylvania corporation that serves as the parent body for the various legal entities owning property for Jehovah's Witnesses.

Watch Tower Society   *short* for Watch Tower Bible and Tract Society.

WBBR   A New York radio station formerly owned and operated by Jehovah's Witnesses.

wedding shower   A social gathering for the purpose of bestowing gifts on an engaged couple or a future bride—one of the few acceptable occasions for JWs to hold a party.

¶

week   *noun* 1. As in common usage, a seven-day period. 2. In JW prophetic interpretation, a seven-year period in some contexts and a seven-thousand-year period in other contexts.

where the need is great   J.W.ese for "where there aren't enough active Witnesses to cover the territory at least twice a year." JWs who relocate their families to serve "where the need is great" are viewed as heroes.

wild beast(s)   *noun* Human governments under the control of Satan the Devil.

wild beast out of the abyss   The League of Nations, and then later the United Nations organization, according to Watchtower interpretations of Revelation 17:8.

wild beast out of the sea   *noun* The worldwide political system of human governments under the control of Satan the Devil, according to Watchtower interpretations of Revelation 13.

wild beast, two-horned   *noun* The Anglo-American world power, an alleged de facto combine of Britain and the United States.

wise men, the   In the JW view of the Christmas story, evil astrologers led by the Devil to seek out the baby Jesus as part of a satanic plot to have the Christ-child killed.

Witness   *noun* A Jehovah's Witness. *verb (not capitalized)* To speak to nonmembers about the JW faith.

Witnesses of Jehovah   A variation of the name "Jehovah's Witnesses," often employed in formal talks.

Word, the   1. Jesus Christ in his prehuman role as the first angel God created and the angel selected as God's spokesman. 2. The Bible.

work   *verb* To cover (a territory, street, etc.) by visiting all the homes in door-to-door preaching activity, as in "We're going to work that territory next week," or "Was this street worked recently?"

work, the   The public preaching activity performed by Jehovah's Witnesses from door to door and in other ways.

world, the   Non-Witnesses, collectively, as in, "Get a shorter haircut, son, so that you won't look like the world!"

world headquarters   The Brooklyn Bethel complex.

worldly   *adjective* Connected with or characteristic of Satan the Devil's evil organization.

worldly expression   A saying inappropriate for JWs to use.

worldly girl   A young non-JW woman, automatically assumed to be immoral and evil.

worldly person   A non-Witness, looked down upon as one who does not merit God's approval.

worldwide work   The operations of the Watchtower Society. This euphemistic expression is used most often in regard to financial contributions to make Witnesses and the people they solicit feel they are donating to "the worldwide work"— God's work that is being done—rather than to a religious institution like others that raise funds.

worship   Primarily field service, but also including other organizational programs and activities.

Writing Department   The division of Watchtower headquarters responsible for generating new literature.

written review   1. A written test administered to all students in the Theocratic Ministry School approximately once every four months. 2. The meeting devoted to administering and self-grading this test. Example: "Tonight is written review, so it might be a good idea to wait until next week before inviting your study to her first meeting."

wrongdoing   *noun* Any offense against God's law—as set forth and interpreted in Watchtower Society publications—punishable through a judicial committee.

WTB&TS   *abbreviation* Watch Tower Bible and Tract Society.

Y

year   *noun* 1. A calendar year. 2. A service year. For example, when a JW pioneer says, "I put in 1,073 hours last year," the time period referred to is the twelve-month period from September through last August.

yearbook   An annual publication in book form reviewing the activities of Jehovah's Witnesses worldwide and focusing on a few different countries each year. Examples: "We'll get our new yearbook in December," and, "I looked up the figures in the *1966 Yearbook of Jehovah's Witnesses." See* JWL.

yeartext   A Bible verse or excerpt selected by the Society for prominent display at each Kingdom Hall worldwide throughout the calendar year.

Youth **book**   The Watchtower book *Your Youth—Getting the Best out of It. See* JWL.

Z

zionism   1. *currently* An evil Jewish political movement that misinterprets biblical restoration prophecies as applying to the modern state of Israel. 2. *obsolete* A divinely approved Jewish movement fulfilling prophecy, encouraged and supported by the Watchtower Society during the presidency of Pastor Russell and the early part of Judge Rutherford's administration.

Zion's Watch Tower   *obsolete* The chief JW magazine, *The Watchtower,* was originally titled *Zion's Watch Tower and Herald of Christ's Presence.*

zone   1. *currently* A group of Watchtower Branch Offices under the oversight of a zone overseer. 2. *obsolete* A circuit.

zone overseer   A Governing Body member or other high-ranking headquarters representative sent out to visit Branch Offices in much the same way that a circuit overseer visits the congregations in his circuit.

zone servant   *obsolete* A zone overseer or circuit overseer.

Breaking the Language Barrier

Perhaps your goal in reading this book is to reach Jehovah's Witnesses with information that will free them from Watchtower mind-control and from the organzation itself. If so, you will find it helpful to understand the role that language plays in keeping them captive, and you will appreciate the insight you have now gained into the meaning of many crucial words that will come up repeatedly in your discussions with them.

You may be tempted to impress the Witnesses with your knowledge of their language by using some of their unique terms yourself. However, let me caution you that this would be a serious mistake. In fact, so that even casual readers of this book will take note and avoid making that mistake, I will state this again in bold print:

CAUTION: You should NOT display your knowledge of "J.W.ese" when speaking with Jehovah's Witnesses.

The reason for this is that JWs are instructed to avoid opposers—knowledgeable non-Witnesses who speak against the sect. The more knowledge you show about the Watchtower organization, the more suspicious and cautious a Witness will become in your presence.

Members are taught that an outsider who knows a great deal about the religion but fails to embrace it must have a wicked heart, a heart that chooses falsehood and evil rather than truth and goodness. (Why else would someone fail to join?) And such a person who actively seeks to converse with Witnesses must be doing so for an evil end. Satan the Devil sends opposers to tempt JWs the same way he tempted Jesus in the wilderness, they believe. If your speech identifies you as a knowledgeable opposer, those brave or foolhardy enough to continue speaking with you will still be placed on guard against whatever you have to say. And if you employ JW expressions in your own speech, Witnesses will want to know where you got those expressions.

If your grasp of the "J.W.ese" language is particularly good, you might even be tempted to enter a Kingdom Hall with the aim of passing yourself off as a Witness. This, too, is definitely not a good idea. Your "accent" will give you away, just as surely as it would if you visited Paris after four years of high school French and tried to pass yourself off as a native. Individuals I have known who have pretended to be Witnesses were found out immediately by those who greeted them as they entered the Kingdom Hall. These, in turn, alerted the elders, who quickly surrounded the interloper and isolated him from contact with rank-and-file members.

If any pretense at all is advisable in reaching out to Jehovah's Witnesses, it is to "play dumb" and *not* reveal how much you already know about their beliefs. You will be able to share a lot more information with a Witness who is allowed to think that he or she is teaching you. That is what JWs are trained to do, so let them do it. Instead of attacking their faith with evidence against the Watchtower organization, ask well-chosen questions to get them thinking. In fact, you can ask them questions that will reveal the same information that you would ordinarily have presented in more direct arguments.

What information should you present? JWs eventually need to face up to what Scripture says, and Christians need to defend the faith, but progress with a JW does not usually begin with Bible discussions. I wrote *Jehovah's Witnesses An-*

swered Verse by Verse to help Christians respond to Watchtower misinterpretations. However, the first step that is usually necessary is to shake the JW's faith in the organization, using the organization's own materials. You may find assistance in doing this in my second book, *How to Rescue Your Loved One from the Watchtower.* It outlines strategies and techniques that have proved successful.

In most cases you could go on endlessly discussing scriptures and doctrines with a Jehovah's Witness, without converting him or causing him to leave the sect. Logically persuasive arguments do not persuade the JW due to the effects of mind-control. The organization's stranglehold on the individual's mind must first be broken before effective teaching can be done from the Bible. (Most Christians I meet find this very difficult to believe. In fact, most refuse to believe it and persist in discussing theology anyway, with no results.) Because the Witness has come to view the organization as God's spokesman, the interpretations of Scripture that it offers *must* be correct, and yours must be wrong. You need to undermine the organization's perceived authority before you can get a JW to reason from the Bible.

It usually takes a lot of solid evidence of false prophecies, back-and-forth doctrinal flip-flops, and outright deception on the part of the Watchtower Society before a JW can even begin to think about Scripture and what it really says. But there are only certain ways that this information can be presented without causing the Witness to fearfully terminate the discussions immediately. My book *How to Rescue Your Loved One from the Watchtower* explains over the course of several chapters what material to present and how to present it most effectively.

Is it really necessary to do that much preparation? Well, anyone can play Bible verse ping-pong with a Witness on the doorstep. Occasionally such discussions bear fruit. You may plant a seed or water a seed that another Christian planted. God can make such seeds grow. But if you are serious about reaching Jehovah's Witnesses, *a lot* of study and preparation is required to do so effectively. The people attending Kingdom Hall receive several hours' training each week in how to persuade, how to use the Bible for support, and how to win arguments. If you go into discussions with them poorly prepared, you are starting out at a disadvantage.

Moreover, I feel the need to caution you concerning the dangers involved. A Pentecostal cult-fighter comes to mind who started studying with two JW elders to lead them to Christ, but who began to fall for the deception himself, and who soon quit his church, renounced orthodox doctrine, and began attending Kingdom Hall—before he eventually came back to his senses. Also, there was an elderly Witness I knew when I was in the organization who had been a Baptist deacon some thirty years earlier. When his wife started studying with two JW ladies, he joined the study to prove them wrong, but instead he and his wife both left the Baptist Church and became Witnesses. And I myself remember saying in 1968 that I "would *never* become a Witness"—only to join the sect a year later, and I stayed trapped in it for the next thirteen years. For advice on how to prevent this from happening in your case, please read the chapter titled "Warning: The Life You Save May Be Your Own" in my book *How to Rescue Your Loved One from the Watchtower.*

Besides study and preparation, you will also need support for your discussions with Jehovah's Witnesses. Your pastor or prayer group may be able to help by praying for you during such meetings, perhaps someone even accompanying you, and by debriefing you after each session. Happily there are also ex-JW support groups and ministries active in many localities, affording the assistance of people with considerable firsthand experience. I am constantly receiving requests from people all over the world asking to be put in touch with such sources of help.

Most important, of course, is the Lord's help. Persons who go into discussions with Jehovah's Witnesses confident in their own strength are often disappointed. But those who rely on the living Lord Jesus Christ and go into such discussions in the power of the Holy Spirit are those who have the greatest success.

The Author's Testimony

My early religious training was in a big, white Unitarian church in rural New England, just south of Boston. I still remember the time when, in my boyish innocence, I expressed to the pastor my belief that God had actually parted the Red Sea to let Moses and the Israelites pass through; he turned to the assistant pastor and said, with a laugh, "This boy has a lot to learn." As I grew older I did, in fact, learn what this church taught. Encountering their pamphlet *What Unitarians Believe*, I read that "Some Unitarians believe in God, and some do not"—and quickly realized the ministers must have been among those who did not believe.

By the time I was fourteen years old, I had reached my own conclusion that religion was "the opium of the people," a convenient thought for an adolescent for who preferred not to have God watching him all the time. And when I went on to Harvard University, I found that atheism and agnosticism flourished there, too. So, between the Unitarian Church and my Ivy League schooling, I seldom encountered any strong pressure to believe in God.

By the time I was twenty-two, though, I had thought through atheistic evolution to it its ultimate end: a pointless existence, followed by death. After all, if humans were nothing more than the last in a series of chemical and biological accidents, then any meaning or purpose we might try to find in life would just be a self-deceptive fiction produced in our own minds. It would have no real connection with the harsh, cold reality of a universe where nothing really mattered. So, I saw myself faced with two choices: God or suicide. Since suicide would be an easy way out for me—I believed there was nothing after death—but would leave those who cared about me to face the pain I would cause, I began to think about God.

Coincidentally (perhaps?), a Jehovah's Witness was assigned to work alongside me at my job. Since God was on my mind, I began asking him questions about his beliefs. His answers amazed me. It was the first time that I had ever heard religious thoughts presented in a tight-knit, logical framework. Everything that he said fit together. He had an answer for every question, and so I kept coming up with more questions. Before long, he was conducting a study with me twice a week in the Watchtower Society's new (1968) book, *The Truth That Leads to Eternal Life*.

In no time, I became a very zealous Witness. After receiving my initial indoctrination and getting baptized, I served as a full-time pioneer minister. This required that I spend at least one hundred hours each month preaching from house to house and conducting home Bible studies—actually a commitment of much more than a hundred hours, since travel time could not be included in my monthly field service report. I kept on pioneering until 1971, when I married Penni, who had been raised in the organization and who also pioneered.

My zeal for Jehovah and my proficiency in preaching were rewarded, after a few years, with appointment as an elder. In that capacity I taught the 150-odd people in my home congregation on a regular basis, and made frequent visits to other congregations as a Sunday morning speaker. Occasionally, I also received assignments to speak to audiences ranging in the thousands at Jehovah's Witness assemblies.

Other responsibilities included presiding over the other local elders, handling correspondence between the local congregation and the Society's Brooklyn headquarters, and serving on judicial committees set up to deal with cases of wrongdoing in the congregation. (I can recall disfellowshipping people for such offenses as selling drugs at Kingdom Hall, smoking cigarettes, wife-swapping, and having a Christmas decoration in the home.)

Although we were not able to continue pioneering after our marriage, Penni and I remained very zealous for the preaching work. Between the two of us, we conducted home Bible studies with dozens of people, and brought well over twenty of them into the organization as baptized Jehovah's Witnesses. We also put the Kingdom first in our personal lives by keeping our secular employment to a minimum and living in an inexpensive three-room apartment in order to be able to devote more time to door-to-door preaching activity.

What interrupted this life of full dedication to the Watchtower organization, and caused us to enter a path that would lead us out? In one word, it was *Jesus*. Let me explain:

When Penni and I were at a large Witness convention, we saw a handful of opposers picketing outside. One of them carried a sign that said, "READ THE BIBLE, NOT THE WATCHTOWER." We had no sympathy for the picketers, but we did feel convicted by this sign, because we knew that we had been reading Watchtower publications rather than the Bible. (Later, we actually counted up all of the material that the organization expected Witnesses to read. The books, magazines, lessons, etc. added up to over three thousand pages each year, compared with less than two hundred pages of Bible reading assigned—and most of that was in the Old Testament. The majority of Witnesses were so bogged down by the three thousand pages of the organization's literature that they never got around to doing the Bible reading.)

145

After seeing the picket sign Penni turned to me and said, "We should be reading the Bible *and* the *Watchtower.*" I agreed; so, we began doing regular personal Bible reading.

That's when we began to think about Jesus. Not that we began to question the Watchtower's teaching that Christ was just Michael the archangel in human flesh—it didn't even occur to us to question that. But we were really impressed with Jesus as a person: what he said and did, how he treated people. We wanted to be his followers. Especially, we were struck with how Jesus responded to the hypocritical religious leaders of the day, the Scribes and Pharisees. I remember reading, over and over again, the accounts relating how the Pharisees objected to Jesus' healing on the Sabbath, His disciples' eating with unwashed hands, and other details of behavior that violated their traditions. How I loved Jesus' response: "You hypocrites, Isaiah aptly prophesied about you, when he said, 'This people honors me with their lips, yet their heart is far removed from me. It is in vain that they keep worshiping me, because they teach commands of men as doctrines'" (Matthew 15:7–9 NWT).

Commands of men as doctrines! That thought stuck in my mind. And I began to realize that, in fulfilling my role as an elder, I was acting more like a Pharisee than a follower of Jesus. For example, the elders were the enforcers of all sorts of petty rules about dress and grooming. We told sisters how long they could wear their dresses, and we told brothers how to comb their hair, how to trim their sideburns, and what sort of flare or taper they could wear in their pants. We actually told people that they could not please God unless they conformed. It reminded me of the Pharisees who condemned Jesus' disciples for eating with unwashed hands.

My own dress and grooming conformed to the letter. But I ran into problems with newly interested young men that I brought to Kingdom Hall. Instead of telling them to buy a white shirt and sport coat, and to cut their hair short, I told them, "Don't be disturbed if people at Kingdom Hall dress

and groom a little on the old-fashioned side. You can continue as you are. God doesn't judge people by their haircut
or their clothing." But that didn't work. Someone else would
tell them to get a haircut, or offer to give them a white shirt—
or they would simply feel so out of place that they left, never
to return.

This upset me, because I believed their life depended on
joining "God's organization." If we Witnesses acted like Pharisees to the point of driving young people away from the only
way to salvation, their innocent blood would be on our
hands. Talking to the other elders about it didn't help. They
felt that the old styles were inherently righteous. But then
Jesus' example came to mind:

"And he went on from there and entered their synagogue.
And behold, there was a man with a withered hand. And they
asked him, 'Is it lawful to heal on the sabbath?' so that they
might accuse him. He said to them, 'What man of you, if he
has one sheep and it falls into a pit on the sabbath, will not
lay hold of it and lift it out? Of how much more value is a man
than a sheep! So it is lawful to do good on the sabbath.' Then
he said to the man, 'Stretch out your hand'" (Matthew
12:9–13 RSV).

If I were truly to follow Jesus instead of men, I saw only one
course open to me. I personally violated the tradition of the
elders by letting my hair grow a half inch over my ears. My
reasoning was: How can they pressure a newcomer to get a
haircut, now, with one of the elders wearing the same style?

Well, the other elders reacted the same way the Pharisees
did when Jesus told the man to stretch out his hand. Scripture says they "went out and took counsel against him, how
to destroy him" (Matthew 12:14 RSV). It took them a while to
react, but the elders actually put me on trial, called in witnesses to testify, and spent dozens of hours discussing a half
inch of hair.

Grooming was not the real issue, however. For me it was
a question of whose disciple I was. Was I a follower of Jesus,

or an obedient servant to a human hierarchy? The elders who put me on trial knew that that was the real issue, too. They kept asking, "Do you believe that the Watchtower Society is God's organization? Do you believe that the Society speaks as Jehovah's mouthpiece?" At that time I answered *Yes* because I still did believe it was God's organization—but that it had become corrupt, like the Jewish religious system at the time when Jesus was opposed by the Pharisees.

It was what I said at the congregation meetings that got me into real trouble, though. I was still an elder, so, when I was assigned to give a fifteen-minute talk on the book of Zechariah at the Thursday night Theocratic Ministry School meeting, I took advantage of the opportunity to encourage the audience to read the Bible. In fact, I told them that, if their time was limited and they had to choose between reading the Bible and reading *The Watchtower* magazine, they should choose the Bible, because it was inspired by God while *The Watchtower* was not inspired and often taught errors that had to be corrected later.

Not surprisingly, that was the last time they allowed me to give a talk. But I could still speak from my seat during question-and-answer periods at the meetings. Everyone was expected to answer in their own words, but not in their own thoughts. You were to give the thought found in the paragraph of the lesson being discussed. But, after I said a few things they didn't like, they stopped giving me the microphone.

With the new perspective that I was gaining from Bible reading, it upset me to see the organization elevate itself above Scripture, as it did when the December 1, 1981 *Watchtower* said: "Jehovah God has also provided his visible organization. . . . Unless we are in touch with this channel of communication that God is using, we will not progress along the road to life, no matter how much Bible reading we do" (page 27, ¶4). It really disturbed me to see those men elevate themselves above God's Word. Since I could not speak out at the meetings, I decided to try writing.

That's when I started publishing the newsletter *Comments from the Friends*. I wrote articles questioning what the organization was teaching, and signed them with the pen name 'Bill Tyndale, Jr.'—a reference to sixteenth-century English Bible translator William Tyndale, who was burned at the stake for what he wrote. To avoid getting caught, Penni and I drove across the state line at night to an out-of-state post office and mailed the articles in unmarked envelopes. We sent them to local Witnesses and also to hundreds of Kingdom Halls all across the country, whose addresses we had obtained from telephone books at the town library.

Penni and I knew that we had to leave the Jehovah's Witnesses. But, to us, it was similar to the question of what to do in a burning apartment building. Do you escape through the nearest exit? Or, do you bang on doors first, waking the neighbors and helping them escape too? We felt an obligation to help others get out—especially our families and our students that we had brought into the organization. If we had just walked out, our families left behind would have been forbidden to associate with us.

In February 1982, I wrote an article drawing parallels between the world of George Orwell's novel *Nineteen Eighty-Four* and the world I lived in as a Jehovah's Witness. I used Orwell's "Newspeak" word "facecrime" to describe the instructions issued at that month's circuit assembly to the effect that "Sisters should not express disagreement with judicial decisions of the elders *even by their facial expressions.*" (First I phoned the District Overseer who ran the convention and had him verify for me that those instructions were actually found in the "Theocratic Subjection" talk outline supplied by Brooklyn headquarters, not an imaginative addition ad libbed by local Witnesses.)

To accompany the article, which I published in the March 1982 issue of my newsletter *Comments from the Friends*, I reproduced illustrations of a family studying together taken from the March 1, 1981 *Watchtower* and the March 8, 1982 *Awake!* magazines—illustrations that were identical except that the father's and son's hair was cut considerably shorter in the 1982 version to reflect "new truths" requiring theocratic hair styles cut above the ears so that Witness males would look different from the world. The altered illustration could easily have come from the desk of Winston Smith in Orwell's novel, since he had the job of altering periodicals and illustrations to bring them in line with Party policy under Big Brother.

The remainder of my article reproduced astonishingly similar quotes from *Nineteen Eighty-Four* and the December 15, 1981 *Watchtower* attributing to the Party and to the Society respectively the right to dispense "truth" to followers. And it concluded with a comparison between the JW teaching that twelve symbolic numbers add up to a literal number of 144,000 in Revelation 7:4–8, and a Party functionary torturing Winston Smith until he admits that $2 + 2 = 5$ if the Party says so.

But, after a few weeks a friend discovered that I was the publisher of the newsletter and turned me in. So, one night when Penni and I were returning home from conducting a Bible study, two elders stepped out of a parked car, accosted us in the street, and questioned us about the newsletter. They wanted to put us on trial for publishing it, but we simply stopped going to the Kingdom Hall. By that time most of our former friends there had become quite hostile toward us. One young man called on the phone and threatened to "come over and take care of" me if he got another newsletter. And another Witness actually left death threats on our answering machine. The elders went ahead and tried us *in absentia* and disfellowshipped us.

It was a great relief to be out from under the oppressive yoke of that organization. But we now had to face the immediate challenge of where to go and what to believe. It takes some time to rethink your entire religious outlook on life. Before leaving the Watchtower, we had rejected the claims that the organization was God's channel of communication, that Christ returned invisibly in the year 1914, and that the great crowd of believers since 1935 should not partake of the Communion loaf and cup. But we were only beginning to reexamine other doctrines. And we had not yet come into fellowship with Christians outside the JW organization.

All Penni and I knew was that we wanted to follow Jesus and that the Bible contained all the information we needed. So we really devoted ourselves to reading the Bible, and to prayer. We also invited our families and remaining friends to meet in our apartment on Sunday mornings. While the Witnesses gathered at Kingdom Hall to hear a lecture and study the Watchtower, we met to read the Bible. As many as fifteen attended—mostly family, but some friends also.

We were just amazed at what we found in prayerfully reading the New Testament over and over again—things that we had never appreciated before, like the closeness that the early disciples had with the risen Lord, the activity of the Holy Spirit in the early church, and Jesus' words about being born again.

All those years as Jehovah's Witnesses, the Watchtower had taken us on a guided tour through the Bible. We gained a lot of knowledge about the Old Testament and we could quote a lot of Scriptures, but we never heard the gospel of salvation in Christ. We never learned to depend on Jesus for our salvation and to look to him personally as our Lord. Everything centered around the Watchtower's works program, and people were expected to come to Jehovah God through the organization.

When I realized from reading Romans 8 and John 3, that I needed to be "born of the Spirit," I was afraid at first. Jehovah's Witnesses believe that "born again" people, who claim to have the Holy Spirit, are actually possessed by demons. And so I feared that, if I prayed aloud to turn my life over to

Jesus Christ, some demon might be listening; and the demon might jump in and possess me, pretending to be the Holy Spirit. (Many Jehovah's Witnesses live in constant fear of the demons. Some of our friends would even throw out furniture and clothing, fearing that the demons could enter their homes through those articles.) But, then I read Jesus' words in Luke 11:9–13. In a context where he was teaching about prayer and casting out unclean spirits, Jesus said: "And I say to you, ask, and it will be given to you; seek, and you will find; knock, and it will be opened to you. For everyone who asks receives, and he who seeks finds, and to him who knocks it will be opened. If a son asks for bread from any of you who is a father, will he give him a stone? Or if he asks for a fish, will he give him a serpent instead of a fish? Or if he asks for an egg, will he offer him a scorpion? If you then, being evil, know how to give good gifts to your children, how much more will your heavenly Father give the Holy Spirit to those who ask Him!" (NKJ).

I knew, after reading those words, that I could safely ask for Christ's Spirit (Romans 8:9) without fearing that I would receive a demon. So, in the early morning privacy of our kitchen, I proceeded to confess my need for salvation and to commit my life to Christ.

About a half hour later, I was on my way to work, and I was about to pray again. It had been my custom for many years to start out my prayers by saying, "Jehovah God, . . ." But, this time when I opened my mouth to pray, I started out by saying, "Father, . . ." It was not because I had reasoned about the subject and reached the conclusion that I should address God differently; the word "Father" just came out, without my even thinking about it. Immediately, I understood why: "God has sent forth the Spirit of His Son into your hearts, crying out, 'Abba, Father!'" (Galatians 4:6 NKJ). I wept with joy at God's confirmation of this new, more intimate relationship with him.

Penni and I soon developed the desire to worship and praise the Lord in a congregation of believers, and to benefit from the wisdom of mature Christians. Since the small group of ex-JW's was still meeting in our apartment on Sunday mornings for Bible reading, and most of them were not yet ready to venture into a church, we began visiting churches that had evening services. One church we attended was so legalistic that we almost felt as though we were back in the Kingdom Hall. Another was so liberal that the sermon always seemed to be on philosophy or politics—instead of Jesus. Finally the Lord led us to a congregation where we felt comfortable and where the focus was on Jesus Christ and his gospel, rather than on side issues.

Penni teaches fifth grade now in a Christian school that has students from about seventeen different churches. She really enjoys it, because she can tie in the Scriptures with all sorts of subjects. I continue publishing *Comments from the Friends* as a quarterly newsletter aimed at reaching Jehovah's Witnesses with the gospel and helping Christians who are talking to JW's. It also contains articles of special interest to ex-Witnesses. Subscribers are found in a dozen foreign countries, as well as all across the United States and Canada. I have also written a number of books on Jehovah's Witnesses. Besides writing on the subject, I speak occasionally to church groups interested in learning how to answer Jehovah's Witnesses so as to lead them to Christ.

We also provide a phone-in recorded message for Jehovah's Witnesses. Twenty-four hours a day, JW's can call 508-584-4467 and hear a brief message directing them to the Bible and helping them disprove Watchtower teachings. Some Witnesses even call during the middle of the night, so that family members will not observe and report them to the elders. So far, we have received approximately twenty thousand calls. At the end of each message the caller is invited to leave his or her name and address, to receive free literature in the mail—and many do.

Our website at http://www.webshowplace.com/Comments provide material that has helped liberate many JWs.

The thrust of our outreach ministry is to help Jehovah's Witnesses break free from deception and put faith in the original gospel of Christ as it is presented in the Bible. The most important lesson Penni and I learned since leaving the Jehovah's Witnesses is that Jesus is not just a historical figure that we read about. He is alive and is actively involved with Christians today, just as he was back in the first century. He personally saves us, teaches us, and leads us. This personal relationship with God through his Son Jesus Christ is so wonderful! The individual who knows Jesus and follows him will not even think about following anyone else: "A stranger they will not follow, but they will flee from him, for they do not know the voice of strangers. . . . My sheep hear my voice, and I know them, and they follow me; and I give them eternal life, and they shall never perish, and no one shall snatch them out of my hand" (John 10:5, 27–28 RSV).

Comments, corrections, changes

The language of Jehovah's Witnesses undergoes constant change—so much so that one who misses meetings for a while can often be picked out by verbal errors. If you note any entries in this volume that should be updated or corrected, please e-mail the author at *comments@ultranet.com* or write:

David A. Reed
P.O. Box 819
Assonet, MA 02702

Key to Abbreviated References

AJWSBS = *Answering Jehovah's Witnesses Subject by Subject,* David A. Reed, Grand Rapids: Baker Book House, 1996.

INDEX = *Index of Watchtower Errors,* David A. Reed editor, Grand Rapids: Baker Book House, 1990.

JWAVBV = *Jehovah's Witnesses Answered Verse by Verse,* David A. Reed, Grand Rapids: Baker Book House, 1986.

JWL = *Jehovah's Witness Literature: A Critical Guide to Watchtower Publications,* David A. Reed, Grand Rapids: Baker Book House, 1993.

RESCUE = *How to Rescue Your Loved One from the Watchtower,* David A. Reed, Grand Rapids: Baker Book House, 1989.

David A. Reed publishes and edits *Comments from Friends,* a 16-page quarterly on sharing the Gospel of Christ with Jehovah's Witnesses. He also serves as a contributing writer of *Christian Research Journal,* the principal publication of the late Dr. Walter Martin's Christian Research Institute. And he is president of Gospel Truth Ministries, Inc., which maintains a free lending library offering materials on Mormons, Jehovah's Witnesses, and other cult groups.

David has authored over a dozen books:
Jehovah's Witnesses Answered Verse by Verse
Index of Watchtower Errors
How to Rescue Your Loved One from the Watchtower
Behind the Watchtower Curtain
Jehovah's Witness Literature: A Critical Guide to Watchtower Publications
Mormons Answered Verse by Verse (with John Farkas)
How to Rescue Your Loved One from Mormonism (with John Farkas)
Worse than Waco
"No blood!"
Answering Jehovah's Witnesses Subject by Subject
Blood on the Altar

Mormons–How to Witness to Them (with John Farkas) —as well as numerous booklets, tracts, and articles appearing in *Comments from the friends, in The Gospel Truth,* and in *Christian Research Journal,* and reprinted in several other periodicals.

Personal Bible reading led David and his wife Penni to leave Jehovah's Witnesses and receive Christ in 1982. They are currently members of East Freetown Congregational Christian Church in Freetown, Massachuetts.

David studied at Harvard University (Class of '68) on a National Merit Scholarship. He is a member of the Authors Guild.